Conversations With
PRINCIPALS

*This book is dedicated to my loving wife, Jane,
and my daughters, Lauren, Erica, and Katie.*

*It is also dedicated to my New York family;
my sister Judy, my brother-in-law, Michael; my
sister-in-law Judy and my nephews and nieces;
to the Wheeler family; and of special note, to Priscilla Wheeler.*

Conversations With

PRINCIPALS

Issues, Values, and Politics

Andrew E. Dubin
San Francisco State University

SAGE Publications
Thousand Oaks ■ London ■ New Delhi

For information:

Sage Publications, Inc.
2455 Teller Road
Thousand Oaks, California 91320
E-mail: order@sagepub.com

Sage Publications Ltd.
1 Oliver's Yard
55 City Road
London EC1Y 1SP
United Kingdom

Sage Publications India Pvt. Ltd.
B-42, Panchsheel Enclave
Post Box 4109
New Delhi 110 017 India

Printed in the United States of America

Library of Congress Cataloging-in-Publication Data

Dubin, Andrew E.
Conversations with principals: Issues, values, and politics/Andrew E. Dubin.
   p. cm.
Includes bibliographical references and index.
ISBN 1–4129–1635–6 (cloth) — ISBN 1–4129–1636–4 (pbk.)
   1. School principals—Professional relationships—United States.
2. School principals—United States—Interviews. 3. First year school principals—In-service training—United States. 4. School management and organization—United States. I. Title.
LB2831.92.D83 2006
371.2′012—dc22   2005020169

This book is printed on acid-free paper.

06   07   08   09   10   9   8   7   6   5   4   3   2   1

Acquiring Editor:	Diane McDaniel
Editorial Assistant:	Erica Carroll
Project Editor:	Beth A. Bernstein
Copy Editor:	Tom Lacey
Typesetter:	C&M Digitals (P) Ltd.
Indexer:	Judy Hunt
Cover Designer:	Janet Foulger

Contents

Acknowledgments   xi

Introduction   xiii
    The Role of the Principal   xiii
    Connecting the Principal to the Reader   xiv
    How the Principal Interviews Were Formulated   xv
    Organization of the Book   xvi
    Connecting Across Interviews   xvii
    Matrix of Principal Interviews   xix

Part I: Elementary School   1

1. Changing the School Culture: The Community Activist   3
    Profile of the Community Activist   4
        School Context   4
        School Characteristics   5
        School Climate   5
        School Organization   5
    Interview   5
    Analysis   22
    Discussion Questions   23
    Student Activities   23
    Interview Question   24
    Simulations   24
    Developing a School Culture   24
    Principal Leadership Applications   25
    Questions Related to ISLLC Standards   26
    Readings and Resources   26

2. Personal and Professional Belief Systems: The Ethicist 27
    Profile of the Ethicist   28
        School Context   28
        School Characteristics 29

	School Climate	29
	School Organization	29
	Interview	29
	Analysis	42
	Discussion Questions	43
	Student Activities	44
	Interview Question	44
	Simulations	44
	The Ethical Balance	45
	Questions Related to ISLLC Standards	45
	Readings and Resources	45
3.	Maintaining Stability and History: The Traditionalist	46
	Profile of the Traditionalist	47
	School Context	48
	School Characteristics	48
	School Climate	48
	School Organization	48
	Interview	48
	Analysis	65
	Discussion Questions	66
	Student Activities	66
	Interview Question	67
	Simulations	67
	Maintaining Tradition	67
	Principal Leadership Applications	67
	Questions Related to ISLLC Standards	68
	Readings and Resources	68
4.	Social Exchange and Power: The Balancer	69
	Profile of the Balancer	70
	School Context	70
	School Characteristics	71
	School Climate	71
	School Organization	71
	Interview	71
	Analysis	81
	Discussion Questions	82
	Student Activities	83
	Interview Question	83
	Simulations	83

Developing Effective Negotiating Abilities 83
Principal Leadership Applications 84
Questions Related to ISLLC Standards 84
Readings and Resources 84

5. The Lens of Decision Making: The Intuitive Leader 85
Profile of the Intuitive Leader 86
School Context 87
School Characteristics 87
School Climate 87
School Organization 87
Interview 88
Analysis 100
Discussion Questions 101
Student Activities 102
Interview Question 102
Simulations 102
Developing Effective Decision-Making Abilities 102
Principal Leadership Applications 103
Questions Related to ISLLC Standards 103
Readings and Resources 103

Part II: Middle School 105

6. Leadership Focus and Planning: The Sage 107
Profile of the Sage 108
School Context 109
School Characteristics 109
School Climate 109
School Organization 109
Interview 110
Analysis 124
Discussion Questions 125
Student Activities 125
Interview Question 125
Additional Assignments 126
Simulations 126
Developing School Trust 126
Principal Leadership Applications 127
Questions Related to ISLLC Standards 127
Readings and Resources 127

7. Evaluation and the Political Arena: The Politician   128
    Profile of the Politician   129
        School Context   130
        School Characteristics   130
        School Climate   130
        School Organization   130
    Interview   130
    Analysis   145
    Discussion Questions   146
    Student Activities   146
    Interview Question   147
    Simulations   147
    Creating a Manageable Work Environment   147
    Principal Leadership Applications   147
    Questions Related to ISLLC Standards   148
    Readings and Resources   148

8. Students in Transition: The Wise Veteran   149
    Profile of the Wise Veteran   150
        School Context   151
        School Characteristics   151
        School Climate   151
        School Organization   151
    Interview   151
    Analysis   162
    Discussion Questions   163
    Student Activities   164
    Interview Question   164
    Simulations   164
    Developing an Organizational Awareness
        of the Changing Middle School Child   165
    Principal Leadership Applications   165
    Questions Related to ISLLC Standards   166
    Reading and Resources   166

Part III: High School   167

9. Perceptions and Assumptions:
    The Multitasker   169
    Profile of the Multitasker   170
        School Context   170
        School Characteristics   171

       School Climate   171
       School Organization   171
   Interview   172
   Analysis   188
   Discussion Questions   190
   Student Activities   190
   Interview Question   190
   Simulations   191
   Structuring a School Environment   191
   Principal Leadership Applications   191
   Questions Related to ISLLC Standards   192
   Readings and Resources   192

10.   Addressing Organizational and
     Personal Needs: The Philosopher   193
   Profile of the Philosopher   194
       School Context   195
       School Characteristics   195
       School Climate   195
       School Organization   195
   Interview   195
   Analysis   211
   Discussion Questions   212
   Student Activities   212
   Interview Question   212
   Simulations   212
   Creating a Consistent School Philosophy   213
   Principal Leadership Applications   213
   Questions Related to ISLLC Standards   214
   Readings and Resources   214

11.   Group Dynamics and Multinationalism: The Internationalist   215
   Profile of the Internationalist   216
       School Context   216
       School Characteristics   217
       School Climate   217
       School Organization   217
   Interview   217
   Analysis   232
   Discussion Questions   234
   Student Activities   234

Interview Question   234
Simulations   235
Developing a Supportive School Environment   235
Principal Leadership Applications   235
Questions Related to ISLLC Standards   236
Readings and Resources   236

Part IV: No Child Left Behind   237

12. A Principal's Approach to the No Child Left Behind Act   239
     Profile of NCLB: The Principal   240
         School Context   241
         School Characteristics   241
         School Climate   241
         School Organization   241
     Interview   242
     Analysis   259
     Principal Leadership Applications   259
     Questions Related to ISLLC Standards   260
     Readings and Resources   260

13. A Superintendent's Perspective on NCLB   261
         Goals of the No Child Left Behind Act   262
     Profile of NCLB: The Superintendent   262
         County Context   263
         County Characteristics   263
         County Climate   263
         County Organization   264
     Interview   264
     Analysis   277
     Readings and Resources   277

Appendix   278

References   287

Index   289

About the Author   295

Acknowledgments

I wish to thank all the K–12 site principals and other administrative leaders at the county and district levels who graciously contributed their valuable time and honest perspectives regarding their leadership experiences. My work was totally predicated on their willingness to talk to me. Indeed, their candor and insights about their administrative work was offered without qualification to better understand the complex nature of leadership and also help and support those aspiring to become leaders in our K–12 schools. I am not at liberty to mention them by name due to the confidentiality of their remarks; otherwise I would certainly do so.

A special gratitude is extended to San Francisco State University, which supported my work to conduct this ethnographic research. As well, a thank-you to Professor Jack Fraenkel, my friend and colleague, for assisting in the methodological design, which explains my research approach. I am also indebted to my colleague, Dr. Mary Ann Sinkkonen, for always being available for feedback and reflection on what I hoped to convey and capture in these interviews. Her support and availability were unqualified and of tremendous value.

Much appreciation is extended to the very expert and honest reviewers who helped direct and shape my writing pedagogy geared for graduate students studying leadership practices. Their comments and suggestions were particularly helpful throughout the conceptualization and writing process. Specifically, I would like to express my thanks to J. D. Jones at Marshall University Graduate School, Charles W. Elliott at Bridgewater State College, and Ernest Johnson, Ed.D., at the University of Texas at Arlington. Appreciation is also due to Joyce A. Dana, Ph.D. at Saint Louis University, Norman Dale Norris at Nicholls State University, Mark D. Myers at Indiana University Purdue University Fort Wayne, Wayne White at the University of North Carolina at Charlotte, Brenda G. LeTendre at Pittsburg State University and Mary Lou Yeatts at Murray State University. My reviewers read and reread my many drafts, resulting in a clear and personalized interview series that truly captures the reality of K–12 school leaders.

I also want to thank Diane McDaniel, my editor at Sage, as well as her production staff, for their support and guidance throughout this process. Diane's focused and expert literary perspective helped navigate our discussions so that the book captured my intentions while balancing it with a cogent and pedagogically sound research and content approach for the readers. This process requires skill, time, tact, and a sensitive hand that was both enjoyable and very effective.

Finally, I also want to thank my wife, Jane, whose professional expertise in psychology provided yet another lens for me to view and understand these findings.

Introduction

The Role of the Principal

The most common community center, institutional organization, and bastion of cultural understanding that we all hold as part of our collective traditional heritage is the public school. It is perceived to be the most understood institution. We have lived, breathed, and grown together through this national institution. It has been, continues to, and will always be the focal point for personal and professional development for our citizenry, responsible for effectively maintaining and perpetuating our collective democratic vision while evolving and incorporating a changing and growing population. It involves all human dynamics, social and organizational structures, and environmental features. It embraces all disciplines of the soft and hard sciences and increasingly engages the international world around us. And it is the principal, and no one else, who ultimately assumes the responsibility for the school's effectiveness.

Yet, when one considers the all-transcending and perceived understandings we all share, there is no document, no blueprint, no formula from which we can draw that provides a road map for an effective educational process in all situations. It is no wonder that we are always in a quandary as to the reasons our educational system is so problematic, and also infinitely successful. It speaks clearly to the complexity of the schooling enterprise and the enormous influence of the principal.

Within this context, it is the principal who is the critical person orchestrating the movements of all the players in the school. The principal makes the decisions that affect people's lives, directs considerable sums of money, creates a climate that impacts the community, and projects the appropriate philosophy and practical vision that propels a school forward. The principal, in essence, is a critical player in balancing and promoting the progress of our society.

These leaders coordinate and direct a system whose purpose involves a paradox: create innovative movement in the development of human behavior and intellectual and physical prowess, while instilling socially acceptable moral and ethical values. These school leaders are responsible for initiating a progressive, fluid, and responsive organizational system while maintaining its steady state, its stability and equilibrium necessary at the current moment in time. Educational leaders are without question as important a professional group of contributing members of our society as any. They face the daunting task of overseeing, directing, and protecting the lives of our children within our schools.

Schools have the companion responsibility of developing young people's capabilities, while socializing them to conform to societal needs and expectations. In order to accomplish this Herculean task extraordinary leadership is required. How does leadership actually function at the school site? What types of real decisions are a part of their daily experiences? How do they make these decisions? A review of the literature in educational administration will reveal volumes of conceptual material that attempt in large part to present all the component parts that underscore the rationale behind leadership behavior. This theoretical underpinning is essential to providing students of the discipline a grasp of the larger picture, the modus operandi for the craft of school leadership.

While all of us have had a range of experiences within the school, either as a student, parent, educator, or community member, unless you have assumed the leadership of a school, it is difficult to understand what is involved in taking on this role. This book is an attempt to bring to view in a simple, straightforward, and honest manner the realities of the principalship as experienced by those who assume this role.

Connecting the Principal to the Reader

An extremely effective and potent method of understanding this professional discipline is eliciting commentary from those in school leadership positions, the principals themselves. In *Conversations With Principals: Issues, Values, and Politics*, I have direct discussions with these principals, which offer a clear and cogent description of the actual school leadership setting for the reader, thus capturing the irrefutable and pure reality of the experience. This is different from other approaches taken by leadership texts because it is a personal dialogue between the principals and the reader.

While case-study presentations are very effective in capturing the realities of the site experiences, they are presented from the standpoint of the writer and therefore have been somewhat skewed and unavoidably interpreted before the reader has an opportunity to assess the case personally. A verbatim exchange between interviewer and interviewee presents the situation with virtually no prejudice or bias and thus open to the interpretation of the reader. It is a pure account of the principal's experience, thinking, and reflection.

Having taught educational administration for more than 25 years and worked as an administrator on virtually every leadership level nationally and internationally, I have found that the stronger the connection between the reality setting, that is, the school, and the academic classroom, the think tank, the more potent the information and worthwhile the experience and preparation for the student. That is why the pedagogy of *Conversations With Principals: Issues, Values, and Politics* is so effective in the graduate classroom. Without exception, students feel that they know the principals, understand what they are experiencing, and are more sensitive to the considerable demands required of the position.

How the Principal Interviews Were Formulated

My primary objective in *Conversations With Principals: Issues, Values, and Politics* is to develop the connection between the students of leadership and those practicing in the field.

The principals were randomly selected and representative, rather than exemplary, although the more experienced principals I interviewed had been award winners. They all wanted to make a contribution to the field and arranged their schedules so that the interviews were conducted when they were not preoccupied with school matters. Some were phone interviews, others were done in person, some during the week, others on weekends. All the interviews were tape-recorded and then transcribed for analysis. The principals were told that the information would be treated anonymously, and in some instances changed somewhat, to further maintain confidentiality. They all had an opportunity to read and edit their interviews.

When I first approached them, I also indicated that I wanted honest comments, feedback that would reflect and capture their experiences in the schools. I requested that they not hesitate to cite political, emotional, social, or otherwise controversial issues that generally might cause inhibition and restraint. It was their candor that would be so important and potent in conveying their positions and experiences as principals.

For each interview, a structured schedule was utilized with probe questions. A purposive sample was selected because I intended to represent a wide variety of levels, experiences, and backgrounds; hence the qualitative nature of the research.

The demographic information about each principal presented in the beginning of the chapters, as well as the series of initial questions focused on their backgrounds, was particularly useful in developing a general profile about the principals, that is, experience in teaching, prior administrative work, types of previous schools, age, and so on. I have found that graduate students need this information to compare their professional and personal situations to those who are assuming the role of principal. It provides a very important point of reference as they consider their career paths, background, and timing. It also helps them better understand that particular principal as he or she is involved at and responds to that specific school site and situation.

Organization of the Book

Each interview in this book conveys a different school experience. While there are administrative connections throughout each interview, as one might expect given the discipline and applied skills, there are distinct differences as well. Although, on one hand, it is important to identify those characteristics that each leader must possess, as evidenced by their comments, there are rich data here that make each experience different and unique to that particular individual and site. This demonstrates the complexity of the profession and breathes life into the prospect that each individual can apply his or her particular imprint on an organizational situation. That specific vision or philosophy has power and is real. Candidates soon discover that principals can make a difference.

The elementary principals, while representing the same grade-level student populations, deal with different organizational issues and utilize distinct leadership styles. These school levels are highlighted in order to demonstrate the uniqueness of each school situation while also capturing the overlap of elementary-school demands and expectations. This reflects the complexity of the schooling enterprise and also emphasizes the leader's role and contribution to his or her school. Specifically, each elementary principal reflected his or her own personality and particular school need in the following ways: systematized testing and uniformity in the curriculum; community dysfunction and staff alienation; maintaining stability and consistency; creating equilibrium and predictability; and, finally, utilizing personal, gut feelings as a part of the decision-making formula.

The middle school principals rather dramatically delineated the very distinct leadership orientations that drove their decision making and defined their schools. On one hand, while politics was the significant thread that linked the schools together, the particular school ethos and backdrop that affected the middle school principal's leadership and application to their schools was wholly different. Emphasis on board encroachment, committee-shared decision making, and focused planning all were part of these respective schools, as indicated by these interviews. While politics was a part of all the school processes, it was specific to the school site.

Finally, the high school interviews were still another vehicle of consistency and also were idiosyncratic to the respective schools. And again, these issues ranged from international students and cultural conflict to continuation schools and organizational coherence and the grounding necessary for management control and authority.

The titles of the leaders were designed to more easily identify the more salient aspects of their personalities and of the issues derived from the interviews. While other titles could likely describe these principals as well, these were selected in the attempt to capture the issue and more easily identify the principal and school.

The pedagogy that follows each interview asks the reader to think very carefully and substantively about the interview. It also asks the reader to be more actively involved and engaged on a cognitive and visceral level. It is extremely important to exercise a physical practice as part of the development of leadership abilities. How you behave, that is, your comments, movement, interactive skills, and so on, must be practiced. Language, voice, diction, and general physical presence require training.

Finally, the pedagogy in Connecting Across Interviews as well as in the Matrix of Interviews below asks students to see outside of each situation so that the thematic issues and cross-pollinated leadership traits are realized.

Connecting Across Interviews

In all the interviews with the principals, what leadership styles can you identify? If we assume that the spectrum of leadership philosophies or approaches can range from authoritative to laissez-faire, how would you define the **Philosopher** (Chapter 10) as compared to the **Balancer** (Chapter 4) or the **Traditionalist** (Chapter 3) as opposed to the **Ethicist** (Chapter 2)?

If you were to compare the lessons learned by the **Intuitive Leader** (Chapter 5) to the insights of the **Sage** (Chapter 6), what would they be? If you recall, the **Intuitive Leader** was principal at two sites and reflected on her initial experience as helping her when she assumed her second principalship. What had she learned and were there similarities with the **Sage**'s approach?

All the principals were asked about loneliness or the sense of isolation. How did the **Wise Veteran** (Chapter 8) respond to that as compared to the responses of both the **Community Activist** (Chapter 1) and the **Traditionalist?**

How did each principal address the need for support in the field? The **Sage** identified specific ways in which she was supported. What did she say and how did her experiences compare to the **Traditionalist?**

The **Philosopher** stressed the need to be prepared for the position, administratively and physically. What specifically did he indicate about his philosophy and how he applied it? The **Sage** was also quite clear in how she prepared for the opening of the school in the fall. How did she prepare the faculty and what did she do during the summer before meeting the students?

In each of the interviews, the need to approach the diverse student populations in each school was central to their discussions, but with a different accent. How was the diversity issue evidenced by the **Internationalist** (Chapter 11) as compared to the **Politician** (Chapter 7)? How did their approaches contrast with the **Multitasker** (Chapter 9)?

In terms of priorities, how would you compare the **Balancer** with the **Community Activist?** They both spoke of their initial experiences with a new school, a new student body, faculty, and parents. How did their experiences compare?

Keeping things in perspective must be a significant characteristic for a principal. How was this identified in the interviews? What did they say about how they handled pressure?

What did the principals state about their respective districts? What role should the district play regarding their support of principals? The **Balancer** assigned very specific responsibilities to her district. What were they?

The principals were very candid when they spoke of frustrations, problems, issues that were particularly difficult. What specifically did the **Ethicist** identify regarding his school and curriculum that was most distressing to him? What changes in the curriculum did the **Community Activist** identify that related to discipline? How was she going to change that?

The school site implementation of the No Child Left Behind Act was the focus of Chapter 12. Did you find this principal's general philosophy and leadership style to be similar to any of the other principals interviewed?

Table I.1 Matrix of Principal Interviews

Chapter	Relevant ISLLC Standards	School Levels	Interview Focus	Primary Leadership Topics	Secondary Topics
1	1, 2, 4	Elementary	• Socialization • Trust	• Low academic achievement·Changing school culture	• Professionalism and respect • Community acknowledgment· • Student and faculty esteem
2	5	Elementary	• Ethics	• Relevant and meaningful curriculum	• Diversity· • Formula curriculum· • Expert/novice teachers
3	1	Elementary	• Leadership styles	• Maintaining tradition • Culture	• Bureaucratic insights • Leadership development· • Role security
4	1, 2, 6	Elementary	• Exchange· • Power	• Mutual needs for all stakeholders	• Professional reflection • Administrator/teacher interaction
5	3	Elementary	• Decision-making models	• Reflective decision making • Recognizing and utilizing staff· • Internal "gut" decisions	• Classroom management • School constituent needs • Teacher observations • Parent conferences
6	1, 4, 5	Middle	• Trust	• New leadership· • Efficient planning • Shared leadership	• Whole schoolwide review • Money allocation • Program assessment • Support teams • School communication

(Continued)

Chapter	Relevant ISLLC Standards	School Levels	Interview Focus	Primary Leadership Topics	Secondary Topics
7	3, 6	Middle	• Burnout	• Politics and supervisory evaluation • Testing	• Parent responsibility • Teacher management and Accountability
8	1, 2, 3	Middle	• Family systems	• Adolescent development	• Change agent for high school
9	1, 2, 5	High	• McGregor X/Y Theory	• Literacy education • At-risk students • Assumptions and expectations	• Behavior management • Shared decision making • Teacher efficacy • Academic achievement
10	1, 2, 3, 6	High	• Maslow-Self-understanding	• Efficient and predictable school management· • Personal and professional equilibrium	• School and societal expectations • School structural changes
11	1, 3, 4, 6	K–12	• Carl Rogers • Hawthorne studies • Human relations	• Multicultural education • Leadership development	• School culture • Administrative authority • Board politics
12	1, 2, 4, 5	K–8	• NCLB Impact on school philosophy and morale	• High/low academic achievement	• Parent involvement • Communication • Short-, long-term planning
13	6	K–12	• NCLB impact on county/district/school operations		

PART I

Elementary School

1

Changing The School Culture: The Community Activist

Instilling a sense of pride, respect, and hope for students, faculty, and community is the focus of this chapter. How can students be reoriented to think they are cared for and capable when schools have been unsupportive throughout their school experiences? How can teachers begin to contribute their talents and energies to schools that have been unresponsive and authoritative in the decision-making process? What are effective strategies that can be utilized by principals to meet students and faculty where they are in order to change a school and create a healthful and positive environment?

Themes addressed in this chapter:

- Creating school pride
- Developing shared decision making
- Acknowledging success
- Overcoming obstacles and roadblocks
- Remaining positive and projecting leadership stability
- Being consistent

Profile of the Community Activist

Principal: female

Age: 45+

Ethnicity: Latina

Experience: 1st-year principal; one year as intern assistant principal; 3 years related administrative experience

School: elementary; student population: 500

We were standing around talking, speaking Spanish, and finally ended up talking about why the kids in our school were not succeeding . . . really a very deep dialogue. It happens all the time. People come and sit in my office and they comment, "When have I ever done this?"

These kids don't have a tomorrow. The cost of failure is so high. It's so urgent. It's a whole prison population is what it is. I struggle with that every day.

I often ask the mom what type of support she has for her child so I can advocate for her. She may be a single mom or whatever, so I continually ask what I can do to help. Half the time when I stay late, I call parents and I make it a point of telling them something that their child did that was good.

I love this job. People ask me how I feel. I tell you that I love it. I absolutely love it. People are so surprised! Well, you know . . . I consider myself a very positive, natural, "organic" person and personality. But I really do love it. I've taken to it like a fish to water. However daunting this school is and as much as I had great reservations initially, I am in the right place.

School Context

All new principals have the daunting responsibility of providing effective leadership relevant to their constituents, while, at the same time, first learning about their school needs. This is a very complex dichotomy for any new leader and requires immediate yet measured action. On one hand, a leader must move deliberately so that she can make thoughtful and effective decisions; on the other hand, she must be immediately responsive to the situation. First impressions are quite powerful and affect perception, which can remain for a long period of time. Our newly hired principal in this elementary school assumed the principalship from a principal who was unable to relate to her parent community and was unresponsive to her faculty, causing considerable resistance.

The school was in an inner-city environment where crime rates were high and drugs and gang-related problems were prevalent. This was her first position as principal. Prior to this assignment, she had been an administrative intern in a high-achieving school with a very seasoned and successful principal as her model.

School Characteristics

The school consisted of approximately 500 students: 60% Latino; 33% African American; 6% Samoan; 1% Chinese, and a few others. On an API (Academic Performance Index) scale it was a 1/1 school, the lowest academic rating. The school achieved the lowest absolute test scores as well as the lowest scores relative to those with similar demographics.

School Climate

The previous administrator was extremely unprepared to deal with the considerable needs of the school. She was also very concerned about safety issues and made decisions that greatly restricted access to the school by the faculty and school community in order to provide a more secure environment. Upon her assignment to the school, she had requested that she not be placed in this administrative position and be transferred to another school. Her request was refused by the district office. There was considerable antipathy between her and the school personnel.

School Organization

The school district had a student population formula that would provide administrative support, such as an additional assistant principal, if there were a sufficient number of students. With an attendance of approximately 500, the school would have been assigned an additional administrator. But this elementary school had fewer than the minimum number of students, so only one administrator, the principal, was responsible for the oversight of the school.

Interview

The following interview was conducted during the principal's 1st week on the job.

Dubin:

Could you tell me a little about your background, preparation, and training?

Principal:

Well, I was trained as a bilingual teacher. That was my initial teaching credential. I worked as a teacher for about 15 years in a large unified school district. As a teacher, I always took a leadership role in my school. One year, my principal was sick and I assumed the TSAP (teacher serving as principal) position for that year and served for 2 years as principal/administrator. Then the district started the internship administrative program, and they begged me to and insisted that I enroll, although I really wanted to go back into my classroom. I was placed in a school with 500 children in a very high-performing school, one of the highest-performing schools in the city. It served extremely well in terms of my training. . . . In fact, while I was there I didn't realize what training I was getting. But now that I am an administrator and have been placed in one of the lowest-performing schools in California, I can see that last year's training was really influential.

This is my 1st year, not as a principal intern, but as the principal. I stand alone.

Dubin:

Tell me about the school you are currently in.

Principal:

Certainly. It is 60% Latino, 33% African American, which leaves approximately 7% Samoan, Chinese kids, and very few others. There are close to 500 children. On an API (academic performance index) scale it is a 1/1 school. That is the lowest possible score. The first category is academic, but the second category is a matched score with similar schools, that is, similar composition, parent education, student population, etc. That is the more distressing score. I'm far more concerned about that score than the academic one because there are many schools which achieve a 1 academically, but the second score compares us to similarly ranked schools, yet we're still a 1.

We have mostly black and brown children, a strong bilingual program, strong teachers. There are more National Board teachers in my school than any other school in the city and six more are going to qualify, or starting the process to become nationally certificated. I'm really thrilled about that. The staff is deeply committed, but it's a hard population of kids. They are bused in and are the product of a very compromised life situation. They're melting down. They're really melting down. Not only must I deal with the overwhelming number of children, but as the only site administrator I must manage a lot of staff: 36 certificated teachers, 10 paraprofessionals, special education, the list goes on and on. There are just so many people.

Dubin:

In light of this being your 1st year, although as you've indicated you've had some experience, what would you say your priorities are for this year (this being within the context of the 1st month of the school year)?

Principal:

It's interesting because my priorities certainly shift from week to week. I have to give you a little more background on what has happened in this school in order to understand my priorities. This is a school that has had a high teacher-turnover rate. That is one of the problems with under-performing schools. It's called a STAR school, if they're at that under-performing level. One of the unfortunate characteristics with STAR schools is that teachers do not stay. Hopefully, I have a group now that is committed and will be the majority. But one of the other problems is consistent leadership. They've had three or four different principals in the past 5 years; three in the last 3 years. The last principal, before me, was placed here 2 days before school opened. She hated it and went to her supervisors and asked to get out of the school within 2 days of working. They refused her. The staff really disliked her (perhaps hated, although that is a strong word). It was horrible. She did things . . . well, let me explain.

It's in a marginal neighborhood; day laborers up and down the street. She had a different background from this population, not Latina or African American. She was not used to the neighborhood. Before school opened, she went into the school before the teachers came back from summer break and changed all the locks. When they returned, the doors were completely locked, and throughout the year she never provided the teachers with a key. They were pretty much locked out for the whole year. They could only be there when she was there. They arbitrated. They went to the superintendent over and over. She even locked the front door of the school. The parents had to take their baby carriages to the back in order to enter. She maintained that it was for security purposes. There was such bad blood.

Dubin:

That gives me a better sense of what transpired prior to your interviewing for the job.

Principal:

Again, I did not want to interview for this school. I thought it was too big of a challenge for me to take a STAR school with 500 children with no assistant principal. Presently, I'm doing double, triple, quadruple the job my colleagues are doing. During the interview for an administrative position, I knew this was a possibility and I didn't want it. I was dismayed when I was offered the position, but the school insisted that they have me.

The superintendent agreed and supported the school request. So I walked into a situation where teachers were not treated professionally, nor with consistent leadership, for many, many years. All the previous principals have come down in a very heavy-handed way, top-down management: "It's 'my way'; this is the way we do things." Well, the change for the people in the building has always been abrupt and hard.

Dubin:

So, with this incredible background and emotions so stark, how did you identify your priorities?

Principal:

My priority, therefore, has been to build community, although I do not see that changing much this year. They need trust; they need to feel that I trust them. I need to treat them like professionals, and this is a staff that really, really needs to feel like professionals again. They've been in such a bad situation.

The children were also aware of this. When I visited them in the spring last year, they knew of the problems with the principal. During the interview period and during my visits to the school, the children would run up and hug me and say, "Would you be our principal?" As you can imagine, it was very charged and emotional.

So it's really a process right now of building community. That is my focus, my overriding focus, for the year. It's not just building community for the teachers but for the students also. There must be an entire community enhancement regarding teaching and learning because they've been a fractured staff and student body.

Dubin:

That's a clear and focused response, and I appreciate how that need overrides everything else.

Principal:

Overrides everything else because I won't be able to do anything unless I can create that bond. And the first thing I did was to tell the teachers that I was here to stay. I told them that I would not leave after this year unless they take me out. I'm not leaving. I've made a commitment to stay for at least 3 years even though it's a great challenge. I come from the teaching ranks and have seen what happens to professionals. Listen, we're not paid very much, our worth anyway. But the one thing that can happen is that I can treat them like professionals. Over the years, these teachers went to conferences and paid for them by using their sick days. They wanted to learn. They wanted to improve. They made every effort on their own, without administrative support or acknowledgment. The place just wasn't run professionally. And that's my biggest priority.

There is, though, another important priority that focuses on teaching. I'm referring to the very low test scores. This school has been pounded on the hand, over and over, to raise the scores . . . raise the scores. . . . They keep throwing administrators in here to raise the scores. Well, one of the things that has happened in the school is that the teachers have been very conscientious and carved it down to needing to work on the basics, that is, reading, writing, and arithmetic. At the moment, they're just doing math and reading. We have three reading recovery teachers here, and unfortunately, but necessarily, everything else is falling by the wayside, for example, arts, music, science, social sciences. The end result is a concentration on improving test scores, but I feel that the soul of the school is missing.

Dubin:

So the whole psychology of the school is undergoing a metamorphosis.

Principal:

Yes. Let me say something else that may help to clarify my feelings.

Fun. The school is not fun. It's not that beautiful, wonderful place it should be. You just don't see that. So my second priority, not even second really, in addition to building trust is to build structures. Put things in place that give children success, something they can be successful at.

Dubin:

I see.

Principal:

I know that when they're failing at reading and failing at math and they have nothing else all day, they do not have a chance to be successful. One of the ways I'm dealing with this concept of fun is at recess or at lunchtime. I have five or six big soccer games going on or basketball games. And, let me tell you, I don't have nearly as many fights in the yards as before because they are being successful. I have to build in successes into their day so they have some hope so that when they finally get to reading and math they can successfully do something. I started a sing-along every 2 weeks; I get the entire school into the auditorium. We all sing together, and it's been very successful.

Something very interesting happened this past Friday. I had a teacher who used the sing-along as a punishment and decided not to bring her children to the auditorium. They were acting up, so she said that they couldn't come. It was the first time I used my administrative authority. I told the teacher that she could not use the sing-along session as a punishment. You can bench them, give them homework, "time-out" them, but not this. I knew that this one small thing, this singing together, was hitting so many bases. We are giving them something that they felt successful about, something they felt good about. We are creating community; we are creating a happy place.

I feel very strongly about this. I must give these children success and build community through school structures. And I'm trying to do this in every instance. Everything I can see . . . because these kids need to be successful at anything because they've been so unsuccessful. It's been such a downward spiral.

Dubin:

I understand the rationale behind it. You're trying to make it holistic and deal with the complete child. You're trying to provide the base that they unfortunately don't have.

Did you get back to that teacher and tell her what you were thinking?

Principal:

Yes. I told her that she was not to use the sing-along in this way. In retrospect, I may have been a bit abrasive, and she may have needed more of a rationale. Still, I went on to explain about the children's need for success, that we've got to have these things in place, and why she couldn't use the sing-along in this way. She understood, but let me add something about her. She is not a credentialed teacher. She's struggling with a highly impacted student population. But, nonetheless, she seemed to understand.

I thought about this exchange with her a lot. I haven't stopped thinking about it. I'll probably write a letter today (Sunday morning), asking to talk to her about it. I really do think she understood, but she also needs to understand the deeper issues involved with these children.

These kids live in the projects (lower-income housing), and I have often driven to their homes. I've been out there many times. It's abysmal where these kids are coming from. She needs to understand all of it.

Dubin:

I see. And so you are really trying to provide the foundation, giving these students support and also focusing on what might be helpful in reinforcing some of the academic expectations of the district.

In several ways you've stated how you're going about doing that. Could you tell me more about those strategies?

Principal:

One of the things that happens in a school like this relates to discipline. The school is so out of control that discipline almost becomes the curriculum. It becomes like a curricular task. When the teachers wrote their academic plan last year, discipline was their overriding focus, and it looked like a subject. It actually competed for funds and time. I'm very concerned about that and how it can effect the time spent on academics. I was a good teacher and I know that discipline can really come through your curriculum. It does not have to be a subject unto itself. It should be embedded in the subject area. This school has struggled so hard with discipline it is competing as a curricular area. I need the teachers to look at differentiated instruction. They need to look at the population, in a cultural context, so that the techniques they use will be more relevant, for example, more hands-on, more kinesthetic, more time out of their seats.

The classes where I have the deepest concerns are where you have rows, rather than centers, and the children are looking directly at the teacher. The teacher is so worried about discipline and order and that everything could fall apart. As I mentioned, I'm trying to get rid of discipline as a curriculum. Recently, in this district, a new math adoption was accepted, and I'm trying to use it as a vehicle to train and refocus on instruction. Everyone has to be engaged in it. I also have an instructional reform facilitator; STAR schools receive such support. This is a person who encourages, models, and pushes curriculum. It's a perfect situation for me since I am a new person: an "open-door" principal. He's a peer, they respect him, and I'm using him as a vehicle to get the curriculum to the teachers. I can say that he and I have had discussions and we need to look at the standards, benchmarks anchored to the curriculum. This happens in all schools, even high-performing schools such as the one I had worked in last year.

Questions have been raised about whether the standards would be too hard for these kids. Well, at low-performing schools where students are two or three grade levels behind, it is understandable that questions will be raised asking whether or not the students are up to it. I have to constantly say that the students can do that; yes, they are able to attain those standards.

We had to differentiate the curriculum and scaffold and strategize to get those kids there. Now, we're not there yet because, as I said, we're analyzing the data. I do not know completely what the data will reflect, but we (the staff) need to pick one standard that we all can focus on, for example, math and/or reading, and hooking something to one standard and learn how to use the standard to anchor and develop benchmarks. I think it's a good strategy to work on just one.

But I must say that it is extremely difficult for me to handle it alone. I'm just so darn busy. While I understand this is my curriculum leadership role, I spend 15 to 16 hours per day doing something else that has to be done as opposed to curriculum leadership, which is what I love. I utilize three literacy specialists, and the upper grades are being trained on a very good reading program. Next year everyone will get it.

Dubin:

What about observations and evaluations of teachers?

Principal:

Unfortunately, at this school, no one's been evaluated in several years. I have 27 people to evaluate this year. Imagine, asking a new administrator. . . . My colleagues, that is, my friends who are principals, well they have about 12 or 13 people on their staffs and only one-third need to be evaluated. Twenty-seven people is a little overwhelming. But I am going to use the evaluation process for me to leverage some kind of coaching or instruction and focus on two to four different areas. I will focus on science and math. I see the evaluator role as a person like a lead teacher or expert teacher, a coach to help them see what their best teaching practices are or where they need to go. Constructive criticism, not a top-down approach. I'm going to take that tact because I have so many observations to do. I'll use this as another vehicle to focus on instruction.

You know, when I say that the kids have little in which they are successful, let me tell you, though, these kids are incredibly successful in science. Science units adopted in this district are all hands-on; they are super-engaging. I have never seen teachers use it properly and children not succeed and be engaged. It's the same concept as the assemblies I mentioned earlier. We have many manipulatives . . . those things that somehow became discarded in the past and those things I want to bring back. I want to ensure that these things are deeply embedded in the school day. You know, when I was in the high-performing school, that's exactly what I saw.

Dubin:

Let me step back for a second because you've raised so many important points that I want to touch upon. You mentioned that you have around 500 students in the school, and you're the only administrator.

Principal:

Can you believe it?

Dubin:

In light of this school and its history and its need, and you being identified as the person that they really wanted to provide the necessary leadership . . . and, as an example, one of your assignments is to evaluate the 27 staff this year, on and on, is there any way for you to negotiate with the district for additional support? You mentioned the curriculum facilitator/collaborator as someone to talk with, but that seems almost happenstance, that is, the new textbook adoption and that's why that person is there. Is there any mechanism for you to be more supported in the light of this overwhelming task?

Principal:

No. This summer I wrote a letter to the superintendent, but unfortunately the school must have a population of approximately 500 children, and we fall beneath that number [$n=474$]. If we exceeded 500 children, we would be eligible for an administrative intern. I tell you, I wonder whether it would be good for me and/or good for an administrative intern training with a new administrator. It would not be the best spot for an intern. But I knew . . . another physical body . . . when I tell you I'm doing 14 to 16 hours a day on things other than visiting a teacher's classroom and dealing with curriculum. People line up at my office door . . . "Can I get a minute?" It's insane. It looks like a darn doctor's office. Let alone all the paper. No. There's no more support. There's no more support. There's no more I can do. I wrote a letter to the superintendent and I explained the situation regarding this under-performing school and that it's been a hellhole.

Listen. You see, the district went to a new budget based upon the per capita child. It's based upon what the child brings, so to speak. For example, if the child is a special education student, or English language learner, you get a certain amount of funding for each child. Now these funds used to be disbursed centrally, but now they're at site. It is the site decision to staff your school. So if you want an assistant principal, for example, you have to buy it out of your site money. Last year, the staff purchased another teacher to reduce class size for Grades 4 and 5. This was a very good strategy. On the other hand, I've spoken with middle school administrators who have two administrators; four counselors and have 500 kids. You can't believe it. Do you see what is going on?

Dubin:

Yes. I understand.

Principal:

And so I wrote a very impassioned letter. Unfortunately, it was ignored. I desperately need somebody else out here.

And even the physical plant. It's a three-story building. It's huge, immense. If anything were to affect my ability to remain in this job, it would be the physical demands from walking up and down these steps, 20 or 30 times a day. I tell you that my feet, the soles of my feet hurt, physically hurt, because of the building. In fact, that's what the last principal said.

Also, it's totally out of compliance. It does not have an elevator. I can't tell you how difficult it was handling the adoption of the new textbooks. It was the worst hell in the world. It is physically daunting just to move textbooks from floor to floor, and I'm here by myself.

Dubin:

So, in other words, this formula, which in one respect gives you the opportunity to make decisions, might be a good strategy, although there are so many needs it simply can't be spread around. Clearly, you need another administrator or someone who can assist you, yet it is understandable that getting another teacher to reduce class size is perfectly reasonable also.

Principal:

Absolutely. Both.

Dubin:

Let me ask you about this. The pressure is daunting. How do you deal with this personally, knowing the magnitude of the work?

Principal:

I love this job. People ask me how I feel. I tell you that I love it. I absolutely love it. People are so surprised! Well, you know . . . I consider myself a very positive, natural, "organic" person and personality. But I really do love it. I've taken to it like a fish to water. However daunting this school is and as much as I had great reservations initially, I am in the right place.

Dubin:

This is clear. Not only do you bring focus but also an expertise and a psychological balance that you really need to have for this kind of job. This is also what I was leading to for my next question. How do you make sure that you maintain this equilibrium and not be burned out because this is obviously a burn-out job with all the things that you've mentioned. And what would you say to another administrator, a new one, who would also be challenged in the same way you are?

Principal:

I would say to prioritize and have a backup plan. For example, there's no way I could do this in 8 hours. There's just no way to do my job in 8 hours, but I've decided to stay late, perhaps 1 or 2 nights. But I won't go in on

Saturdays or Sundays. That was something of a rule I established, although not a hard-and-fast rule. In fact, before school started this summer, I spent 30 consecutive days at school and many Saturdays. But it's just something I do want to adhere to. I mean I've stayed until 10 and 11 at night. Administrators are like that because at that hour they're alone and can get things done. But again, that's why you have to prioritize.

Also, for new administrators, I think it's important that they do something important for them. I leave my office and I know that things are not done. You do the things that you have to do: downtown paperwork that's due; you can't get behind on your deadlines. Some of it you just cut out, but it's really difficult to answer that question because I'm still a new administrator and learning. That's a question for a real seasoned person in a school like mine. What is it that they do?

I'll tell you that you must have a good emotional perspective. If you're a person who is a perfectionist and must get everything done and have things in order, well, it's not going to happen. It's not going to happen. You have to know that it's totally spontaneous, and when you get some things done, consider it a real accomplishment.

Dubin:

You've really answered the question well. You've identified that you must set up priorities and also that you can't have expectations that are unrealistic. You also must be able to walk away from the job even though it may be incomplete, and that it's OK.

Principal:

Yes.

Dubin:

What you've said is that there might be something we understand intellectually but emotionally may not be able to follow through on.

Principal:

Right. Right. Right. Right. Well, it doesn't feel good. I'm not young. I've had four kids and I understand this stuff. I can see how the district hires some young type-A guys, and they're in their offices every night until 11. They don't have the maturity to understand that you need to be flexible and roll with the punches. I think that raising my family gave me that. I learned that if something turned out a different way from what I thought and not as I expected, I managed. I do think it takes maturity more than anything in order to understand it emotionally and deal with it.

Dubin:

You're not saying anything that seasoned administrators, whom I've interviewed, aren't saying. You're really hitting the mark with that. In fact, one administrator mentioned that it's important to know yourself, having that maturity, a balanced perspective, knowing when to say no and yes. You're really restating much of what has been articulated by veteran administrators and supported in the literature.

Principal:

Good.

Dubin:

Let me ask you a question based upon your earlier comments about people lining up outside your office. You said that people are lined up outside your office and that's where you spend so much of your time troubleshooting, as opposed to some of the other areas such as instructional leadership. Why are they lined up? What is it that they need so urgently, and so many, that requires your immediate attention?

Principal:

The custodian needs to talk with me. I have two. They'll ask which one is to clean the cafeteria at 3, that it's so-and-so's job, not his. Someone else has to talk to me about keys, or someone needs to talk about someone's kids, or there's the SST or a parent wants to talk to me about not wanting her daughter drinking milk. I have mentioned that it is important that children drink milk. Then a teacher will want to talk to me about a mother who is driving her crazy and getting all the other mothers worked up. Or the new teacher needs to speak to me about her growth development plan. . . .

I'm trying to recreate my day this past Friday for you, to give you a little snapshot.

Dubin:

You've captured it very nicely.

On a different topic you alluded to when you talked about the district letter, when we talk about politics, would you consider the principalship to be a political position? If so, in what way?

Principal:

Hugely, hugely, hugely. It's political and so complex. It's political in so many arenas. For example, it's political with the community. Last year things were problematic with the administrator because she didn't speak

Spanish. This year because I speak Spanish I have better control over the kids, although it's not totally because I speak Spanish.

Also, there are many different constituencies, and so you have to politick. I suppose it's not different anywhere else. You have to work them. It's very political downtown. They are either with you or against you. They're with you if they see that you are working . . . also if they know you. There is the good old boy's network. Last year when I was the administrative assistant, my principal was able to get things done because they knew her, how she worked, and they did her favors. For me, I can't get a quarter of those things done because they don't know me. But I have another technique. I sort of throw myself on people's mercy with my openness and ask for help, ask them to visit my school and that I'll be so grateful.

I'm trying to work on my personality, but what politician doesn't?

Dubin:

In other words, knowing your constituencies, understanding their needs, and making inroads into the district as to how to get into that network as quickly as you can.

The other thing that you talked about earlier was isolation. That comes up often with experienced administrators and those first taking on this role. Could you speak a little bit to this feeling and that reality on a practical and emotional level? How do you deal with that?

Principal:

Well. I'm too busy to think about it right now. In my daily situation I'm too busy to actually think about it or worry about it. I'm just not feeling it. You know what I mean? I'm way too busy. There's a whole lot of stuff for me to know. It sort of has me in this wonderful spot. I don't know that there's a huge pressure coming down on me. I don't know who has the hammer in their hand because I'm new. I'm sort of learning things. It gives me a little break. As far as the loneliness, being a Latina helps and going into a school with this type of population with Latino teachers, going into a school where they desperately wanted me. I had the best situation of anybody in the sense that this was a school that was really messed over. Their previous administrators did not have the necessary skills, that is, writing, management. Fortunately, I have many of those skills. So that, combined with their really wanting me—my personality, my vision—these are people who are so much like me, that is, speaking Spanish. It was the perfect fit. They have envisioned an administrator like me, so they are incredibly cooperative, warm. They hang out in my office. I have a wonderful relationship with them all. As I mentioned, I have an instructional reform facilitator who I have a strong relationship with. I am not a top-down management person; I am very, very engaged.

Another thing. I try to visit every classroom as often as I can: twice a week. I have a notepad with me to give them feedback. By the time they come down to their mailboxes, I've already written comments to give them feedback, for example, the children are engaged, expectations you've communicated are clear, relevant, and so on. I'm trying to be encouraging. I'm trying to create the air of professionalism so that when we are working in other areas that require a commitment and focus, this is the groundwork to creating that responsibility. I say that word 10 times a day: professional. In this way the community is with me.

Dubin:

Yes. You are so connected with this community immediately, in their ability to relate to you and, in this context, your ability and sense that you can connect to them has provided a bond at the very beginning. This has placed that isolation on the side, which is somewhat unusual. That fit appears to be a very healthy thing.

Principal:

Yes. Absolutely. In fact, I was thinking of that this past Friday. We were standing around talking, speaking Spanish, and finally ended up talking about why the kids in our school were not succeeding . . . really a very deep dialogue. It happens all the time. People come and sit in my office and they comment, "When have I ever done this?" Well, a lot of this has to do with the fact that I'm Latina. You know. Especially with the parents, although the African American parents like me too, perhaps because I'm very direct. I often go over to their house. I drive right over to their house.

I'm very clear about my intentions and I communicate that to the parents. I speak very candidly, and I may be up in your face. "Understand, I'm advocating for you and your child." I understand. I tell them that I'm just as concerned for their child as they are. I often ask the mom what type of support she has for her child so I can advocate for the child. She may be a single mom or whatever, so I continually ask what I can do to help. Half the time when I stay late, I call parents and I make it a point of telling them something that their child did that was good.

You see, many of these problem students are around the office at the end of the day because of bus problems, whatever, and they're phoning their parents. This gives me an opportunity to tell them about their kids. If there was something that happened that was good, I tell this to the parents . . . "Calvin was exceptional today. He did everything right. I am so glad that he is here." You see, I know those parents only get the "negative" call over and over from schools that know that he is failing, know that he is acting badly.

It makes a difference and it makes a difference in my loneliness level. A few weeks ago I went to a dance with one of the teachers. Where I go my staff also goes. We're the same community. We always have been. That's making a big difference, a huge difference in terms of my loneliness.

Dubin:

Let me follow-up with a quick question: How sensitive/effective do you think you're going to be, or are thinking about, in providing the feedback to those whom you are obviously developing an unusual closeness with? Will it be difficult to be objective in order to help them develop in areas where they need to be stronger? Might that be a more delicate process when you need to tell a friend in a sense, but clearly someone working on behalf of the kids, that they need to improve?

Principal:

Yes. Absolutely. Already I have a teacher; someone who is a really nice guy; really great, but he could be a great teacher somewhere else.

Dubin:

Somewhere else?

Principal:

Yes. Somewhere else. You see, we're so impacted. You can't be a nice guy. There is no room for missionaries and nice people, nice guys, nice women. These kids don't have a tomorrow. The cost of failure is so high. It's so urgent. It's a whole prison population is what it is. I struggle with that every day.

But, let me tell you, emblazoned on my forehead is to always think about the children, think about the children. In this way, I can also say to the teacher who may not have the best teaching practices to take it off them, the teacher. The focus and driving force is the kid. Think about the children. We always need to think about the children and take them (the teachers) out of it. It makes it a lot easier for me if I keep in perspective why we are here. . . . It makes it easier for me to evaluate a teacher. It also makes it easier for them to hear it if I've put it in that perspective.

Dubin:

It's great and important that you have that kind of clarity. I would think that it is always important to hold onto that because there will be times when you'll be torn.

Let me ask you if there's anything else you'd like to add.

Principal:

Well, I would like to say that, about community, these children I'm work-ing with are similar to my own children. I think that it's really, really impor-tant for there to be a match between the administrator and the school, just as I thought there should always be a match for a teacher.

In fact, I would often say to new teachers not to take the first job they're offered. They need to wait to get the job at the school they like. How many teachers talk about problems at the school or not liking the administrator? It's not like another job won't come. There is some picking and choosing. For an administrator it's so important to have that fit, to feel that there's a fit. That loneliness that we talked about. I could never have done this job if that staff had not stepped up to cooperate. I could not have figured out the schedules. I didn't know what they were talking about. I didn't understand the building. They were talking about the east yard and the west yard. They have cooperated the whole way because they want me; they're willing to help me through this. I think it's very important for there to be a fit because it won't function if there isn't.

The last administrator told me that she will never return to administra-tion. She was always locked in her office, always locked in her office. Her staff didn't like her, the parents didn't like her, and the entire political thing with the district.

It's really important that there's an organic fit, but when there isn't, it's your first job to find things that have similarities, find places where there are commonalities. You need to find a way to bridge the community or the cultural gap, whatever it may be. I'd also like to say that you'll know when there's a fit. You'll feel it. The job will be easier to do. Your job will be eas-ier to do.

Dubin:

Yes. That mutual need. Essentially, you're saying that we're all in this together and for the same reason. After, you need to deal with the issues, but you have to be at the same starting point. That's important to discern as you take that job.

Principal:

There's one other thing that is really disconcerting regarding the loneli-ness of the position. I'm evaluated on test scores, qualitative test scores. I need to identify that the school will raise its scores 15% with the African American population, for example. I'm evaluated on a very alien, disconnected way as to what I'm actually doing at this school. And there's no one there to really tell me how I'm doing, except perhaps my secretary. And I'd like to hear it. I've always been a person who can hear that. The only reason I'm in leadership and am good at leadership is because I've always been willing to reflect and look at myself critically and push myself. That is part of my personality, part of my joy. I'm competitive with myself all the time and just like to push, not with other people, but with myself. How far can I go? How much can I change? How can I get my core beliefs moved further along in my life? It's a personal thing. But there's nobody there to tell me, ever, how it's working. So I have to look into people's faces. It's that politicking thing. I have to see. Do the kids look happy? Am I putting these things in place? Is it working? By sort of evaluating the entire situation, I internally evaluate myself. But that's a hard thing, not having anybody else. . . .

Dubin:

Yes, that's so important and it also speaks to the idea of isolation, that is, there is no one who is available to provide information, even basic information on how things function. The emotional component of simply having someone as a support person is a second component, and the third aspect is how you are doing to get some feedback that makes you feel that you are being successful. You believe you are, and you are strong enough and confident enough to have your own gauge, but everyone needs someone to say, "Good job."

Principal:

Yes. Last year, when I was mentored by a very effective administrator, working together, that was a situation where there was another intelligent person doing the exact same job. That was wonderful. We could talk to each other. But without having another person on my level . . . well, of course, I can network and I have meetings and such and that's the point of that. But it is really isolating. It's sort of serendipitous. I don't know all of my job description. Everything I do, you couldn't write it or explain it.

Dubin:

Thank you so much. You have covered the waterfront. I really appreciate the time you have taken on a Sunday. Your assignment for the rest of the day is not to think about work. Go do something else.

Analysis

This newly placed principal was responsible for organizing and redirecting the activities of a school that was in disarray and under-performing. She needed to implement an alternative decision-making process that would speak to the needs of her school constituency. She had to build trust in her staff and a supportive and nurturing environment for the children. She also had to begin integrating herself into the politics of the district in order to garner needed resources for her school. During the interview she addressed many of the general leadership areas involved in administration, for example, school goals and priorities, personnel, budgetary decisions, participatory management strategies, politics, ethics, personal goals and frustrations, as well as a host of other leadership considerations specific to her school.

Reorienting students' and teachers' perceptions about themselves addresses the concept of socialization, that is, the shaping of values, ethics, belief systems, social mores, and dispositions through formal and informal organizational mechanisms. This is an extremely important function of the school and one that this principal understood as she began to change the organizational process and activities impacting her students and teachers. We are aware that the process of socialization begins at birth; social interaction is an extremely important feature of this social phenomenon. The social biography of an infant, that personal history which individuals have by virtue of their birth into a family with a definite social status, provides a basis for identifying who the important socializing agents will be and how they will affect the individual's growth and development.

Individuals are constantly confronted with varying and diverse definitions that encompass economic, historical, cultural, social, and scientific dimensions. The social biography of school-age children includes their experiences and associations with their families and teachers, and these experiences will also be profoundly influenced by the social and economic conditions of the family.

By viewing the leadership of this principal in the context of this underlying socialization and conceptual framework, it is easier to understand what motivated her to develop specific school activities. While there were many conditions out of her control, she had hoped the school would begin to provide the environment to change the children's perceptions of themselves and to develop different attitudes and belief systems to make them more capable and successful in school.

By the same token, this socialization concept is not limited to young children. Adults also continue to experience processes of socialization. The variables remain the same. We know that many institutions that involve adults serve the same function, that is, to change behavior. We need but look at military academies, medical schools, law schools, or any vocational training institution to find evidence of organizational controls that affect people's values and perceptions of themselves. In this elementary school, the principal hoped to provide respect, acknowledgment, and professionalism to her faculty in order to gain their confidence and willingness to commit to the school mission. Obviously, this will require time, but she indicated in her interview a willingness to serve for 3 years at the school, realizing that to change behavior there had to be a sufficient amount of intense and focused involvement.

Discussion Questions

1. What are some of the key issues this administrator raises in this interview?

2. What is the tone of this interview?

3. Can you identify the changing role of the parents in this community?

4. What is her perception of the district's educational philosophy and what drives that perception?

5. Could you justify the position this principal has taken regarding curriculum and overall school climate?

6. What political changes have transpired in this district, and why?

7. What changes would this administrator recommend that would significantly change the effectiveness of teachers?

8. Do you find her comments consistent with other schools and/or districts you've experienced?

9. If you were appointed principal in this school, what would some of your first-year objectives be?

Student Activities

1. Write a letter to the superintendent requesting additional administrative support.

2. Write a letter of introduction to the community indicating your philosophy, background, and goals for the upcoming school year.

3. Write a letter of introduction to the staff regarding your philosophy, background, and goals for the upcoming school year.

4. Write an agenda for your first faculty meeting at the beginning of the school year.

5. Identify funding sources you would pursue to support your school program.

Interview Question

What additional interview questions would you direct to this administrator?

Simulations

Role-play the employment interview of the principal that was conducted by the community of parents, teachers, and district personnel. Develop a series of questions that each role-playing member would have asked that addresses the following areas:

1. What would you expect her objectives to be, short- and long-term?
2. What would you expect her leadership style to be?
3. In what area of leadership would you expect her to be most expert?
4. How would she handle disciplinary issues?

Role-play a parent information night where you need to explain the testing results from your third- and fourth-grade classes to the parents. Included in your presentation should be information about

> curriculum articulation, vertical and horizontal
>
> test comparisons with other schools
>
> school patterns and trends for the past 3 years
>
> identified learning gaps per grade level
>
> class-size impact on test scores
>
> instructional material used and newly adopted texts
>
> home support strategies
>
> report card design and information source
>
> federal expectations regarding No Child Left Behind

Role-play a different leadership style that addresses national testing preparation of students to

> veteran teachers
>
> inexperienced teachers
>
> parents who are opposed to testing
>
> parents of "gifted and talented" students

Developing a School Culture

The principal identified several strategies that would help improve the culture of the school.

Consider the following:

How do you define school culture?

Is there more than one culture that operates in a school? Please explain.

What additional strategies would you employ to change the culture of this school?

How would you know you're successful at changing the school culture?

Do you think it's important for the principal to be of the same ethnic background as a significant portion of the student and/or teacher population?

Principal Leadership Applications

At one point in the interview, the principal talks about having to reprimand one of her teachers for using the assembly as a penalty for students if they did not behave. The principal was adamant about not using the assembly for this purpose. She explained how she had approached the teacher and indicated her strong feelings about the desired use of the assembly and potential impact on the children.

Do you feel her approach was correct? Why?

Is there another way she could have communicated this to the teacher?

Role-play the conference with the teacher utilizing a direct leadership style and one that is more consultative.

Which do you find more effective, and why?

During another exchange in the interview, she talked about creating an emotional balance, considering the incredible demands placed on her by the students, parents, and teachers.

What suggestions did she make regarding remaining in control and not out of emotional balance, considering the demands of the job?

How would you handle this level of pressure if you were the principal of this type of school?

What advice did she offer the inexperienced administrators that would help them cope with these demands?

Another very important message of the conversation was delivered when she spoke of the need to separate her professional role from her personal relationship with her teacher colleagues.

How did she reconcile the relationship between herself and her teachers?

How was she able to maintain her professionalism and still develop strong personal ties with her faculty?

Do you feel that this would be a difficult role for you in assuming the principalship?

Questions Related to ISLLC Standards

1. How did this principal address Standard 1? Based upon the interview, cite at least one example that demonstrated that this standard was met.

2. How did this principal address Standard 2? Based upon the interview, cite at least one example that demonstrated that this standard was met.

3. How did this principal address Standard 4? Based upon the interview, cite at least one example that demonstrated that this standard was met.

4. Did you find that she also responded to other ISLLC standards? If so, which ones would you say she addressed and please cite specific examples.

Readings and Resources

Kozol, J. (1991). *Savage inequalities*. New York: Crown.
A powerful critique documenting the disparities that exist in school systems in the United States. This penetrating commentary focuses on the economic and social imbalances between social and racial groups.
Nisbet, R. A. (1965). *Emile Durkheim*. Englewood Cliffs, NJ: Prentice Hall.
A critical review of the renowned social scientist that captures his understanding and perception of people and their role in society today.
Rothstein, S. W. (1993). *The voice of the other: Language as illusion in the formation of the self*. New York: Praeger.
A critical analysis of how language affects the perception of social status and role definition in society.

2

Personal and Professional Belief Systems: The Ethicist

Reconciling one's own value system with that of a school organization requires an understanding of the differences between expectations and beliefs. Schools are responsible for transmitting and reinforcing ethical belief systems that reflect different points of view with equal representation. The balance or imbalance between these perspectives represents the school culture. It is not uncommon for these ethical orientations to be different from community to community. When these ethical considerations are in conflict, leaders must decide whether the dissonance created is manageable and acceptable to them personally or professionally. What is acceptable for a school culture may not be consistent with the ethical perspective of a school leader. The focus of this chapter centers on the ethics involved in leadership decisions.

Themes addressed in this chapter:

- Testing and assessment
- District policy and oversight
- Educational philosophy
- Ethics reflected in society, school, and individual
- Ethical hiring and faculty retention policies

Profile of the Ethicist

Principal: male

Age: 50+

Ethnicity: Caucasian

Experience: 1 year as principal; 3 years as assistant principal; 4 years as elementary school teacher

School: elementary; student population: 850

Well, the issues themselves are overwhelming . . . they're overwhelming in this district. For me, what has changed is that [the district] has put its foot in the door as to what is going on in the classrooms. It's affected the control that we have, how we handle teachers and everything . . . trying to get the scores up in our district. Well, the scores went up a little bit in elementary but went down in middle school and down in high school. So the district is all over us. What's happening in elementary school is that they're telling us when to teach, what to teach, and how to teach it. For me that's unacceptable, but I'm living with it because I'm working here. Basically, it's the experience. I understand where things are coming from and how to do things. The times I've gotten hammered I've gotten up and not done it again or done it differently. It's experience. It's experience. I'm not like a deer in the headlights anymore. . . . Well, I think it's part of being a human being. There are teachers who have been in the classrooms for 10 years and still can't teach. I don't know how to explain it. Perhaps it's innate. It's part of being in the world and growing and changing. It's not being afraid of taking a position. It's not being afraid of trying to see how it happens and making the school work.

For new people coming in, you need to build up a network of those people you trust, who you can work with. You need to be as reflective as possible, well-versed in all aspects of the school. You simply can't walk in and take over a school and expect things to happen. You need to have resources and sources and a lot of patience and an attitude that you're going to work hard.

School Context

A basic tenet of leadership is to know oneself. Every school advocates for a principal who can articulate his vision and apply it in a meaningful and well-coordinated manner. When competing forces prohibit principals from applying their visions to students, significant problems can arise.

The principal in this elementary school had a very clear sense of self and school vision. He was personally vested in the education of children and had a definite sense of what was right. While feeling highly committed to providing a strong educational program, he recognized obstacles that prevented him from achieving his goals. The school was very challenging, a highly at-risk population that stretched him as an instructional leader and tested him as to his ethical sense of meaningful education for his students.

School Characteristics

The school consisted largely of African Americans and Latinos. Many of the students were second-language learners.

School Climate

The administrator tried to involve the faculty in decision making, although there was limited administrative support available to him. He was very concerned about the teaching competence of his faculty. He also felt that "downtown," the district office, had been a constraining weight against which decisions were made, so the sense of continued poor decisions regarding curriculum reform and personnel was ever present.

School Organization

The school had a principal and one assistant principal.

Interview

The following interview was conducted during the 1st month of the school year.

Dubin:

Tell me a little about your background, experience, and training in administration.

Principal:

I first started as an elementary school teacher for 4 years. I've been a high-school vice principal, a middle-school vice principal, and an elementary principal and vice principal. I also teach graduate courses on the university level in the teacher education program.

Dubin:

With respect to your current school, could you tell me a little about its makeup, student population, and so on?

Principal:

Sure. It's a Title I school: 65% Latino; 25% African American students; the difference being Asian and Caucasian children. The population has been changing: 10 years ago it was mostly White, then African American, and within the last 2 or 3 years or so, Latino children.

Dubin:

Tell me, what does Title I mean? You referred to this term earlier on when you were defining your school.

Principal:

Yes. Title I refers to our being a low economic population. All our children receive free lunches.

Dubin:

Does it have to do with low reading test scores?

Principal:

No. It's solely based on socioeconomics.

Dubin:

We are in the 2nd week of the school year. Could you tell me a little bit about your priorities for the school year?

Principal:

Yes. Based upon their test scores in reading and math, we're working on a new reading series so our focus will be on literacy and math. With our changing populations, our scores went up a little bit, but we're still low on the API (academic performance index). We're 1 and 1, which means socio-economically we're Level 1 on our testing, which is about the lowest on the scale. We're working on those two areas to bring the scores up.

Dubin:

You referred to API. What does that designate?

Principal:

It's the state-assigned value as to their rating of the schools.

Dubin:

With respect to administration, how would you say you allocate most of your time? Let me suggest a few categories that you could consider when you respond to this question. It could refer to working on reports, that is, bureaucracy duties and functions or school facility and plant issues, that is, room allocation, safety, personnel, instruction, community relations, budget, politics. If you could, identify what areas you spend your administrative time and focus.

Principal:

This year the focus will be on the classroom. I've been in most of the classrooms. We're trying to get the teachers set up to do a better job. We're working on more small-group instruction with them. I've done several in-services on that, so most of my time lately has been in the classroom.

Budget is obviously a very important part of my work as well as community relations. We have several faculty and community meetings coming up, for example, the SSC (student site council), but the focus for the beginning of the year, because we have this new reading and math series, has been in the classroom to get the teachers to be more ready to teach effectively.

Dubin:

You mentioned several committees you identified with initials. Could you tell me what they mean?

Principal:

These are our community groups: The SSC is the student site council. Basically because of our Latino population, we're starting these committees next week to get parents involved. Essentially, these different committees run the school and are charged to get parents involved. What we have found out is that the more parent involvement we have in the school and the more effective our relationship is with the community, the better off the kids are and the better the school is. It makes a big difference.

Dubin:

I'm sure it does. How about some of the other areas you mentioned? Obviously, the school-community relationship is important. You mentioned instruction and a different reading series. You alluded to budget. Could you tell me a little more about any of these areas? Could you also tell me more about your perceptions about the politics of either the school or the district?

Principal:

The budgets are extremely important. We have about $1 million, which needs to be specifically placed. We have a lot of programs, and each funding calls upon a different set of teachers to do different things, which require specific parameters. It is a constant battle with downtown to figure these things out. Often the language of the budget areas is not clearly defined.

As far as the school goes, that is, politics, our school population is changing. Unfortunately, we have two schools in one now. We've got our AL, alternative-language school kids and our regular kids and we've got two sets of teachers: those who teach only in Spanish and those who teach only in English. What's happening is that we have two different communities. We've two different sets of books and different teachers, and it's a constant battle in terms of funding to make sure that our AL students are funded as well as our EO students (English-only).

The politics have certainly popped its head up this year. We're having political problems because parents are upset that various things aren't getting into the program. We're short books in the AL program because it hasn't been done properly. So it's become a real political problem.

Dubin:

You mentioned AL and EO. What do these terms mean?

Principal:

Alternative language and English-only. You see, not all parents want their children in bilingual programs, they want them in the alternative-language program or strictly taught in Spanish and then English added, whereas the bilingual program is more English than Spanish. It does, though, raise another problem. We don't have teachers who are qualified to teach and, in this school, we usually have 1st- and 2nd-year teachers who are just starting because we're an inner-city school. We have problems with delivery; we have problems with preparation. It's a struggle. It's a struggle.

Dubin:

Would you say these are typical administrative issues in inner-city schools?

Principal:

In many ways, yes. The changing student populations, community involvement, teacher preparation, budgets are important issues in inner-city schools. They're important issues for any school.

The critical problem here does deal with teachers. We've had three teachers here who were placed from other schools. They had tenure but were terrible teachers, according to feedback I've received from the other schools, but were never bumped out. That's a problem.

Also, another problem is dealing with parents and downtown, with the district, because you never get any support. So I've learned that you need to spend time with someone in the district to find out who you talk to and how to handle certain issues if something comes up. If you don't know the politics, you get your head handed to you around here. If you don't know who to call and how to handle the problem, it will always be a problem.

Dubin:

Would you impress upon a young administrator that it is very important to understand the politics? Should they anticipate some of the problems you mentioned about teachers and issues about preparation and supervision?

Principal:

Yes. Let me go on. How to supervise, how to run your parent meetings, how to handle problems with parents, are some of the areas to understand. What's the best way to do this and how to have a system set up to handle these kinds of parents . . . who to go to downtown.

Another concern: books. . . . We don't have all our books in, so it would be important to discuss what the process is for books. . . . Who do you go to?

Maintenance and operations are other areas. We've got bathrooms out, toilets not working . . . all the day-to-day problems. You need to know who to go to . . . when to scream, when not to scream, where to scream.

Dubin:

Yes. I understand. In light of all these issues a new administrator has to encounter, would you set up weekly meetings or opportunities to ventilate and help clarify some of the confusion?

Principal:

Yes. What we've started this year is a breakfast for new administrators. So once a month they come in and have an opportunity to talk about the issues and problems, what's ongoing and what can be handled immediately. Everyone gets up and has a chance to talk and discuss these things.

Dubin:

How do you find them to be?

Principal:

Well, the issues themselves are overwhelming . . . they're overwhelming in this district. For me what has changed in this district is that it has put its foot in the door as to what is going on in the classrooms. It's affected the control that we have, how we handle teachers and everything . . . trying to get the scores up. Well, the scores went up a little bit in elementary but went down in middle school and down in high school. So the district is all over us. What's happening in elementary school is that they're telling us when to teach, what to teach, and how to teach it. For me that's unacceptable, but I'm living with it because I'm working here.

Dubin:

I certainly understand your frustration. Is the district moving into a different kind of program that is more generalized, more uniform?

Principal:

To the minute degree. . . . They are telling you what page to be on and what day to be on it!

Dubin:

Really?

Principal:

Yes. It's terrible. It's terrible. For me, the art of teaching, well it goes against everything I believe in. It has taken effect particularly in the elementary school. They're in the classrooms. You have to do this on a certain day, you have to do this on a certain day . . . this is what you're going to teach the kids today. . . . Well, it's almost obstruction, not instruction, not really teaching anymore.

Dubin:

How are the teachers reacting?

Principal:

Well, it's like anything else. Everyone complains, but they all go along because they're worried about their jobs and lives. You do what you can within the requirements. But there's no art, no music, no science, no creativity.

Dubin:

You say that there's no art, no music, no creativity. Is that because they're putting this aside to focus on improving test scores?

Principal:

You've got 2½ hours of literacy and 1½ of math mandated by the district. It does not leave you time to do anything else.

Dubin:

So to understate it you would say that it's imbalanced?

Principal:

That would be understating it.

Dubin:

With respect to veteran and newly appointed administrators, what would you say to them about things that you've learned? How would that conversation go?

Principal:

With newly appointed administrators, they need to focus on how they get things done . . . how do you implement this? With veterans it's more of a creative venture . . . how do you get this into a school, how do you handle this, not so much nuts and bolts. You see, it's more philosophical with veteran administrators in the sense that they understand these problems and all know that they exist. How do you add luster to the school? How do you bring parents into the school that I haven't tried? . . . This hasn't worked. How would I do this differently?

Dubin:

If you were asked, what makes you better today that you were 5 years ago?

Principal:

I weathered the storms. Basically, it's the experience. I understand where things are coming from and how to do things. The times I've gotten hammered I've gotten up and not done it again or done it differently. It's experience. It's experience. I'm not like a deer in the headlights anymore.

Dubin:

What makes you not like a deer in the headlights? There are many administrators with years of experience that are like deer in the headlights. They are still paralyzed under these circumstances.

Principal:

Well, I think it's part of being a human being. There are teachers who have been in the classrooms for 10 years and still can't teach. I don't know how to explain it. Perhaps it's innate. It's part of being in the world and growing and changing. It's not being afraid of taking a position. It's not being afraid of trying to see how it happens and making the school work.

Dubin:

Earlier on you mentioned that the position was a political position. Could you touch upon that a bit more? What makes it political?

Principal:

Especially with the different populations that we have in school today, it is extremely political and you have to be aware. Last year we had a battle between our African American parents and our Latino parents. We had some funding that was to come to the school and they both wanted it. So we had a principal positioned in-between these two groups and the district. When he asked for advice from downtown, they said that they didn't know.

You see, you must make decisions about how to run the school in light of all these contending cultures. It's a battle now. You have the bilingual program, the English-only kids who just speak English, kids who barely speak English, and kids who want to speak their primary language and slowly. You've got many groups contending for the same bucket of money.

Dubin:

Would you say it's a budgetary environment as much as a social environment that an administrator has to contend with?

Principal:

Absolutely. And the administrator can only be spread in a limited number of places. The administrator has to deal with this group and with another group and yet another group. In each case, you must spend an equal amount of time with each competing group. You have three different sets of books to manage. Basically, you have different sets of teachers and in some cases in my district, many bilingual teachers who barely speak English coming from Spain, and that's a different group with a different program.

Dubin:

Are these teachers credentialed?

Principal:

Yes.

Dubin:

I'm sure you're aware of a federal mandate that requires teachers to be credentialed and not teach with emergency credentials.

Principal:

Yes. It's been crazy around here. We've had teachers here who we had to fire because they were teaching under emergency credentials.

Dubin:

And you had to fire them.

Principal:

Yes. Unless they were in a specific program, they couldn't stay in school.

Dubin:

I see. That's an extremely difficult situation.

Principal:

I had a person with a doctorate in chemistry. Because she had the doctorate, she assumed she didn't need to worry about the credentialing program. Well, we had to let her go. She was a great teacher.

Dubin:

That must have been very frustrating in light of how difficult it is to recruit teachers in general.

I don't know that I've asked you, but in this elementary school, how many students are there?

Principal:

850 students.

Dubin:

How is that usually broken down in terms of administrative appointments and support?

Principal:

Well, [if you have] over 600 kids, the district allows you a vice principal.

Dubin:

OK. I just wanted to clarify that.

If I could ask you a different question: if you were to consider a particularly tough issue you had to face in your career, for example, it could be about a student, a teacher, a parent, a district matter, what comes to mind?

Principal:

The biggest issues for me are issues that focus on the classroom, that is, quality of teaching, tenure, for example. It's mediocrity which upsets me, and I find unfortunately that the district supports this. It's getting people to budge off of what they do, to consider best practices and teach better. If the teachers were operating with this attitude, I can take care of the rest of it. The school has programs that work well. I've got money, but what goes on in the classroom is where it falls apart for me.

Dubin:

Would you say then, if you were to restructure, you would provide more time for training administrators who understand instruction and pedagogy, to have the time to work with teachers?

Principal:

Absolutely. That is so important. Yes, and again, the teachers that are coming from these institutions are ill-prepared to go into the classroom. They are simply not prepared.

Dubin:

Would you consider changing the entire credentialing process?

Principal:

Absolutely: We've got teachers who are part of internship programs and basically are thrown into the classrooms first and taught afterwards. I've got six or seven new teachers now I'm spending time with, and they have no idea. They don't know how to teach to the intellectual spread of the kid, the small-group instruction, academic foundations. I don't understand it. They get into the classroom and most of them teach to the entire class. They don't break them up into groups. They don't individualize the instruction, differentiate questioning. I don't see any of that going on. It's extremely frustrating.

Dubin:

I see.

Principal:

And it's endemic.

Dubin:

Are districts prepared to take on some of that responsibility if the schools of education are not responding to the need or preparing teachers adequately?

Principal:

I wouldn't do it districtwide. As far as I'm concerned, I feel that this district is ineffectual. For example, in response to the struggles in the classrooms, they are not attempting to better prepare the teachers. This is what they are not doing. Rather, they are approaching it by telling the teachers how and what to teach. So their answer is less theory and more practicality, in a sense taking away all of the art of teaching. They don't allow teachers to be creative, to try anything. You do it this way or you get out.

Dubin:

It sounds as though what they're doing is restricting teachers who might have promise to limit what and how they deliver.

Principal:

And they're doing the same thing with the kids. They're restricting the creative and intellectual kids who can really stretch if they're given a chance because what's being dictated to the teachers is, in turn, being dictated to the children.

Dubin:

Are you seeing a reaction from the kids in terms of their responsiveness to this type of curriculum?

Principal:

No, I haven't. The kids are not aware. And this school, over the past 3 or 4 years, well, has really settled down. I don't have the problems I had before. I've had one referral and I haven't had a single suspension. The school runs well, but there's no qualitative change in the classroom. It is all superficial as far as I'm concerned.

Dubin:

What would you say has changed in the kids that has reduced the disciplinary issues?

Principal:

After-school programs. We really work with the kids. We've brought in outside groups to work with the teachers to do classroom management. Also, the population is stable. We've settled the teachers down so that we don't get such a big turnover anymore. The school population we had begun in second and third grades are now in the fourth and fifth grades. They have had the same process, how to deal with things, expectations, and so forth. So they've settled down. They know when they come to school what they have to do. It makes a big difference and it takes time. It takes time working with the kids.

Dubin:

There are many factors. You have the program. You have money, student stability, and consistent faculty. You have a curriculum that is pretty locked in where they are following things, one step at a time.

Principal:

Lockstep. Basically, lockstep.

Dubin:

Another principal I interviewed mentioned about how isolating the position was. Is there a feeling of isolation as principal, that is, being in a leadership position?

Principal:

Middle management . . . we have everyone beating up on us. We have upper management screaming and yelling at us, for example, timelines to do this and that . . . teachers pulling at you from the other side. You have parent groups. Isolation? Absolutely, and especially in elementary school. If you don't have a vice principal, you've got no one to talk to. Everyone is the enemy . . . not in a formal sense, but you have to watch your back at all times because everyone is watching. In education, when it hits the fan no one is around. You do have to watch yourself.

Dubin:

How do you deal with that?

Principal:

Well, again, the only thing I can do here is reflect enough to think about how it is going to work out. Again, I think that because of my experience, I keep myself out of trouble by doing things that are, in a way, not going to get me "out there." When I do make decisions, they are based upon a lot of conversations with other people and what I think is best for the school, much process and reflection.

Let me give you another example of recent parent activism. The district was sued last year by the NAACP. So what's happened now is that for most of the kids who are in trouble and, unfortunately, African Americans, parents come in with a different attitude. Now that it's hit the paper that the NAACP is suing the district, I, as the administrator, become the target. I'm stupid . . . and I'm this and that. They do not realize that these are things I cannot control. I have to learn to deal with that too. It's made a difference because the parents are much more proactive in terms of their kids. They're downtown a lot more, so it's a different world.

Dubin:

Well, this has its plusses and minuses. They're more involved with their kids, which is what you want them to be, but it also raises issues of encroachment, where they're coming on too strong, too much.

Principal:

Yes. Absolutely. And the problem is, when it comes to the individual child, we've lost perspective. It's become the school's fault. The school's not doing this, and I'm not doing that. So for those parents who have kids in trouble, basically the responsibility has been taken away from them. It's different.

Dubin:

Final question. Is there anything you'd like to add? Doing research on decision making and educational issues, new administrators and those who have been actively involved, as they read some of your thoughts, are there any final ideas or insights, philosophically, educationally, or otherwise you'd like to communicate?

Principal:

For new people coming in, you need to build up a network of those people you trust who you can work with. You need to be as reflective as possible; well-versed in all aspects of the school. You simply can't walk in and take over a school and expect things to happen. You need to have resources and sources and a lot of patience and an attitude that you're going to work hard.

Dubin:

Would you say it's important to have an opportunity to exchange ideas in the field?

Principal:

I would like time to talk informally; roundtable discussions with principals and teachers to discuss these kinds of day-to-day problems in the school, which essentially are glossed over.

Dubin:

In other words, emphasis on people in the field, speakers coming and talking about programs that have worked or otherwise, or just an exchange of what goes on and having a chance to talk about it with practicing administrators.

Principal:

That would be a tremendous help for everybody, not just veterans but beginners too.

Analysis

This experienced and seasoned principal was responsible for organizing the activities of an under-performing school based on a curriculum reading and behavioral model to which he was opposed. While he recognized the need to improve the academic skill levels for his students, he felt that the approach being mandated by the district was antithetical to his belief system. He felt ethically conflicted between his own sense of what the essence of teaching was compared with the practical pressures exerted by the district.

He also felt that the district and, consequently, the schools were victims of outside community pressures that would force schools to respond to educational initiatives that he felt were counterproductive to effective education. He viewed schools and curriculum with a more progressive and holistic approach and spoke to the needs of the whole child. While identifying problem teachers who were ineffectual with students, he also recognized the frustration of many of his teachers who also saw their roles in a more creative way and were extremely limited by a structured curriculum. Nonetheless, they followed the edicts of the district.

During the interview, he addressed many of the general leadership areas involved in administration, for example, school goals and priorities, personnel, budgetary decisions, participatory management strategies, politics, ethics, personal goals, as well as a host of other leadership considerations specific to his educational philosophy.

The issue of what role ethics plays in developing school policy and making appropriate decisions at the school site is one that administrators grapple with every day. How do we define ethics, and can it be categorized or formalized to accommodate every situation? When we consider the decisions that school leaders make regarding special education, testing and assessment, disciplinary policies, resource allocation, recruitment, and a host of other issues, the value system of our administrators frequently factors subtly, yet dramatically, into these decisions.

Ethics can be defined as value-laden screens reflecting the particular points of view of different segments of the school and community in general. To offer a framework or ethical roadmap, we then can identify several areas that might be differentiated, representing several vantage points in which ethical decisions can be reviewed. For example, personal ethics involves one's own particular view of right and wrong. This orientation comes from one's personal history and experiences. There are organizational ethical screens which, in schools, address those policies that reflect that particular district's philosophy that is made operational at the school site. There are professional ethics that reflect the standards of the profession, that is, for administrators, teachers, counselors, and so on. Of course, there is the greater society, which imposes its general view of ethics through the media and the broader political arena. Finally, there are the means, or pragmatic ethical screens which constitute the practical reality of decision making. When all these ethical considerations are interwoven, the ethical "recipe" from which a decision is determined is complete. In the context of the principalship, this process is most often undertaken subtly, often unconsciously, as the decision is made. In this particular case, the principal had a very definite educational perspective and clearly assigned a personal judgment to the curriculum and pedagogical application mandated by his school district on his student population. His ethics were in direct conflict with those of the district.

Discussion Questions

1. What are some of the key issues this administrator raises in this interview?

2. What is the tone of this interview?

3. How does he identify the new role of parents in this community?

4. What is his perception of the district's educational philosophy and what drives that perception?

5. Could you explain this principal's philosophy regarding curriculum?

6. What is his political view of the principalship?

7. What changes would this administrator recommend that would significantly change the effectiveness of teachers?

8. Do you find his comments consistent with other schools or districts you've experienced?

9. If you were appointed principal in this school, what would some of your first-year objectives be?

Student Activities

1. Write a letter to the superintendent requesting a review of the mandated curriculum.

2. Write a letter of introduction to the community indicating your philosophy, background, and goals for the upcoming school year.

3. Write a letter of introduction to the staff regarding your philosophy, background, and goals for the upcoming school year.

4. Write an agenda for your first faculty meeting at the beginning of the school year.

5. Identify funding sources you would pursue to support your school program that would represent an alternative to the current curriculum. Indicate a rationale for this new curriculum.

Interview Question

What additional interview questions would you direct to this administrator?

Simulations

Role-play the employment interview of the principal that was conducted by the community of parents, teachers, and district personnel. Develop a series of questions that each role-playing member would ask that address the following areas:

1. What would you expect his objectives to be, short- and long-term?
2. What would you expect his leadership style to be?
3. In what area of leadership would you expect him to be most expert?
4. How would he handle conflict?

Role-play a back-to-school night where you need to explain the testing results from your third- and fourth-grade classes to the parents. Included in your presentation should be information about

Curriculum, textbooks, and instructional approaches

Test comparisons with other schools

School patterns and trends for the past 3 years

Identified learning gaps per grade level

Class-size impact on test scores

Home support strategies

Report-card design and information source

Federal expectations regarding the No Child Left Behind Act

The Ethical Balance

The principal reflected upon many school factors that were very difficult for him. He indicated that the teachers were not prepared to work with children whose needs escaped the training these teachers brought into the classroom. He indicated that policy and credentialing mandates adversely affected the hiring and retention of teachers who were very successful with the students. In light of these issues, consider the following:

1. What alternative strategies would you recommend to employ more effective teachers?

2. How can he better manage his feelings regarding his ethical dilemma regarding curriculum?

3. What other tact could he employ to address the district regarding the curriculum?

Questions Related to ISLLC Standards

See Appendix for ISLLC Standards.

1. How did this principal address Standard 1? Based upon the interview, cite at least one example that demonstrated that this standard was met.

2. Did you find that he also responded to other ISLLC standards? If so, which ones would you identify he addressed and please cite specific examples.

Readings and Resources

Behrman, J. N. (1998). Values underlying capitalism. In J. N. Behrman (Ed.), *Essays on ethics in business and the professions*. Englewood Cliffs, NJ: Prentice Hall.

Colby, A. & Kohlberg, L., et al. (1987). *The measurement of moral judgment*: Vol. 2. Cambridge, England: Cambridge University Press.

Fullan, M. (1997). *What's worth fighting for in the principalship?* New York: Teachers College Press, Columbia University.

3

Maintaining Stability And History: The Traditionalist

Predictability and order are the benchmarks of a stable and controlled school environment. This perspective is central to a newly appointed principal's charge as she assumed the leadership position of a small elementary school. How does an inexperienced young principal provide strong leadership that continues a rich tradition? How does she introduce her own style while maintaining the accepted leadership approach of the former administrator? How does she gradually introduce change? What types of relationships must be developed that acknowledge past practices while introducing new ideas and approaches? These are some of the central issues identified in this interview with her.

Themes addressed in this chapter:

- Overcoming the leadership learning curve
- Starting up a school
- Keeping perspective
- Developing administrative support groups
- Accepting limited success

Profile of the Traditionalist

Principal: female

Age: 40+

Ethnicity: Asian

Experience: 1st-year principal; 1-year as intern assistant principal; 3 years related administrative experience; teacher, mentor

School: elementary; student population: 200

. . . I brought a certain kind of vision that attracted them, which was consistent with the principal who served before me. She had been here for a long time and had built up this school. She was here from the 2nd year it was built and the school is 19 years old. I believe the reason I was selected was because my vision was very similar to what she believed. So, in coming into this school, my priority was maintaining that vision, the same culture, the same kind of decision-making process.

I think they were very interested in what my beliefs were . . . my priorities are to remain true to what I had communicated to them in terms of my style and beliefs. I keep hearing that they liked what I said during the interview . . . they were impressed with that. I really want to maintain what is here in the school and also carve my own niche here and continue to move forward. It is a very successful school, in terms of the test scores and general reputation of the school. I want to continue what has been successful, stay true to my vision, and be in line with what came before.

I knew that this was going to be a little scary for me. As a result, most of my time has been trying to navigate to get the school started. I have spent so much time trying to get a secretary in place; even now it hasn't been resolved. How do I interview people, how to get personnel established, how to get teachers in place . . . how to set up the paraprofessionals.

Things like getting the bells to work after summer school was over. Well, we couldn't get them working again. I came to school the 1st day after a principal's meeting and the phones were dead. I had to go to another site to call to find out how to requisition for repairs. I spent so much time finding out what to do . . . and then doing it and following up on it to make sure it got done. The way central office appeared, from my perspective, seemed that everything was up in the air and a mess. You couldn't count on what one person told you because someone else would tell you something different. That's how I spent most of my time during the first 2 or 3 weeks I'd been here.

School Context

Assuming a leadership position successfully must be approached by having a clear understanding of the complex needs of the school and community. This newly hired principal was mentored by the principal who was about to retire. It was a school that sought a leader who would continue the school traditions and exercise a leadership style similar to the previous principal. While it is important to establish one's individual decision-making strategies, it is also necessary to move at a pace and style sensitive to school needs and expectations. It takes time to first recognize and appreciate tradition and then deliberately and thoughtfully to initiate more individual goals for the future.

The principal in this small elementary school entered the position with limited administrative experience. She had a fairly clear sense of what her charge was and how she was going to achieve her goals, based upon her apprenticeship with the departing school principal. The school was extremely well-structured, predictable, had high student success, and was well supported by the community.

School Characteristics

The school consisted largely of Asian second-language learners: 65% Asian, 35% White. It was considered an alternative school, which required that parents apply to the school through a lottery system. There were approximately 250 students. It had a history of few disciplinary problems. Faculty and administration had a cooperative working relationship.

School Climate

The previous administrator involved the faculty in decision making but in a limited way. She had been the principal at the school for many years and had a very definitive approach and leadership style that was well-accepted by the faculty and community. She had strong connections with downtown.

School Organization

The school had one principal and no additional administrative support because of the limited number of students enrolled.

Interview

The following interview was conducted during her 1st week as principal.

Dubin:

Could you tell me about your educational background and administrative experience prior to assuming the principalship?

Principal:

I spent over 15 years as a classroom teacher in this and a neighboring district. After becoming involved in many district leadership positions and community activities, I decided to take a sabbatical and go back to graduate school to earn my preliminary administrative services credential and master's degree. Mind you, this was after 20 years that I decided to return to school and get my master's degree in educational administration. Before that, what got me interested in leadership and administration was my work with the mentor teachers program. Because I had been mentored by many teachers, I decided to get involved in the mentor teacher program and the BTSA program, a beginning teacher support association. I started to support new teachers and got involved in teacher-training activities. I was really interested in doing more of that, which is why I went into the leadership aspect of education.

After I received my master's, I entered an administrative internship program that the district had just established when I returned from my sabbatical. At that point I was at the end of my master's program and ready to do an internship and so I applied with the school district. They were establishing these positions to support elementary schools that had a student population of over 500. In lieu of the district giving them assistant principals, they wanted to establish an internship program in order to give the school more support. I spent last year at one of the elementary schools in the district, as an administrative intern.

In that capacity I had a great deal of opportunity to work with parents and more students, in general, outside the classroom. I also did a lot of school-wide programs, that is, student council, conflict manager programs, and was more involved in that way. I was able to work with teachers, getting more experience with student success teams and IEPs (individual education plans). I was learning more about those kinds of processes.

My internship gave me a great deal of insight as to how a school runs and the dynamics involved. After that ended, I was actually ready to go back into the classroom because I wasn't sure if I wanted to continue in administration. I had to make some tough decisions. As it turned out, I was requested by the school district to interview for a principalship, and I did. Ultimately, I was chosen by the principal selection committee at the school, and that's where I am now. I was selected and offered the position.

I decided to go ahead and pursue it, even though it wasn't my original intention. It's a good school, nice and small. It's got a good community and teachers. It was something I decided that I would try out to see if administration was something I wanted to continue. I'm a new administrator in this school.

Dubin:

Yes. Would you say that your year in the internship was well spent as a quasi assistant principal?

Principal:

Oh yes. It was definitely worthwhile. I really liked the fact that I was able to work with a principal who was nurturing and supportive. I didn't feel as isolated as you might feel if you were to go right into a principalship on your own. That allowed me to ease into that role a lot better. I was able to work and get advice from her. She was right there. She helped me tap into resources and people that I could talk to and learn from. In that way, it really helped me in the transition in moving into this role. Incidentally, I was actually called the assistant principal, and we worked really well as a partnership. She dealt with the bureaucratic aspects of running a school, while I was more able to work hands-on in the school program. It made it a good partnership. We supported each other. We each had our own different areas where we were involved. We also had different strengths. That gave me a good taste of working with many different communities and trying to pull them together and move the school forward.

As an intern, I was able to learn a lot about the nuts and bolts of administration. I was able to learn a good deal about the community at large and be able to multitask, that is, get involved in many areas, different kinds of activities at the same time. In a way, it was very hard, but I think it was a real learning experience for me and quite gratifying.

Dubin:

It sounds like an excellent opportunity to really get exposed to administration where you did make decisions in many respects but also had the safety net of someone who really had the ultimate responsibility.

Principal:

Yes. That's right. There was always somebody you could always look to, to take the lead. You don't always have the same perspective or you may not have the same opinion. But in many ways it is important to see how other people react in certain situations and be able to step back and observe. You don't always have the opportunity or luxury to do that if you're in a school, running it by yourself. So in that way it was very good, and, as you pointed out, it was a safety net. Again, it was a partnership, and she was the final authority. She was the person who had the final approval, so you could always defer to her because she had the experience and knew how to react in a given situation. She had the knowledge and a certain kind of wisdom. You can use that experience and grow from that.

Dubin:

The opportunity for prospective administrators to have that extensive training experience as you've had is quite limited. This is something everyone would recommend to candidates considering administration.

Principal:

Unfortunately, there aren't as many opportunities.

Dubin:

Tell me a little about this school.

Principal:

Well, this is an alternative school. In other words, we don't necessarily draw from the neighborhood although many of our students live nearby. You need to apply and be selected in order to be enrolled in the school. During the enrollment period, they choose to come to the school. It's a very small school population relative to other urban schools. It's only about 250 students. It's not as diverse: 65% Asian, about 30 to 35% White, and the remaining number are a mixture of other ethnicities. We're very heavy in the Asian population. We don't have any bilingual programs; most of the classes are general education, although we have a high population of English language learners. We have 14 classrooms. We usually have two classes per grade level from K–3 grades. Then we have fourth and fifth grades. We have two special day classes, K–2 and K–3 and Grades 3 to 5. We have special day classes of severely impaired students, mostly two to six students, so it's a very specialized program for our special education children.

Dubin:

Is there an active parent group?

Principal:

There's a very strong parent community here. There's a parent-teacher organization (PTO) rather than a PTA, so they don't have to pay national dues, although they pretty much operate autonomously. There is a core group of parents that run that organization. They're dedicated to the school and do a great deal of fund-raising. The money they raise goes to the enrichment programs for the school, so even though we're a small school, we have a lot of outside resources that come in, for example, consultants.

The students have a lot of opportunity to get involved and do things outside of the classroom. We have a music consultant who comes in and works with our kindergarten and up to our third-grade classes. We have members of the ballet who work with our third, fourth, and fifth grades. We do a lot of theater and dance. We have instrumental music. Now we're exploring the idea of bringing in consultants to support the PE program. We do have a lot of things happening in the school. We also have an art consultant who works with all the classes and provides them with studio art and various activities. So there's actually quite a lot that's going on in the school. Juggling all the people that come in and use the resources has been a challenge.

Dubin:

Yes, I'm sure. You said earlier on that the PTO generated a good deal of revenue through fund-raisers. Could you tell me a little more about that?

Principal:

Yes. The parent organization usually takes responsibility for the fund-raisers, as far as I know. They don't have a membership, that is, they don't charge membership dues, so everything they do, all their activities, all the money that they generate is through their fund-raising. The first thing they're doing right now and are planning to do is a direct appeal where they send out flyers to all families throughout the school, requesting that parents make direct donations. That's one way they raise money. They also have candy sales. Another big event that they have is a carnival, which I believe they will do in the fall this year. That carnival sets up games and attempts to enlist people in the community and neighborhood. In the spring they have a silent auction. They get donations from the community, and parents are involved in that as well, trying to get donations. I don't have a good feel yet as to how that works, but that's another way they raise money.

Dubin:

Well, I'm sure with time you will. This is a very unique time for you in your career. You're beginning as a principal and you're now concluding your 2nd week. What would you say your priorities are for your school for this school year?

Principal:

My priorities. Well, I think that because I was selected by the school I brought a certain kind of vision that attracted them, which was consistent with the principal before me. She had been here for a long time and had built up this school. She was here from the 2nd year it was built, and the school is 19 years old. I believe the reason I was selected was because my vision was very similar to what she believed. So in coming into this school, my priority was maintaining that vision, the same culture, the same kind of decision-making process.

I think they were very interested in what my beliefs were. I think that my priorities are to remain true to what I had communicated to them in terms of my style and beliefs. I keep hearing that they liked what I said during the interview . . . they were impressed with that. I really want to maintain what is here in the school and also carve my own niche here and continue to move forward. It is a very successful school in terms of the test scores and the general reputation of the school. I want to continue what has been successful, stay true to my vision, and be in line with what came before.

Dubin:

So, in order words, continuity is one of the key priorities for you, to maintain what has been a highly functional, healthy, successful, and well-supported school. Over time, you would like to begin to identify areas that you could be more active; as you say, carve your own niche.

Principal:

Right.

Dubin:

How would you say you spend most of your time? Would it be report writing, or the management of the plant, or with personnel, budget and so forth? Where would you say you are devoting most of your time?

Principal:

Well, I would say that I am devoting most of my time trying to navigate through the bureaucracy in the school district. I had felt this when I came into the school; that is, the principal had retired and was unavailable and the secretary, who was the backbone of the school, transferred to another place.

Dubin:

That makes it much more difficult.

Principal:

Yes. So I knew that this was going to be a little scary for me. As a result, most of my time has been trying to navigate to get the school started. I have spent so much time trying to get a secretary in place; even now it hasn't been resolved. How do I interview people, how to get personnel established, how to get teachers in place . . . how to set up the paraprofessionals. You see, last year the district began a new procedure called [the] weighted student formula so the schools could be more autonomous with their budgeting. The school would get more money directly and more decision making as to how to spend their money. With regard to the paraprofessionals, for example, trying to establish more positions and extend ours within the limitations of the budget was something I was unfamiliar with. When I came into this school, those were some of the things I really had to work on to make sure that those things were in place when school began. That's where I say I spend so much time, so I'm familiar with those kinds of processes. I needed to spend time on the phone, calling people, finding out who I'm supposed to talk to, what I'm supposed to do, what I'm supposed to submit and try to follow-up on. I did not anticipate that it would take me as long as it did.

Dubin:

That can be very frustrating, not being familiar with these new processes.

Principal:

Yes. Things like getting the bells to work after summer school was over. Well, we couldn't get them working again. I came to school the first day after a principal's meeting and the phones were dead. I had to go to another site to call to find out how to requisition for repairs. I spent so much time finding out what to do . . . and then doing it and following up on it to make sure it got done. The way central office appeared, from my perspective, it seemed that everything was up in the air and a mess. You couldn't count on what one person told you because someone else would tell you something different. That's how I spent most of my time during the first 2 or 3 weeks I'd been here.

Now that school's begun, much of that has been resolved. Of course, now there are other challenges which started coming in. Initially, most of the time was getting the school started, that is, getting people in place so that the school was ready. Personnel issues are a little bit more resolved, although I still don't have a secretary.

Dubin:

What is happening now?

Principal:

Now I have many more parents coming to me and talking about their needs and what happened in the past . . . what needs to be done to continue to move forward. The dynamics are starting to change now that school has opened. It was pretty intense before school started. I really wanted to quit the 1st day of school. The 1st days were so frustrating because I spent hours feeling so unproductive. There were many moments like that.

Dubin:

Obviously, this is a very rich time in your career to stop and reflect upon what is happening as you begin your administration. What would you say to a new administrator facing those things you've identified in your initial experiences?

Principal:

Well. Someone first assuming this position could be very frustrated unless you come into it with a state of mind that you will get through it a little at a time. You also have to keep your sense of humor. You have to have the fortitude and the will; you have to have both. If you don't come into it knowing that you need both, it can really get to you very, very quickly.

I think that that's what got me through it in the beginning. I came into it with a certain mindset; that whatever was going to happen I was going to get through it and keep moving. I wasn't going to let one thing or a group of things get me down. I don't know if this is advice that someone can take; it's more willful determination to be able to overcome these obstacles. I'm not sure that you can tell anyone that. I think it has to be a mindset. To put into words, to communicate verbally to someone else this need for a mindset seems trite or doesn't seem appropriate. It seems that it needs to come from within.

Dubin:

That is very important to each individual to explore whether or not they possess those inner feelings and strengths that you've described. Each prospective administrator must explore those insights before they are in that position.

Principal:

Even if you have the fortitude, you need to have the will to do it. You have to go into it knowing that this is something you want to do, or you're determined to do, or at least try. I don't know if that can be taught to anyone.

Dubin:

As you've suggested, these inner strengths are realized in a different way from person to person, but listening to you reflect is a very powerful message that everyone can get something out of. . . .

On a different note, do you think that the principalship is a political position, and if so, in what ways?

Principal:

I think it is. I can look at it in two ways: politics is one thing, as opposed to having to be a politician where you have to be able to talk to a lot of different people and take in what they say . . . to make some kind of determination, decision. It is political because you need to balance all the different needs and wants and desires of everyone who comes into the school. I think that's the big responsibility. I don't know if you can call it a political position or not.

I'm more of a forthright person. I say what I feel, but in this position I can't always do that, and in that respect you have to put on a politician's face. You do have to listen to people and take all of that in but not always give up too much information until everything has been processed. In that way it is political.

It is political with respect to advocacy. Oftentimes, if you're an advocate for students or for teachers, you do have to get involved politically. This is not always an easy thing to do in the school district. While you are told to represent the school district, you also have your own feelings about how things are run and done. You need to put on a certain face for the public or to parents.

I'm not certain I'm responding to the question, but when you say politics, sometimes I think of making a balance of everything around you, having to put out that message to people because you represent some higher being. You're not here on your own. You can't always say what you feel or what you think.

Dubin:

That's a very good answer. You're saying that you must be sensitive to the many needs and forces that present themselves, that is, district, community, being an advocate for the kids as well as having a particular feeling that you have yourself, of a particular point of view. That is political posturing . . . and sorting out your own ethical balance in all of it. Being able to balance everything so everyone is served reasonably, equitably, fairly, ethically. That's the art of it.

One other note, has there been a particular issue that you've faced, in your administrative career this year or prior experiences, that is, district, parent, student . . . a tough career decision?

Principal:

Well, because I haven't been the leader of a school for very long, I think I can refer to my experience last year as an intern. There was a situation where I had a lot of internal conflict. My prior school had an excellent reputation, highly desirable, parents were quite active, and students were very successful. The new principal with whom I worked followed a previous principal who had been there for many years and had built up its reputation. When I entered that situation, the dynamics in the school had already been changing. The student population was beginning to change. The teachers at that school were engrained in the culture of the past and it was difficult for them to make changes.

There was a new administration. It was a big challenge for me to be involved in that kind of situation, coming into a school undergoing real transition with considerable resistance to these changes. There were forces that you could and could not control. There were students that were very challenging, volatile. I don't think the school culture was ready to deal with those kinds of students. That certainly was a challenge. The students had their own needs and, I believe, constituted your first priority, making sure that they got what they needed, that their situations were taken care of, their personal situations were stabilized. As an administrator, you worry about working with the students and their families.

Dubin:

Where was the conflict?

Principal:

On the one hand, you had teachers who were not able or equipped or trained to deal with these students who break out of the mold. We had teachers who came to us for leadership and follow-up to deal with a lot of these things. They wanted students to be suspended or expelled. They wanted students out of the school, but we felt that the focus should have been to help kids adapt to transition, to do well in school. That year was quite a struggle for me to balance the teachers' perspective, yet I was functioning as an administrator. So going from that role as a teacher, empathizing and trying to understand their situation, but then as an administrator trying to look at things more globally in terms of the families and what kinds of resources were available.

Dubin:

What do you think the teachers' expectations were?

Principal:

Teachers wanted the situation to be handled immediately. They wanted the kids moved away. So, I certainly think that this was a challenge dealing with the entire climate in the school; change, transition, turmoil . . . for a while.

Dubin:

What strategies did you consider?

Principal:

The way we tried to resolve this was by trying to bring in different programs into the school. We would do more community building and add more structures in the school; processes and procedures were established. Teachers who needed support were able to get support.

Dubin:

That certainly was a challenge . . . school change and how difficult that is. How many years do you think it would take to make that kind of change, that is, the new administration, new demographics factoring in the historical context . . . the need for teachers to make these adjustments or changing some of the faculty? How long would you say it takes, realistically, to develop a sense of equilibrium in a school like that?

Principal:

We started getting things in motion last year after we identified the issues and did some planning. I would think that it would take at least 2 or 3 more years. Actually it might be sooner because by the end of the year when I left, eight teachers had retired. They had been there for a long time. So there are already many changes going on in the school because of the new people coming in. There's an opportunity to build your own school and enact changes and put your own programs in place. It's already in motion right now.

Dubin:

I would agree and, as you've indicated, what might accelerate it is the change of faculty, new blood, new vision, less baggage, and more direct input regarding faculty hiring. This would really develop the nucleus that you're looking for.

Principal:

Yes. In fact, right now they'd gone through some very intensive training before school began and so the processes have begun to start. I'm hoping that after 2 years or so, things will really turn around there.

Dubin:

A new administrator can't do this overnight. It takes time and you have to be realistic. A common problem with new administrators is they want to do things so quickly, and it's just not really feasible.

On yet another note, I wanted to ask you something that has come up with other interviews I've conducted. It deals with isolation. It is a feeling that you're there and somewhat alone. Tell a little bit about that feeling, which is probably a part of what you are experiencing right now.

Principal:

Oh yes. When you walk into a school as a new administrator, or just the fact that it's a new school situation, you feel isolated the minute you walk in. It's because of the role that you are in. You're not a teacher anymore. People see you differently. I think I perceive myself differently although what I want and strive to do is continue to keep the perspective of a teacher. But, you have to deal with things that go beyond the classroom that teachers don't realize. Understandably, they don't realize what it takes to run a school. So, in a way, I feel isolated because I don't have anyone to support me and here I don't even have a secretary. I have a temporary person, and we're trying to get through all of this together. We're trying to learn things together. As I mentioned, we're both new and I try to convey to her that we're partners. She runs the front office.

We try to maintain a learning environment, make it easier for the teachers to deliver instruction. So it is isolating. You're the person who hears about everything and you're the person who needs to make sure that things happen. You can't pass it on to anyone else. There isn't anybody else. By the nature of the position itself, it already isolates you, no matter the personality or what your other perspectives are. You're the boss. You're the person who is going to be able to tap into things for teachers. They look to you for those kinds of answers. Sometimes I just don't feel comfortable that I'm the authority. I don't want to be the person they come to for little things or big things, but there's nobody else.

Dubin:

Are there other sources for you to explore for support?

Principal:

If I do feel isolated I call someone. There is a support structure out there that I've established personally. I have friends who are principals and all very good about supporting and giving me advice. If necessary, I try calling the central office and getting through to those people and tell them that I am new. I seek out help. But frankly, there is a sense of isolation. But I felt that when I was in the classroom, even though I worked well with other people.

Dubin:

How would you compare the two?

Principal:

When you're in the classroom you actually function alone, and it's up to you to be able to reach out to your colleagues and other teachers and collaborate with them. I am that kind of person who does reach out. Collaboration has been something that has sustained me in my career. So in this principalship, I have to find a new way of reaching out to people because people are not here on site that I can commiserate with and get support from and who are in a similar situation.

Finally, my own personal determination to reach out and network with other people will help me stay less isolated.

Dubin:

Would you say that it would be advisable to have something of a mentorship program, support system that would allow young administrators necessary information or just to convey questions or provide resources? You obviously have taken it upon yourself and developed your own network, which will serve you extremely well. Would you say that there should be a general procedure or policy that a district should initiate?

Principal:

Well, that's what my expectation was when I came on board as a principal. I thought I would get some support. I knew that they had mentors for principals in the past, that is, retired principals who would come back and work with new principals, and so I was expecting something like that would be in place when I came in. That hasn't happened yet, and I hope that they still plan to do that, but as of yet, they haven't.

Sometimes you just don't want to bother other people about certain things. If the person is there on site you can actually work with, then they could show you things. That would be great. I would have loved a mentor who would have helped me open up the school. I walked into the school not knowing what to do. How do I get class lists? How do I communicate with parents? No one told me any of that. Just the nuts and bolts would really have helped me through all of that. I'm not even talking about the support of having someone to talk to . . . the therapeutic aspect.

Dubin:

In another interview, a weekly breakfast was organized for this support opportunity. How about something as simple like a breakfast once a week? Or a time, some place you could just gather. You do have principal meetings, but that sounds more like business than support.

Principal:

What I have found out about those principal meetings . . . I had attended them last year as an intern. They really tried to establish a network of people. They put you in collegial teams so that when you went there you sat together with the same team all the time. In that way you were supposed to build relationships and share information with the same people. But, for some reason, that didn't work for me. I find that interesting because as a teacher when I went to a workshop or in-service and they did some community-building activity, I really enjoyed doing that, sharing information and collaborating with people. Yet, when I went to these administrator meetings they tried to do the same thing.

Dubin:

Why do you think it didn't work?

Principal:

I believe it didn't work because of the low morale of the people in that room; you could feel it. The district facilitators made you sit and read an article or jigsaw, or sit and reflect on what was happening at your school site. They really made an effort to do that kind of sharing, but because morale I found was so low, people really resented going to those meetings. They resented engaging in those kinds of activities because they had better things to do. They had to leave in the middle of the day to go to those meetings. They had to leave their school sites. Your mind was on other things. I don't get as much from those kinds of activities as someone coming out to my site and working with me. I found that last year I sat with the same group of people all year long and yet I actually didn't really get to know them on a personal level.

I think it was the time and atmosphere which was so difficult. You just felt the morale; it was so low. I don't know how effective these meetings can be because it doesn't take away from the burdens of your job, rather it seems to add more, to make people come to a breakfast or make people come to some kind of meeting where you try to get them to build connections and collaborate. I don't enjoy that as much as I thought I would because I always had enjoyed and appreciated it as a teacher.

Dubin:

It is a dilemma. On the one hand, I think everyone would appreciate support and being mentored and having an opportunity to just ventilate. Yet, if it is not done well, people see it as additional stress, artificial, and a waste of time.

Principal:

Well, what they had done at the beginning of the school year at the time I tried to get the school started was to assign a person from central office to all the sites. That person was supposed to be the conduit or the support person to help move things along . . . to identify what you needed . . . to tap into the appropriate resources. So I was very happy when they told me that this person was going to contact me and help support me and get me what I needed. What ultimately happened was that this person faxed me a list and asked if I had my staffing, with a yes/no checklist. Was my building ready? Yes/no. I had to check it off and I had to fax it back to her. So I was kind of disappointed that it was done in that way. She did finally contact me by phone and gave me feedback as to what I was doing and told me that everything I was doing was absolutely appropriate. I would ask her a few questions about whom I should contact and whom I should call. So in a way, even though there was an attempt to try to provide support, it didn't seem to be meaningful or helpful. I don't know how it can be improved, but it was disappointing the way it was done.

Dubin:

What about a retreat for a day or a weekend where you actually meet other principals before you open the school . . . a time when you can actually talk about those items that were faxed to you . . . share ideas in that way?

Principal:

That would be a good idea. They are trying to establish a cohort of new principals, and we actually did meet once. But that was after we had been trying to open school. It was a few days before school opened, and we were already at our sites. To develop something like that prior to actually stepping into the school and trying to get into all the nitty-gritty of trying to open the school . . . if it were planned out well, a retreat like that would really be good. If a person could come in and talk about how to get your class list; how to navigate through human resources to get your staffing in place . . . how to get through all of that. Not all the principals have to hear this, but we [new administrators] do. The assumption is that you have to get started, and later on you'll get the support you need to get you through it. But by then, I'm already into my job, and my mind is going to be on a lot of other things. I don't know how engaged I could be.

So what you had mentioned about a retreat is really a great idea. What they did attempt to do, prior to the opening of school, was have a 3-day principal's institute. They had a lot of people come in and talk about leadership and how to get through the new processes that were to be in place. I really appreciated that but I was really worried about how to open school and get a new secretary. At that time I was not interested in being an educational leader because my mind wasn't really on that aspect of the job. I know that they were trying to inspire us and get us off on a positive note. But, for some of us like me, who was new, I wanted to know how to access information about my budget . . . how I needed to get supplies into the school. If they could start that sooner, people would feel a little bit more confident and assured as they went into the school situation.

Dubin:

The practical things of starting a school earlier, before you're actually there, when you can talk with other people and develop that network. Then, what would be equally as important is having that connection, not through e-mail, but a real person on the other side of the phone who could even come out to the site and see how things were progressing . . . follow-up. It seems that trial by fire was the modus operandi.

Principal:

I'm afraid that it is the norm rather than the exception.

Dubin:

Final question, and after this interview I want you to get home to your family.

Principal:

And not stay over the weekend?

Dubin:

Exactly. That could come but remember it's important to balance all this, as you know. As we conclude this interview, are there any last comments or thoughts you want an aspiring administrator to consider regarding leadership and the principalship?

Principal:

Well, if you're coming from the position of a classroom teacher role, I think that jumping into an administrative role cold is going to be very difficult. I think it's important to engage in a lot of other administrative activities, beyond the classroom, before going into administration. It will give you a more global perspective. I think that that is what happened with me. If I had gone from the classroom into administration directly, I don't think I would have survived. Because I had other experiences and making a transition and exploring other areas, I was able to see other kinds of programs in education. I think that that kind of exposure was very important. Getting involved in district kinds of activities, getting on committees, university programs, community programs, and so on . . . just trying to get into different aspects of the profession beyond the classroom gives you a lot more information and perspective as you move into educational leadership. Again, that's very important.

At times, when I work with new teachers, they've commented that they want to be a principal. They might be teaching for only 2 or 3 years and yet they say they want to go into administration. On the one hand, I really admire that. But, on the other hand, I believe that they need experience and also a kind of wisdom in working in education and working on different levels and arenas. I think that it gives you an advantage, building that kind of knowledge base. I think that people considering educational leadership should try to engage in other kinds of activities beyond their school site to see if that's really what they're interested in.

Dubin:

Thank you very much. Obviously this is a journey that is not for everyone. Of course, ultimately, they are the final authority on that decision, but the more exposure they have on the myriad of administrative tasks, the more realistic they will be in matching their skills and interests to the demands of the job.

Analysis

This young and inexperienced principal was responsible for maintaining and perpetuating the climate of a small, well-performing elementary school. She understood her mandate and planned to focus on program continuity before determining what, if any, changes were necessary regarding the direction of the school. She also wanted to continue the effective decision-making process already in place at the school.

She had to build trust in her staff and provide her own legitimacy to the role, since she was assuming the principalship in the wake of a seasoned and well-tested principal. She also had to acclimate herself to the school, since she had only just begun. While she had experience at that school site, the role would be different and dramatically impact the previous relationships she had enjoyed with her parents, faculty, and students. She also had to become familiar with the district and the important decision makers downtown. During the interview, she addressed many of the general leadership areas involved in administration, for example, school goals and priorities, personnel, budgetary decisions, participatory management strategies, politics, ethics, personal goals, as well as a host of other leadership considerations specific to her educational philosophy.

In any leadership environment, understanding who you are, the community of constituents with whom you need to work, and the organizational needs are paramount. As this principal began to unravel these elements of her school, she was in the discovery phase of applying an appropriate leadership style suitable to the situation and her school members. What type of leadership style was appropriate as she assumed the principal role in the beginning of the school year could be quite different from the one she demonstrated as the year progressed. This would be dependent upon the needs of the school as it evolved and the appropriateness to the people with whom she worked. This is generally a rather fluid situation and requires considerable insight and adaptability.

When we explore the many leadership styles and behaviors, there are some basic approaches that can be identified and adapted to accommodate various models. From a sociological point of view, Max Weber speaks of leadership in terms of authoritative, legal, traditional, and legitimate roles. That is to say, a leader, by assumption of the role, has certain presumptive traits bestowed upon him or her by virtue of the position. These traits or characteristics represent the historic perceptions people place on those in decision-making and leadership roles. These translate into the acknowledgment that leaders assume the legal mandate of our system, the legitimacy of history, the parental role of tradition, and the authoritative force of power and control.

Another, more practical leadership definition speaks to different styles; for example, authoritative, directive, consultative, and laissez-faire leadership behaviors. These are realized in a specific style with the authoritative approach being somewhat autocratic; the directive more of a dialogue but with intent and a clear agenda; consultative or participative with a balanced exchange with all members; and finally, the laissez-faire, which is open-ended and allows for autonomous decision making.

Discussion Questions

1. What are some of the key issues this administrator raises in this interview?

2. What is the tone of this interview?

3. Why does she not identify or stress the role of parents in this community?

4. What is her perception of the district's effort to support young administrators and what drives that perception?

5. Could you explain this principal's philosophy regarding mentoring?

6. What was her political view of the principalship?

7. What changes would this administrator recommend that would significantly change the effectiveness of beginning school leaders?

8. Do you find her comments consistent with other schools or districts you've experienced?

9. If you were appointed principal in this school, what would some of your 1st-year objectives be?

Student Activities

1. Write a letter to the superintendent requesting additional administrative support.

2. Write a letter of introduction to the community indicating your philosophy, background, and goals for the upcoming school year.

3. Write a letter of introduction to the staff regarding your philosophy, background, and goals for the upcoming school year.

4. What agenda items would you include for your first faculty meeting at the beginning of the school year?

5. What funding sources would you pursue to support your school program?

Interview Question

What additional interview questions would you direct to this administrator?

Simulations

Role-play a meeting that the principal convenes with her staff in the beginning of the school year. What leadership style would you convey that demonstrates your knowledge of the school and a vision for the upcoming school year?

What leadership style would you initially utilize to your staff? How would this be different from leadership styles you would demonstrate individually, to each faculty member?

In light of the problems that she described when the school was opened at the beginning of the year, how would you approach your staff explaining some of these difficulties? What type of dialogue would you expect to transpire between you and your teachers?

If a parent approached you and was concerned about the communication between the school and the community, particularly at the beginning of the school year, how would you respond? What communication mechanisms would you recommend that could address future issues?

Maintaining Tradition

This young principal stated that she wanted to maintain the climate that had been established by the previous administrator. She also indicated that, in time, she would take the initiative to establish her own leadership philosophy and direction.

1. Do you think this is a good strategy?

2. Would you wait or initiate change more rapidly?

3. What are the advantages and disadvantages to either approach?

Principal Leadership Applications

The principal mentioned that the PTO was a very effective and powerful organization in the school. Did you feel she knew enough about the organization? Consider the following:

- How would you acquaint yourself with the parent group?
- Would you allow the group to work autonomously or would you set the agenda?
- Is it important to establish a greater pool of volunteer parents? Why?
- Why would parents want to maintain the status quo of the PTO?
- What other ways of generating funds for the school would you propose?
- How would you create a support system that would provide important feedback and guidance during your 1st year as a principal?

Questions Related to ISLLC Standards

See Appendix for ISLLC Standards.

1. How did this principal address Standard #1? Based upon the interview, cite at least one example that demonstrated that this standard was met.

2. Did you find that she also responded to other ISLLC standards? If so, which ones would you identify she addressed and please cite specific examples.

Readings and Resources

Dubin, A. E. (1991, Spring). The power of the second in command. *The San Francisco State School of Education Review, 3,* 43–46.
The following article focuses on the power that is vested in the assistant principal position, not necessarily by intent but by placement in the organizational structure. At times this position may be more powerful than the principalship.
Leithwood, K. A. (1992). The move toward transformational leadership. *Educational Leadership, 49*(5), 8–12.
This article focuses on the need to create opportunity for a school to gradually move toward change, reshaping its priorities by exercising an all-inclusive leadership approach.

4

Social Exchange And Power: The Balancer

S ocial interactions between members of a school organization are extremely important in determining the school atmosphere. What transpires between an administrator and her personnel affects all decisions. This exchange is constantly shifting and rebalancing in order to maintain these relationships. Another way of looking at this is in terms of power and authority. Through her relationships with her faculty and parent groups, the principal attempts to create an ethos at her school to allow teachers to feel comfortable, supported, and active members of the school community.

Themes addressed in this chapter:

- Creating an atmosphere of trust and mutual respect
- Fostering an atmosphere of professionalism and growth
- Maintaining balance and equilibrium among school members
- Generating leadership definition and vision
- Working with district leadership for support

Profile of the Balancer

Principal: female

Age: 45

Ethnicity: Filipina

Experience: 1st-year principal (current); 7 years prior principalships; related administrative experience

School: elementary; student population: 410

It is a very political position because it involves power. It deals with power. The relationship with the staff demonstrates the dynamics of power. I think a wise principal will know how to communicate the concept that power need not be used at the expense of others or to oppress others. Power should be used in order to build together.

In the beginning of the school year, I talk about the school vision. It's really a long process and it's not something you can impose upon people. It's the whole concept of school vision; it's something that is owned and accepted. This is my 1st year in this school so I've talked to them about it and why I believe it's important for us to have this vision so we could march together.

How to relate to teachers, especially if you are coming into a staff that's already formed and you are the newcomer. I think it's very important to be wise. Leadership is not autocratic but rather authoritative. It is important to listen to them and at the same time gain their acknowledgment of your leadership. You should not be a wishy-washy supervisor on the one hand, even though you listen to them, but the one who makes the decisions; and you stand by those decisions. You are willing to be responsible for your deci-

School Context

Leadership is a shared responsibility. It calls upon a personal philosophy and skill to appropriately apply that philosophy to the school environment. Extending this view to the faculty as you develop a personal and professional relationship requires time and sensitivity.

The newly arrived principal in this small elementary school entered the position with a rich and very diverse background. She was well-experienced administratively and academically, personally comfortable with herself, and had a definite sense of what her charge was and how she was going to achieve her goals.

School Characteristics

The school consisted largely of Filipino students with other populations represented: White, Asian, Latino, and African American.

School Climate

The student population was of a reasonably high socioeconomic level: parents who had been successful professionally, had lived in the United States for a period of time, and had risen to middle- and upper-middle-class levels. In this respect the school community had high expectations for student achievement and performance.

School Organization

The school had a principal and a resource reading specialist position, one part-time librarian, one part-time computer aide, and three to four instructional aides. There were 19 full-time teachers.

Interview

The following interview was conducted as she was assuming her 1st-year principalship in a new district.

Dubin:

Could you tell me a little bit about your background, experience, and training?

Principal:

I was a graduate student in the early nineties in the fields of international and multicultural education. I started my research in bilingual education and went to my school district to observe classes. The more I was exposed to the needs of our bilingual populations of children, the more I wanted to become part of the field, to be involved in their education. So I decided to apply as a teacher. While I was doing my graduate work, I applied as an elementary school teacher. My previous experience had been teaching on the university level in the Philippines and in Mexico before coming to the United States. But because of my desire to become involved in the education of language-minority children in this urban center, I decided to be an elementary school teacher. I wanted to be a Spanish bilingual teacher, having just come from Mexico where I lived for 10 years before coming to the United States.

I was born and raised in the Philippines. I am a Filipina. I married a Mexican and was in Mexico for 10 years before I immigrated to the United States. And so I applied to the district as a Spanish bilingual teacher. When they interviewed me, they decided that I would be better placed as a bilingual teacher in the Filipino education center, which is a newcomer center for newly arrived immigrants from the Philippines.

I was a teacher there for 3 years. Afterward, I was recruited to be the principal of that school. I was specifically recruited by the superintendent at that time and served as principal at the center for 6 years. Last year I was transferred within the district to another school where I was principal. This year I decided to apply to another school outside of the district, was hired, and am currently the principal.

I consider it to be a multicultural population, a K–6 elementary school. The majority are Filipino students: 48%. The difference between these Filipino students and the populations of the Filipino students in my previous district is that these students come from families who have been here for a longer time and have moved up the socioeconomic ladder. They're usually middle-class families. The majority are Filipino American families.

Dubin:

I see. That gives me a clear picture of your background and current situation. With respect to your training, what would you say has prepared you to become a principal?

Principal:

Well. I think that the interaction with other principals. I don't think anything really prepares you fully to become a principal until one is actually there. I think it is experience dealing with parents, children, and supervision. I had hoped that my academic training in the disciplines I loved so much, multicultural education, philosophy, and instructional strategies for language-minority students would equip me strongly as a principal. I really have very little time to practice what I love, to be able to be involved more academically as a principal. I am finding that I spend much of my time dealing with parents and troubleshooting with children. I spend much of my time in a facilitation role with my staff.

Dubin:

Yes, I understand.

Principal:

I wish there were more academic subjects in the preparation programs. Leadership programs focus on dealing with power plays and how to relate to teachers when you are a supervisor and, at the same time as an academic colleague, an instructional leader, which was very helpful. It's always a balancing act for me, needing those skills but also wanting more academic training.

Regarding my faculty, I usually begin the year by emphasizing the focus I would have for the year. I identify a unifying point that would inform them of my priorities as to how I spend my time and energies. This year I have defined my focus to be literacy development and math understanding. When I say math understanding, I don't refer to the book. I really refer to the critical and analytical thinking of the students. I focus on the students' intellectual and psycho-social needs. I divide my time so I'll be an instructional leader in relation to my teachers and their work, a student advocate, and involved with my parents.

I work hard with parent involvement, not only having them volunteer for activities but to understand that they are to be true partners in the education of their children. I also involve other organizations, including institutions of higher education in order to support the focus of literacy development and math understanding of the students in my school.

Dubin:

How do you do that? With all your priorities, which sound very focused and clear, how do you communicate that to the faculty that this is your priority and the direction you're heading?

Principal:

In the beginning of the school year, I talk about the school vision. It's really a long process and it's not something you can impose upon people. It's the whole concept of school vision; it's something that is owned and accepted. This is my 1st year in this school so I've talked to them about it and why I believe it's important for us to have this vision so we could march together.

I also told them it's something I want all the stakeholders to own. I asked them in the beginning of the school year what they wanted the school to be in the next 5 to 10 years. I asked for their input and for them to process this so we can finally, by the end of the first semester, articulate it in a sentence as to what our vision is for our school.

Dubin:

Let me back up for a moment and ask you how many students there are in the school.

Principal:

We have 410 students in the school.

Dubin:

How many faculty?

Principal:

I have 19 classroom teachers; one resource reading specialist; one RSP part-time librarian; one part-time computer aide; and three to four instructional aides.

Dubin:

So, essentially you constitute the leadership of the school: no assistant principal. There is no one else.

Principal:

Yes, that's correct.

Dubin:

When you look at your day, how would you say you spend your time? For example, do you spend your time working on reports, bureaucracy, or working on the management of the plant, safety issues, budget, personnel, and instruction?

Principal:

I would say it varies. At certain times during the year, we have to do a lot of reports and paperwork. For example, at the beginning of the year we need to complete a school site plan, which is time spent heavily drafting and submitting a document. It requires a lot of work with parents and teachers. And so there are peak times during the school year when it's heavily loaded on filling out forms and preparing reports.

Then, during the day, I need to be very disciplined. I have also learned that it is very important to come early. When I do, I can organize more efficiently. For example, our classes begin at 8:30, and I try hard to be here before 8. Actually, my goal is to be here at 7:45, but I have not been able to do that. When I do come here at 7:45, it makes a difference as to how I organize before 8.

I have two office staff here: one, who is my full-time secretary, and also a part-time clerk-secretary-typist. When I can, I talk to them every day about the schedule for that day, the priorities that have to be done during the day . . . especially the daily operations of the office and the school. I never know what will come up for me with respect to troubleshooting, and so at least the daily operation has already been settled. The priorities are established and defined, and my secretary and typist know what they have to accomplish during the day.

Dubin:

I see. When you talk about troubleshooting, could you give me an example of what that means?

Principal:

Of course. For example, today, after I gave instructions to my office staff, I went out to the yard and followed a class to their room because I wanted to talk with them. They are a newcomer class, 4 and 6 grades together, and I wanted to talk with them about a report I received about children hitting each other. At the time I was talking with them about this, I was called about an irate parent who was going room to room bothering the teachers. That's right, from room to room. At the same time I was also told that a new student had just arrived with his parent and there was no desk for him. I had to attend to the irate parent while needing to find a desk for this student. I barely had time to contact the custodian to find a desk for him to bring to the room.

Of course, I cut short my conversation with the parent of the newcomer as well as the class regarding the hitting to go to my office and find the irate parent, who, I was told, was in my office yelling at my secretary. On my way to the office, a teacher had intercepted me and gave me a heads-up about what had happened. Apparently, the parent thought that his child was being bullied by three other kids and wanted to go to each classroom to find the kids who were bullying his child. The perception from my teacher was that the parent was going to discipline each of the children when they were found. The teacher who had intercepted me told me that she had spoken to the man and, fortunately, directed him to the office.

And so I went to the office and when I arrived he was calm. I spoke with him and listened for 30 minutes. I explained to him what our procedures were at our school. I indicated to him that I appreciated the fact that he was trying to take care of his child, but it was necessary for him to follow the correct procedures. I assured him that I would attend to this and his child would be able to do his work but that he needed to promise that he would follow the correct procedures. This is but one example of something that I had not planned to do the 1st hour of my day.

Dubin:

So on the one hand, you try to provide some sort of structure at the beginning, particularly with your secretaries, but in the course of the day you need to be very flexible and spontaneous and adjust.

Principal:

Oh yes, yes. This is an excellent example of troubleshooting. Yet at the same time, I say that this is very much a part of my job. In these situations I really make the parents begin to understand how they must partner with us, but with certain parameters.

Dubin:

Next question is about administrators and those kinds of issues facing them. Although you're new to this school, you've been a principal for several years now. In general, what would you say new administrators should consider as they face their first administrative position? By the same token, what are your thoughts regarding issues facing more seasoned administrators?

Principal:

I know that when I apply for a particular administrative position, I would want to be sure about the school community I am hoping to join. I would want to research the type of community it is in order to determine whether the teaching staff wants to work together and with their leaders.

I would also want to know the type of support I would receive from the district. I think that this is very crucial. I would not want to get caught in the middle of having to be on the front line and not getting the type of backing needed to be an effective administrator. I would want these two things to be clear and acceptable before accepting the position.

Dubin:

So if you were to advise a new administrator about accepting a position, one would be to do the type of research regarding the type of community you were to be involved with.

Principal:

Yes. Another very important part deals with how supportive the superintendent's office would be.

Dubin:

How about those administrators who are more experienced? What would you advise them or share with them regarding issues more common to them?

Principal:

I think it is so important to share notes and victorious practices. We cannot institutionalize all the good practices that are going on, but at least we can share them with each other. There should be open collegiality. This is one thing I really appreciate within this district. I really feel free calling other principals and asking them questions about how they would deal with various issues. I think that those nuggets of wisdom are so important to share and pass on.

I also think another important role is to train future leaders. I think if we notice someone who has the potential of being a leader, we should take that teacher under our wings and walk them through the process. We should encourage them and be more proactive about preparing future leaders.

Dubin:

What would some of the nuggets of wisdom be that you've gained over the years?

Principal:

I think one is how to relate to teachers, especially if you are coming into a staff that's already formed and you are the newcomer. I think it's very important to be wise. Leadership is not autocratic but rather authoritative. It is important to listen to them and at the same time gain their acknowledgment of your leadership. You should not be a wishy-washy supervisor on the one hand, even though you listen to them, but the one who makes the decisions; and you stand by those decisions. You are willing to be responsible for your decisions.

Dubin:

And stand by it. Do you consider the principalship to be a political position, and if so, in what way?

Principal:

It is a very political position because it involves power. It deals with power. The relationship with the staff demonstrates the dynamics of power. I think a wise principal will know how to communicate the concept that power need not be used at the expense of others or to oppress others. Power should be used in order to build together.

Dubin:

So it is definitely a political position.

Principal:

Yes. It is definitely a political position. But I also believe that there is a possibility to use this political position in a proactive and positive way.

Dubin:

When you think about situations that you've had to confront over the years, is there any one in particular that you've had to face in your career, with a student or parent, that you could address?

Principal:

I think that the most difficult situation is one where you are caught in the middle. In fact, I've recently had a discussion with a former principal who is now a supervisor of principals, and she said that the principalship is the most difficult position in the district. She felt that the principal had to deal with so many sectors of the system. The principal is there on the front line yet does not have the last say, the ultimate power, yet they are on the front line.

Dubin:

When you talked about sectors of the system, what are they that the principal has to contend with?

Principal:

Well, the children, the parents, the community, the supervisors, the super-intendent, the maintenance people, the businesspeople are all sectors we deal with . . . the psychologists, the mental health workers.

Dubin:

In several of the interviews I've conducted with a number of principals, they have mentioned the idea of isolation. What are your thoughts regarding this concept?

Principal:

I was thinking of that just a few days ago. I have not had any time whatever to spend time with other principals, to just hang out with them. I'm sure that they're in the same position that I'm in, yet I haven't the time to call them to ask for some advice. We do not have the time just to talk together or study something, to have lunch together. We do not have that luxury. Because this is a new district and new school, I find myself getting home very late, between 7 and 8 every day. Where is the time to socialize or be academically engaged with other principals or even teachers? The situation is different with teachers, but I want to be available, to have intelligent conversations with my teachers. I don't have the time. The time they're together is their free lunchtime, but at that time I'm in charge of the cafeteria so I'm not with them.

Dubin:

With respect to isolation, in one respect not having the time to exchange ideas but also being in this on your own. Because you're the key decision maker, is there a sense that you're operating without any support?

Principal:

Yes. I feel that on a day-to-day basis. In general, though, I don't feel isolated. I think it depends on the district you're working with. I've been here for only 2 months and I've felt support. The 1st day they mentioned that if things escalate to proportions that are more difficult to manage, always call us and we'll be there. And whenever I've called they've been there. They've given me their insights about the situation and also their counsel as to how to proceed.

Regarding the contractual arrangement, I've asked them that if the term of the principal is for only 1 year, what would happen if they become dissatisfied? Would they let the principal go? They've responded that although the contract is on a yearly basis, their intention is to work with the principal they hire long term. This is the philosophy of the district. They work with the principal so it works out at the end. I really appreciate that philosophy.

Dubin:

Well that certainly is something that each principal should have. It also places the concept of isolation in a certain context because you're not isolated. You're feeling supported and linked.

Principal:

Yes. Yes. And to be told that they want my leadership, to be supported by the school constituents, that it is very important.

While I think leadership is very important, I do not think that it is the only factor. I think that it's very important to have a supportive staff that would be willing to march with the leader. It's so important to have the support of the community.

Dubin:

Would you say that the secretarial help is important in the organization of a school, support in a school, control in a school?

Principal:

I really think it's key. It's key because it is one very important support system for the principal. The secretary is the one who is there every day and can help make the plans and priorities for the principal. A good secretary would know how to take on the responsibilities so that the principal can manage other priorities.

I think it takes real vision and heroic commitment to be a real leader in the public school system. Of course, I am not talking about those who want to go on power trips or who want to earn more than a teacher earns. I am talking about someone who really wants to be a good leader. It is a tough job. You have to be willing to sacrifice. And in order for one to be willing, you need to have a vision and a sense of commitment.

Dubin:

I see. Is there anything you'd like to add for anyone to better understand this complex job?

Principal:

Well, I have several messages. I have one for those who want to enter educational leadership. They should do it with their eyes open and, in the same sense, they should be challenged in a positive way. I also would want the message to go to those in a position of support. I am referring particularly to superintendents and those who supervise principals. They can really make or unmake a person, a principal. The type of support or lack of it that they have, or can manifest, can make a considerable difference. In other words, principals need their support and trust in every way; the same type of support I tell myself that I need to give my teachers.

Dubin:

You've discussed so many issues. You've responded very honestly and thoroughly. You've talked about your school and issues that have concerned you and that if you make a mistake, that's OK, and the district will be there to support you.

Principal:

I think all of us need that; in any field we need that. I really hope that we can encourage good people to become principals by giving them the support that they need.

Dubin:

In the light of your experience with this new district, what did they do to groom you and help ease you into this role?

Principal:

It was very encouraging when the new district conveyed to me that they were very impressed with my interview. They seemed as though they were really interested. In fact, they spread this around to the community so when I first arrived at my school, I felt that I came with a good recommendation, even though it was the first time they met me. I think that that was very important.

This is a great favor we can do to new leaders. I would want to do this to someone who would succeed me, for example.

Dubin:

What about an orientation or retreat?

Principal:

Oh yes, yes. I took that for granted. We had that in my former district and we have that here as well. It is so important to just come together to get to get to know each other, to get to know the policies of the district, and be together in identifying the school and district goals and objectives. I think that that is very important.

Dubin:

Thank you very much for your insights and time.

Analysis

This principal was very experienced and felt very strongly about participatory management, that is, shared decision making. She also felt that the principal was the ultimate decision maker and took responsibility for those actions. She planned to build trust in her staff and a nurturing but substantive learning environment for her teachers and students.

She talked about the importance of background and training. She mentioned areas of success and challenges and the need for the district to provide that kind of immediate feedback and support in order to create school continuity. In this way she felt that there would be psychological equilibrium for everyone in the school.

During the interview, she addressed many of the general leadership areas involved in administration, for example, school goals and priorities, personnel, participatory management strategies, politics, ethics, personal goals as well as a host of other leadership considerations specific to her educational philosophy.

All relationships are predicated on an exchange, be it tangible or psychological. Exchange theory is a very useful concept to analyze the transaction between administration and all community constituents because the exchange that is generated between each party defines the relationship and sets in motion further exchanges. Relationships can be either intrinsically or extrinsically rewarding. These considerations draw people together in order to form relationships, and when these associations are found satisfying and rewarding, a bond is created between individuals.

When focusing on the leadership of the school, it becomes more complex, since the social element is interwoven with authority and power so that the rewards escape the boundaries of the social contract. This is why the principal must be able to balance the social nature of the relationship with her school community and with the power she exercises. When she desires to develop a bonding relationship with her teachers, she also needs to create an appropriate balance that defines her role in the school. This reciprocation of exchanges, where the teacher performs her professional role in a supportive environment, will be returned with professional and social acknowledgment by her principal. She may be given a formal letter of commendation and also verbal support, that is, gratitude, appreciation constituting an exchange or transaction. These exchanges are expected by all members and constitute the dynamics of relationships.

Discussion Questions

1. What are some of the key issues this administrator raises in this interview?

2. What is the tone of this interview?

3. What does she identify as the role of parents in this community?

4. What is her perception of the district's educational philosophy and what drives that perception?

5. Could you explain this principal's philosophy regarding her recruitment preparation?

6. What was her political view of the principalship?

7. What would this administrator identify as strategies that would move the school forward?

8. Do you find her comments consistent with other schools or districts you've experienced?

9. If you were appointed principal in this school, what would some of your 1st-year objectives be?

Student Activities

1. Write a letter to the superintendent requesting additional administrative support.

2. Write a letter of introduction to the community indicating your philosophy, background, and goals for the upcoming school year.

3. Write a letter of introduction to the staff regarding your philosophy, background, and goals for the upcoming school year.

4. What agenda items would you include for your first faculty meeting at the beginning of the school year?

5. What funding sources would you pursue to support your school program?

Interview Question

What additional interview questions would you direct to this administrator?

Simulations

Role-play a conversation this principal would have with a veteran teacher. How would she develop the type of balance she relates in her interview? How would she acknowledge her years of experience and expertise?

Role-play a conversation this principal would have with a new teacher. How would she develop the type of balance she relates in her interview? How would she make the less experienced teacher feel validated?

Role-play a conversation with a parent who is a member of the school site council regarding a controversial issue. How would you manage such an exchange? Describe the balancing of power that transpires as you negotiate different elements of the issue.

Developing Effective Negotiating Abilities

Based upon the interview and her philosophy, how would you incorporate her insights within your leadership approach? In other words, what specific strategies would you utilize when

You want your faculty to perform certain tasks beyond their normal work responsibilities

You wish to counsel teachers about an inappropriate lesson you observed without deflating their sense of worth

You are developing long-range planning and have very specific goals but still want to elicit feedback and input from your faculty

Why is the Exchange Theory an important concept in leadership behavior?

Principal Leadership Applications

During the interview, the principal discussed the need to interact with her colleagues. Why do you feel this was important to her? How would it contribute to her effectiveness as a school principal?

The principal stated how important it was for the district to be available and consistent. What impact did her perception of the district have on her and her acclimation to this new school? How would her reaction help support the district in other ways, for example, recruitment and hiring, publicity, retention?

Questions Related to ISLLC Standards

See Appendix for ISLLC Standards.

1. How did this principal address Standard #1? Based upon the interview, cite at least one example that demonstrated that this standard was met.

2. How did this principal address Standard #2? Based upon the interview, cite at least one example that demonstrated that this standard was met.

3. How did this principal address Standard #6? Based upon the interview, cite at least one example that demonstrated that this standard was met.

4. Do you find that she also responded to other ISLLC standards? If so, which ones would you identify she addressed and please cite specific examples.

Readings and Resources

Blau, Peter. (1964). *Exchange and power in social life.* New York: Wiley.

5

The Lens Of Decision Making: The Intuitive Leader

E ffective decision making is the cornerstone ability for any effective leader. What approaches are utilized in effective decision making? Does experience drive all decisions or are there specific strategies that are employed that help guide the process? Do leaders possess an instinctive ability to recognize the problem and act accordingly? This chapter focuses on the principal's ability to approach problems in a variety of ways: from an experiential, retrospective, and intuitive base.

Themes addressed in this chapter:

- Understanding your faculty
- Identifying significant community members
- "Gut reactions" and decision making
- Utilizing experience to recognize distinctions in school organizations and cultures
- Not overreacting; keeping perspective

Profile of the Intuitive Leader

Principal: female

Age: 55

Ethnicity: Caucasian

Experience: 3 years as principal at this site; 4 years in staff development prior to this appointment; 10+ years related administrative experience at the district level; one additional principalship

Schools: elementary alternative K–6; student population: 600; elementary; population: 825

You need to pay attention, to some degree, to everything that is going on until you find out what is happening with all the groups that are related to the school, for example, the PTA, teachers, site council, student council, safe route to school, disaster plan: there's a lot. At some level you have to pay attention to all of it while still getting the big picture. I think that my recommendation going into a job, and I did this and I still think it is quite valid, is try not to go into a situation and rock the boat too much right away. I see it happening so many times. People do that. Be flexible; be willing to change your priorities. Don't be so tight. Be a good listener.

I guess the first principalship was a real eye-opener for me. Although I felt I was very trusting of everyone at the school site, in retrospect I was really doing a lot. In the second principalship, it really gave me the perspective of understanding that I didn't have to do so much. There were a lot of capable people around the school, a lot of empowerment by letting people do a lot.

If you want to change something, make sure it is something several people want, not a few people. Does the staff support this particular change? Otherwise, even though you may have a wonderful idea and it the best thing that should be happening at the school, if the change creates discomfort before you have a level of trust with the people, then you're interfering with their job . . . they'd likely complain about you and everyone else. That is negative energy and you don't need that. So do yourself a favor, buy them some sweet rolls. Give them some coffee, you know. Paint the staff room, do something that they will like, get to know the place, build some trust. Get them to realize that you all want the same thing and that you should do it together. Otherwise, it will just create a lot of animosity and you'll have to backtrack.

You see, there are times when something happens in your school and you'll have a sense of it, for example, with a teacher, student, or whomever. Normally, the best thing is to respond to it based upon this intuitive sense.

Well, it is the best job I've ever had, actually. It is not the same as teaching. Teaching is its own thing; personal, but on a smaller scale. . . . But the site administration, that relationship that you have with those people and school over time, the accomplishments that you can achieve related to the quality of instruction is phenomenal. It's a wonderful and very unique job.

School Context

Principals must be able to balance the many demands of their school. Ideally, they must also have a clear sense of who they are and what priorities are in the interest of the school. To do this they must be responsive to all groups.

The pressure to be a micromanager can be an overwhelming need that inexperienced leaders often bring to their first principalship. They often want to know exactly what is transpiring at all levels at their site and initially do not have a grasp of the abilities of their faculty in order to assign relevant duties.

This principal's first school had no significant behavioral issues. Test scores were quite strong, and parents had high expectations for student performance and success. Prior to this assignment, she had worked at the district level in staff development.

Her second principalship was at a school far more diverse in population. She had also been pursuing her doctorate prior to assuming this position and returned with stronger expertise in school organizations and a more grounded professional understanding of her own capabilities and school operations.

School Characteristics

Her first elementary school consisted of approximately 600 students with a significant White population. There were small populations of Latino, Asian, and African American students.

Her second elementary school was quite diverse with 30% to 40% representing a White population and almost 60% to 70% representing Latino, African American, and Asian students.

School Climate

The administrator explained that in her first administrative position she was highly uncertain about the power bases in the school. It was a very wealthy district, and the children represented a more privileged population. Over time she understood the ethos of the school.

In her second administrative placement, the school was far more diverse and her understanding of her own capabilities and those of her faculty were significantly enhanced by her professional and personal growth due to the additional time between positions.

School Organization

In her first principalship, the district did not provide any administrative support, although she was supported by a lead teacher.

In her second position, there were 465 students, and she had no administrative support.

Interview

The following interview was conducted as a retrospective on her administrative experiences as a principal and educator.

Dubin:

Please tell me about your educational experience in general, as well as your training and preparation to assume a leadership position.

Principal:

Well, currently I work at the university level focusing on teacher credentialing and the administrative program. My formal training after my undergraduate degree was in early childhood education and special education. After several years of teaching, approximately 18 years, I spent 3 years in a staff development project, working countywide in specific school districts with teachers, administrators, school board members, and parents to improve their education programs. After that I went to an elementary school principalship for 3 years after which time I took a leave to complete my doctorate. After receiving my doctorate I returned to the district to assume an administrative position overseeing categorical programs. I worked in curriculum development and categoricals for 6 years. At the same time, I was beginning my career as an instructor on the university level. Currently, I am working full time doing project coordination and teaching on the university level.

Dubin:

With respect to the principalship you served in for 3 years, could you tell me a little bit about that school?

Principal:

Yes. Actually, I served for 3 years at that school and then later on in my career, I was principal at a different school; very different populations at each school. The first principalship was considered an alternative school because students in the school selected the school. It's a school of choice in the district, not a neighborhood school. The population there was very clearly committed to the curriculum and very focused; kind of a back-to-basics approach. However, as time went on, the school became very much like all the schools in the district because the level of what had to be done in

California became more homogeneous. So our school was more and more like any other school. The population was still self-selected.

I guess the first principalship was a real eye-opener for me. Although I felt I was very trusting of everyone at the school site, in retrospect I was really doing a lot. In the second principalship, it really gave me the perspective of understanding that I didn't have to do so much. There were a lot of capable people around the school, a lot of empowerment by letting people do a lot. That was a very big lesson for me between the two principalships. Also, the interim between the two assignments was about 7 years. A lot happened during that time, including the completion of my doctorate. I did a lot of studying in various areas, particularly my area of specialty, intuition and decision making, which certainly affected the way I worked with people.

Dubin:

I see. Could you tell me a little bit more about the school, that is, the size, demographics, the staff?

Principal:

Of course. The first school was about 600 students, Grades K–6. The demographics were primarily White; that is, 90% Caucasian and very high achievers. We were a California "distinguished" school. Our scores compared to the scores of the top schools in California; we were almost always in the top 3%. It was that type of school. My second school was quite different and more closely reflected the population of California: 30% Caucasian; 60% to 70% everything else. The socioeconomic levels of the second school were quite mixed. We had kids who were living in cars under freeways and kids with intact families. That was a very mixed bag, very different schools, and the kids in the schools were quite different. The second school, I found the kids to be much more diverse, more open, warm and friendly; outgoing, not as stressed out. The first school, the kids were more reserved, not so open and friendly, and very high achievers.

Dubin:

Tell me about the staff, administrative support.

Principal:

We had no administrative support in my first school. The second school had about 465 students. At that time the district had changed configuration so that the sixth grade was no longer at the elementary school, and so the second school was a K–5 school rather than a K–6.

Dubin:

Is there any formula for administrative help based upon numbers?

Principal:

Well, various districts had formulas. Our district did have something of a formula. If there were over 600 students, you wouldn't have additional administrative support, but rather a lead teacher released part of the day or possibly, if you could also use categorical money, have that lead teacher full time. This was not an administrator as a support person. I have had friends who, particularly in urban settings, didn't get any additional administrative support unless the student population reached over 1,000.

Dubin:

Incredible.

Principal:

Unbelievable. And those were urban school districts. And here we are in a suburban environment with not nearly the same issues and we're getting the support. It is terribly unfortunate. In fact, I supervise administrative candidates who are in schools where the student populations are about 400 students, and they have administrative support; an actual assistant principal. But those are in very high-wealth schools.

Dubin:

Have you any idea how the formulas are determined? This has come up several times. What is the rationale or thinking on the district level regarding the addition of an administrator? How do they come up with a number?

Principal:

In other words, how is it that an additional administrator can be placed in a school when the student population is 400 or 500 or 600?

Dubin:

Yes.

Principal:

I don't really know. I think it's really arbitrary. I think it depends upon how much the principal and parents in that community complain about the level of attention they are getting. I think that the parent community is the most important factor that could influence the administration, who would then go to the board. I don't believe that there is a real rationale as to the number of kids and what the work load might be. You see, in some settings you could have 400 kids, but the complexity of the issues are such that you need support. Certainly, if there were 1,000 kids. . . . In thinking about another principal I had worked with, well she had 960 students and had to wait until she got to 1,000. That was yet another district.

Dubin:

That was an elementary school.

Principal:

Yes. That was an elementary school.

Dubin:

And she was the only administrator in that school. She was the only one, essentially, responsible for almost 1,000 students.

Principal:

Yes. It's very scary and overwhelming and now especially, because you have the reduction in class size, the K–3 teacher populations which have doubled and the retirees. We also have interns, new teachers to the profession, who are required to have two formal observations before the deadline of March 1 when a principal turns in their evaluations. So when you increase the number of visitations and observations that are supposed to be happening, I do not see how the principals can do it.

My last year at my first principalship there were 22 teachers on the staff, and there was a point where I had 11 who were non-tenured: half of the teachers. I could barely make the required number of visits for those people, let alone the full-time, tenured teachers who simply had to wait after March 1. That was not good. You need to do formal observations starting in October, and it was impossible to do it. Remember, for each observation you had a pre-conference, the observation, and the post-observation. That's a lot of appointments to set up.

Dubin:

It's easy to see how these young principals are overwhelmed, immediately burned-out, and stressed.

Principal:

Yes. We know that many of our very best young administrators don't last more than 2 or 3 years before they find something else to do. A high percentage of them find something else to do rather than continue the principalship.

Dubin:

Let me ask you to reflect back on either principalship regarding your priorities. How did you set up your priorities for the year and how did you communicate that to your various constituents?

Principal:

Well, I think I got better at it over time. The 1st year I knew there were certain problem areas when I came into the school, certain groups that needed to be calmed down. I really had to make that the priority. The group had become very difficult. A group of parents were affecting the work teachers were doing in the classroom. The teachers were concerning themselves too much with what these parents were doing. I wanted them to focus on the kids and what they were doing in the classroom. That was my priority and, as a result, what happened was I overlooked the PTA. In the meantime, a little revolution was forming that I didn't see.

The 2nd year it really came to me. I realized then that when you set priorities you cannot completely devote your efforts in one direction, you have to look at everything. You need to pay attention, to some degree, to everything that is going on until you find out what is happening with all the groups that are related to the schools, for example, the PTA, teachers, site council, student council, safe route to school, disaster plan. There's a lot.

At some level you have to pay attention to all of it while still getting the big picture. I think that my recommendation going into a job, and I did this and I still think it is quite valid, is try not to go into a situation and rock the boat too much right away. I see it happening so many times. People do that. Be flexible. Be willing to change your priorities. Don't be so tight. Be a good listener. I was fortunate in that teachers would come into my office and tell me that they wanted to do this or that. Being able to listen to what people are saying and make adjustments to those requests that seem logical is the right thing to do.

Dubin:

In setting up those priorities, how do you think you spent most of your time? For example, were there district reports that needed to be attended to that required much time, or the management of the plant, safety issues, budget, personnel, and so on?

Principal:

Well, honestly, in the beginning, most of the time I spent was in class-rooms. I just made myself do it. I wanted the teachers to see me as a person who knew what I was doing. I wanted for kids and teachers to be comfortable with me walking in and out of the classrooms. I did that a lot, every day. The other work, reports and such, well I did that before and after school. I was there every day until after 7 almost every night, especially the 1st year.

As I gained more experience I found ways of shortcutting. One of the things I found that I was able to do was, during the classroom observations, I wouldn't leave the classroom until I wrote the draft of the comments. I originally left the classroom with my notes and worked on it in my office, but I was always interrupted. When I had an observation and was in the classroom, the secretary knew not to interrupt me unless there was an emergency. She knew to leave me alone when I was in the classroom. That's where I needed to be. And so I found [that] using the time to write up the observation saved me time later on. Little things like that you get better at.

You also begin to realize that teachers can do a lot. You don't have to do it all. I was very fortunate in both settings that I had teachers who could handle things, for example, the science fair, the technology lab, while other teachers handled a lunchtime program with clubs. Sometimes there was a stipend involved or they were just into it.

Dubin:

As a general rule, your experience allowed you to focus on accessibility, visibility, observations, and so you dealt with curriculum and instruction, essentially, rather than plant management, safety, and so on.

Principal:

Yes, that's right. We did deal with those other things. We added new land-scaping, classrooms repainted, furniture, put in power lines, and so on. Those things did go on, but I really made an effort on doing those other things.

Dubin:

You alluded to this before but, what would you say the major issues are to those first pursuing administration and also to those who had been involved in administration through the years?

Principal:

The requirements from the state, at the moment, the whole emphasis on standards, and the obvious lack of trust from the legislature and on down is dreadful. How can administrators help their staff do their jobs the best they can with this level of stress over the standards? The performance index, which is so public, is a huge deal. It affects people so they're simply not thinking about kids.

The administrative job is to help put that in perspective and to get the job done at the same time. I think if the administrator truly understands the curriculum and knows what good instruction is and has respect for that and the staff's view, I think it could happen, and they would stay in the profession. The issues, whether you are brand-new or experienced, are very similar. The difference is what you bring to it, your level of experience, and how you put it all in perspective. You would imagine that for someone who's done it longer it would be easier, not necessarily better, but with more ease than someone who is first coming into it.

Dubin:

With that new person coming in, if you were to provide some advice, you mentioned earlier about something you had learned, that is, don't rock the boat. Don't try to take on too much too soon. Don't try to initially change things, first get the lay of the land. Is that something you would want to convey to a new administrator?

Principal:

Yes. I strongly recommend that. If you want to change something, make sure it is something several people want, not a few people. Does the staff support this particular change? Otherwise, even though you may have a wonderful idea and it might be the best thing that should be happening at the school, if the change creates discomfort before you have a level of trust with the people, then you're interfering with their job. They would be in the survival mode. Their attitude would not be very good; they'd likely complain about you and everyone else. That is negative energy and you don't need that. So do yourself a favor, buy them some sweet rolls. Give them some coffee, you know. Paint the staff room, do something that they will like, get to know the place, build some trust. Get them to realize that you all want the same thing and that you should do it together. Otherwise, it will just create a lot of animosity, and you'll have to backtrack.

Dubin:

Now you alluded to developing trust first, and you mentioned some examples. Is that what you meant by trust, that is, connecting with them and getting their support? Doing things that would make the environment more pleasant, those kinds of things?

Principal:

Yes. Let them know what you know about curriculum and let them know what you don't know. They have been teaching for a while and have information, and you should be humble. Your staff will be teaching you something, and you're all in a learning environment together. It's important that that be communicated as soon as possible. Your administrative leadership behavior will be communicating that, not what you say. Everybody learns the buzzwords, and you can say the right story, but it's the behavior that people will see. They will know that you're an honest, capable person. The words alone won't be the only thing.

Dubin:

That's usually the paradox with a new administrator. New administrators want to convey knowledge and information but they also need to be honest, open, and flexible about what they know and don't know. Often, these things are at odds.

Principal:

Yes, and they need to be willing to say when they're wrong publicly. I made that mistake. It's modeling and it's what we want them and the kids to do.

Dubin:

Yes. On another topic, it's been said that the position is a political one; if so, in what way?

Principal:

Yes, because you must keep your various constituents happy; it's political. You're juggling a lot of people who are coming at you from different perspectives and with different needs. You have parents, teachers, kids, special-education personnel, cafeteria people, custodians, the superintendent, downtown administrators, the school board members who'll know who you are, the local police and fire people because, more than once, you'll need to call 911. You've got to deal with all those people. You've got bus drivers, yard supervisors, and you've got to balance them all out. You want them all to respect you and help you out because at some point you're going to need their cooperation to run that place. You simply can't do it by yourself. So you've got to buy them some candy once in a while and bring it to the maintenance department, for example. Tell them how wonderful they are and thank them for their help. You must learn to ingratiate yourself, and it reflects on your school. Everything that you do to ingratiate yourself is putting your school in the same limelight, and that's what you want.

Dubin:

Let me ask you this. You said earlier on that your research had a major component dealing with intuition. Could you elaborate on this and how it can be applied so that a new administrator could use it?

Principal:

Certainly. Actually, my dissertation dealt with that topic: specifically, principals' intuition, and I interviewed all the administrators in this county. You see, there are times when something happens in your school and you'll have a sense of it, for example, with a teacher, student, or whomever. Normally, the best thing is to respond to it based upon this intuitive sense. I mentioned earlier about my experience with the PTA when I entered the school that I had a sense of what was going on but didn't respond to it. Well I should have. That intuitive sense was what I was feeling, but I didn't follow through with this sense. I heard conversations in the faculty room; I saw parents talking with other parents outside the office and I knew the conversations were about leadership with the PTA. I heard certain names were going to be involved but I didn't follow through; I stayed out of it.

I really didn't want to stay out of it. I questioned whether or not I should get involved and ask questions. The answer was yes. I should have gotten involved but I didn't follow through because of my sense of apprehension, and it certainly came back to haunt me. I think that people who get a sense of something have to follow through in some way, whether it's having more information by observing it yourself. It could mean checking with people at your site as a reality check; whatever it takes, whatever is appropriate.

Dubin:

You would say it's a gut reaction or a judgment call.

Principal:

Yes, I would say it's a judgment call. Years ago, there was a screening process for administrators, something of an assessment center. There were several tasks, and I remember going there for 3 days and participated in these various activities. There was a rating. They were trying to determine whether you had the potential to be a particular type of administrator. There were characteristics, and judgment was one of the characteristics, that is, when to do what and what was appropriate were very important considerations.

Dubin:

As you reflect upon your career, which spans a considerable amount of time and territory, could you think of a particular or unusual issue or judgment call regarding a student, district, parent, teacher, and so on, that you could comment on?

Principal:

Yes, I can think of an incident. This dealt with summer school. It was the last day of summer school and the students went on a field trip to the beach. They were supposed to return from the trip by 2. At about 1:45, the parents started to arrive at the school to pick up their children, but the bus wasn't there by 2 or even 2:10. The parents were concerned, and I told the parents not to worry; there was traffic quite often, and it was a Friday afternoon. I kept the parents outside and went inside to my office to call transportation to find out about the bus and what was going on.

As it happened, the bus had been involved in an accident in town with a bicycle. The accident had occurred about a mile and one half from the school, but anytime a school bus is involved in an accident, the Highway Patrol has to be called because of state jurisdiction. And so they had to wait for the Highway Patrol and interview all the kids; it was a big deal. You see, I knew the kids were fine but that the bus wouldn't be there for a while. I went outside but I didn't want to tell them the whole story for fear that they'd drive over to the bus nearby and possibly, in their concern, create a problem for the authorities. At that point, the bus was only 15 minutes late anyway. So I went outside and explained that I would be checking with transportation. I reassured them that I expected that all was fine and went back into my office. Ten minutes later, at approximately 2:20, I returned outside and did inform them that there had been a minor accident and that no one was hurt. They had to remain there because the bus driver had to complete a report, and they would be coming shortly. At about 2:45 the bus finally arrived, and the parents took their children home.

In retrospect, I felt that I had made the right decision in parceling out the information to the parents. I felt that it was the right thing to do: There were no injuries, their kids were fine, and I did not want them to worry sooner than they needed to. Again, looking back on it, I still feel it was the right thing to do. If there had been a different circumstance where the kids were injured and the parents needed more information to be more involved, of course I would have told them right away. But I think that this was one instance where I felt the best judgment was not to create panic with the parents. I felt that I had enough information to give them that was accurate.

Dubin:

So that speaks well to the idea that judgment is extremely important and that trust has to be established with the parents so that information you determined would be given, ultimately, would be understood by the parents.

Principal:

Yes. That's right. It's very serious. And that decision making, making these judgments, is so important. Another general example, on-site, is if there are children who might be injured, judgment is so important. Often you read about schools where kindergarten children get in trouble. Well, you know situations happen with children constantly, and unless there is an issue with life and limb at risk, I tend to be very cautious before you rush to judgment and call for suspension or expulsion. You need to really check this out and determine the correct procedure. Of course, if it deals with a potential highly serious matter, that is, weapons and drugs, well that's automatic, that's out of your hands. But when you have a role to play and there's judgment involved, I would be very serious about it and give it some thought. You could produce the most serious consequences. You must really be careful.

Dubin:

So the idea of patience is extremely important and also ensuring that you have all the information before you make a decision.

Principal:

Absolutely. I used to have this thing called the "big investigation." I would always have this big investigation. Sometimes with certain children, you could never get the true story no matter how much you investigate. You simply cannot get to the bottom of it. Usually, after a period of time when I was checking on a student problem or story, I would call the kids to the office and tell them that I couldn't discover the truth because their stories did not align. I would tell them that I was tired and that it was taking too much of my time. I would reprimand them and tell them to think very seriously about their behavior, and there would be other consequences if it happened again. Sometimes you simply couldn't really get to the bottom of it, and it had to be handled in that way.

Dubin:

With respect to these decisions and what we talked about earlier, particularly about numbers and student enrollment, which you felt was arbitrary, would you say that the position of principal was one of isolation? What are your thoughts regarding this perception?

Principal:

Yes. There's no question about it. You have constituents, but it is very vague and very isolating. It's very important to have some kind of a buddy; someone in the district or a friend, someone you could call any time. When I had a decision to make and I was wondering about it, I would call another principal or several in the district, and we'd talk about it, and I'd ask the same question. I always got advice from people in the same position, let alone those in the district office who were in different positions. My boss was a good example. But I always called people who held the same position. I think it is very important to have a buddy. If the district does not set it up for you, I would personally set it up with somebody.

Dubin:

That has come up on several occasions, the need to have some kind of support system because, indeed, it is a position where the buck stops there. Ultimately, you make that decision, but it is important for your own sense of being, sense of perspective to have a range of options from people with whom you can consult.

Obviously, we have covered a considerable range of topics, and I appreciate your breadth of experience. Is there anything else you would like to add that we haven't discussed?

Principal:

Well, it is the best job I've ever had, actually. It is not the same as teaching. Teaching is its own thing; personal, but on a smaller scale. The level of impact expands when you are teaching at the university because you're influencing so many students who are going in so many different directions. But the site administration, that relationship that you have with those people and school over time, the accomplishments that you can achieve related to the quality of instruction is phenomenal. It's a wonderful and very unique job.

It's important to be in the right position, and that it matches who you are. The experiences that I had in different settings were dramatic differences. Except for personal things that were happening in my life at the time, I would have stayed in the second school and requested that I be a principal there permanently because I really liked it. It was great and very different from my first experience. Unfortunately, I was not able to at that time. It can be a very rewarding, energizing, and satisfying job, and certainly was for me.

Dubin:

Is it for everyone?

Principal:

No. No job is for everyone. It has to be a match. Certain characteristics are important. Being organized and being able to "short-order cook." You need to handle a lot at one time, and with a smile. If you get confused, overwhelmed, can't do five things at one time, if you can't answer 86 questions in 1 minute, if all those things drive you crazy, then it would be hard for you to be a principal.

Dubin:

Thank you very much for your insights and candid remarks!

Analysis

This very experienced and seasoned principal reflected on her administrative experiences at two different elementary schools. Her comments were quite rich because she was able to compare these experiences in the light of her professional development and personal growth, which took place between her two appointments. Each school offered different challenges to which she responded with varying degrees of success. Her administrative roles demonstrated the need for her to be flexible and understand the complexities demanded from the different school settings. She needed to implement appropriate decision-making processes. She had to build trust in her staff, provide legitimacy and a supportive and meaningful environment for her students, given their cultural and economic backgrounds. During the interview, she addressed many of the general leadership areas involved in administration: for example, school goals and priorities, personnel, budgetary decisions, participatory management strategies, politics, ethics, personal goals, as well as a host of other leadership considerations specific to her educational philosophy.

Assessing the organizational needs of a school in order to apply an appropriate decision-making process is critical. How do principals make decisions? Are there models that can guide the process? Who should be involved in the decisions of the school and should all decisions be approached in the same way? While these questions are interconnected with leadership style, we can separate the two areas by focusing on decision making in a more concentrated and linear manner.

Decision-making models have been utilized in the organizational literature, which identifies specific steps that effectively address all elements of a decision. Peter Drucker, a pre-eminent organizational theorist, offers a very clear yet basic approach to effective decision making. He identifies six steps in the process: (a) define the problem, (b) analyze the problem, (c) develop alternative solutions to the problem, (d) decide on the best solution, (e) convert decisions into effective actions, and (f) monitor and assess the results.

As we review the interview with our elementary principal, the intuitive sense of decision making falls outside the normal construct identified in Drucker's (and others') model. In one situation she describes, while she did not fully grasp the problem on her school campus regarding community and parent involvement, she sensed that something was amiss. Had she paused for a moment to tap into these feelings and apply a behavioral model of decision making to her sensibilities, the exercise might have proven to be quite fruitful in identifying the problem that confronted her and what ultimately developed into a school issue.

A behavioral decision-making model approaches decision making differently. While the rational Drucker model, as described above, assumes that all solutions can be identified, evaluated, ranked, and ultimately selected, the behavioral model assumes the opposite. For one, it assumes that information will always be flawed or incomplete, and all potential alternatives never fully captured because all the consequences will never be understood and that, finally, evaluations will never be sound because of the insufficient data to begin with.

Both models are extremely useful in assessing decision making and could reasonably be applied to this principal as we examined her many decisions described in this interview.

Discussion Questions

1. What are some of the key issues this administrator raises in this interview?

2. What is the tone of this interview?

3. Did she not identify the role of parents in each of the school settings?

4. What is her perception of the school's infrastructure and how did it affect her leadership effectiveness?

5. Could you explain this principal's philosophy regarding curriculum?

6. What is her political view of the principalship?

7. What changes would this administrator recommend that would significantly change the effectiveness of new administrators?

8. Do you find her comments consistent with other schools or districts you've experienced?

9. If you were appointed principal in either of these schools, what would some of your 1st-year objectives be?

Student Activities

1. Write a letter to the superintendent requesting additional administrative support.

2. Write a letter of introduction to the community indicating your philosophy, background, and goals for the upcoming school year.

3. Write a letter of introduction to the staff regarding your philosophy, background, and goals for the upcoming school year.

4. What agenda items would you include for your first faculty meeting at the beginning of the school year?

5. What funding sources would you pursue with the parent organization to support your school program?

Interview Question

What additional interview questions would you direct to this administrator?

Simulations

Role-play a discussion the principal would have with a colleague where she describes her intuitive sense of what she felt was transpiring with her parent community.

Role-play a conference she had with several of the students she was reprimanding in her office.

Role-play a meeting she would have with her faculty where she recommends a workshop for all teachers dealing with student cheating. Indicate the current research about frequency and what effective strategies have been found to be successful with elementary schoolchildren.

Developing Effective Decision-Making Abilities

Based upon the interview, how would you begin to develop effective decision-making skills?

What decision-making models are most frequently used and in what situations?

What decision-making model are you most comfortable with and why?

Principal Leadership Applications

At one point in the interview, the principal was asked about a tough decision regarding delaying a decision to communicate to the parents about a bus accident. She explained her rationale for delaying that decision.

Do you think she was justified in making this decision? What would you have done differently?

The principal spoke very honestly about the need to approach each school in which she had worked in a different way.

What were these differences in the schools?

What leadership approaches would you use that would mark these distinctions?

How could she have researched the school to better prepare for that position?

Questions Related to ISLLC Standards

See Appendix for ISLLC Standards.

1. How did this principal address Standard #3? Based upon the interview, cite at least one example that demonstrated that this standard was met.

2. Did you find that she also responded to other ISLLC standards? If so, which ones would you identify she addressed and please cite specific examples.

Readings and Resources

Drucker, Peter F. (2002). *The effective executive.* New York: Harper Collins.
A classic organizational analysis identifying rational and irrational decision-making processes. Drucker offers a particularly rich, descriptive, and far-ranging analysis of this process through the lens of a management expert and social scientist.
Zey, Mary. (1992). *Decision-making: Alternatives to rational choice models.* Newbury Park, CA: Sage.
A review of decision-making models that takes into account variations of classic forms of decision making.

PART II

Middle School

6

Leadership Focus and Planning: The Sage

Preparing to assume the principalship of a school requires considerable planning. Conferencing with your faculty, staff, and parent constituencies in order to develop professional and personal relationships as well as to identify school needs as perceived by these critical groups is extremely important. How can a principal demonstrate respect for the history and traditions of the school, support the wishes of the school community, and still incorporate her leadership philosophy and vision for the school? This principal demonstrated such leadership skill in a unique way. Her approach set the tone for a very successful and positive 1st school year.

Themes addressed in this chapter:

- Preparation for relationship building
- Personalizing the school environment
- Short- and long-term planning for program development
- Visibility and availability
- Community outreach
- Financial support

Profile of the Sage

Principal: female

Ethnicity: Asian

Age: 50+

Experience: 5 years as principal; 3 as assistant principal; 5+ years related administrative experience

School: middle; student population: 570

Well, the very first priority was to build trust into the administration; team building. I am a team builder. There was a lot of healing that had to go on. The last year with the former principal, the staff was very divided. You were either pro-administration or anti-administration. There were many cliques. . . . I walked in and I had to do my homework very quickly, that is, team building and looking at what services the school had, including community service.

I then started prioritizing . . . I came to school the entire month of July just to familiarize myself with the school. . . . The next thing I wanted to do was to meet the staff and meet them one-on-one. I also wrote a letter to them introducing myself, my background, my experience and asked them for their resumes. I wanted a history about their experiences at the school; what committees they had served on; what their goals were for next year . . . what administrative support they expected. I mentioned that I would be in school beginning August 6 and for them to give me 15 minutes to one-half hour, to meet with them . . . so we could get to know one another. . . . I had a one-to-one conversation with every staff member before the opening of school. That was a very eye-opening and wonderful experience.

I always interacted with all the children. I personally, well, I am blessed to have a memory for names and so prior to the opening of school, I took the yearbook out and placed all the children's pictures on 3-by-5 cards. I knew at least 150 faces. I knew their names before the opening of school so that I could interact with them. I could go up to all the children and introduce myself. . . . That also was very important to me.

You also need a communication support system, a colleague. There's nobody that understands the role of the principal except a principal. One day I could be mopping the floor and cleaning the toilet, and the next day I could be making a presentation to the board of directors. The job is indescribable. You need to have a colleague and a friend who you could call up and cry, scream, and ask for help; someone to support you.

Another thing: Do your homework. Ask questions. Get to know who in your district can support and help you, who in central office or support staff or what is available. It is a never-ending job. That's what I say to those who are new or two or 3 years down the road. Know how to manage your time and balance yourself.

And do have another life after school.

School Context

All experienced educators and school leaders must adapt their skills to meet the specific needs of the school. This veteran and highly experienced principal entered her 1st year in the principalship with a particular focus on understanding her school ethos and history. It is quite clear from her interview that she grasped the demands of her faculty and staff. She also knew that, while working with her staff, she could not compromise her essential mission: supporting the needs of the students. While she anticipated a certain degree of resistance, she successfully created an environment that helped diffuse that resistance. She personalized her relationships with her teachers by researching the school background and history regarding grants, foundations, committees, and parent involvement. She prepared to meet and connect with her student body by spending her summer familiarizing herself with her student population. This typified her leadership style and was indicative of a school leader who was focused, energized, and involved. This approach and the impressions it created were quite powerful and had a lasting impact on her staff and community during her tenure.

School Characteristics

The school had approximately 60% Pacific Rim students, a large population of Filipino students generated from one area of the city, Chinatown, and a small population of Latino children. Of 570 students only about 70 were African American.

School Climate

The school had a strong educational program and a number of grants that supported the overall school program. The previous administrator had run the school for a number of years and had just retired, which led to a high degree of apprehension on the part of the faculty. They were uncertain of the future leadership of the school. There were deep feelings that fragmented the staff. Some supported the previous administrative arrangements, and others were looking for change.

School Organization

The school district had a student population formula that provided for administrative support for a specific number of students. With an attendance of approximately 570 students, the school also had the benefit of a head guidance counselor.

Interview

The following interview was conducted after the principal's recent retirement from the school.

Dubin:

Could you tell me a little bit about your background, experience, and training?

Principal:

Well, I started teaching in 1968. I was a history major. I started as a fifth-grade teacher and then taught third grade. From there I was a Title I resource teacher for a few years. I worked in the reading department as a reading specialist for 4 years. Then the program was dissolved, and I went to work in a middle school as a reading teacher/specialist for 3 years. After, I served as a Title I program resource teacher again at the middle school level. I went to work for the bilingual department as a language specialist.

I became an assistant principal for a brand-new high school, which opened up, and my major responsibilities were to oversee the math/science technology program. I did that for 3 years and then went on to the middle school as a principal for 5 years.

Dubin:

Could you please tell me a little bit about those schools in terms of population and demographics?

Principal:

All of my 34 years of experience have been in this urban inner-city school district. The populations in the elementary schools I have worked with have been predominately African American, 60% Title I students.

Dubin:

What are Title I students?

Principal:

Title I students are those who fall below the 40th percentile: educationally disadvantaged youth. My middle school, which was inner city, had 60% educationally disadvantaged, and 60% ELL (English language learners). Eighty percent of my students were on free and reduced lunch. The size of the school was approximately 570.

The high school I had worked at was entirely different, in that it was a brand-new high school. It was front loaded every year, so we would get 300 new freshmen. That was a challenge. Every year it seemed as though we would be starting over; hiring new staff, ordering new materials. Sometimes I wondered if it would have been better to open up the school with the entire population. That was an enormous amount of work.

The school started out as a special school in a low-income area to create a new, academic, college preparatory high school. There was a heavy focus on science, math, and technology. When the school was designed, 60% of the students would come from all over the city, that is, open enrollment, and 40% from the neighborhood. The 1st year was filled with students with strong academic backgrounds, ready for college, and prepared for the rigorous academic program. These were students who came from all over the city and a small population came from the neighborhood. The 2nd year and the 3rd year it all changed. Approximately 70% came from the neighborhood, and so it was a major challenge; students were not as academically prepared. It was a big switch so we had to change curriculum. We had to add an academic literacy class, an extra academic math class for those students who were not prepared for algebra as well as other classes. It was a very diverse population.

Dubin:

It sounds like a considerable change, trying to accommodate students in terms of curriculum in the light of what they now entered with. How about faculty? Were there adjustments that had to be made regarding their ability to work with different kids?

Principal:

Yes, there were. The 1st year when we hired teachers, because we were very public and somewhat in the limelight, we were allowed to recruit nationwide; we had a huge amount of applications. We had over 150 resumes to review for only 10 positions. We were very rich in who we were able to select and recruit. The 1st year we had a very young staff. I felt like an old lady. Many were 23 and 24 years of age. Half of the staff came from one of the top universities in the nation and were trained by them. They were truly computer literate; they really knew curriculum. They were trained in best practices, knew their subject matter, but they were very young. That was the 1st year.

In the 2nd year, we needed to get some seasoned teachers because of the new group and balance the staff. They needed to have at least 2 or 3 years of experience in order to come into the program. We had already begun clustering families, coring, and so our freshmen students had been put into families of four teachers. We had class sizes of no more than 25 to a class so that the four teachers would share no more than 100 students. They had common prep periods for the teachers: math, science, English, social studies. That really helped in working and preparing the students for a rigorous program.

Dubin:

You were there for 3 years after which time you went to the middle school. Tell me about that school but tell me why you decided to leave at that point in your career.

Principal:

I didn't really decide. I had worked for 8 years prior at this middle school and then worked for the bilingual department in the district. I saw a middle school advertisement for the principalship at this school and noticed that the previous principal was retiring. I thought that it was a nice school, excellent location, 60% Pacific Rim children, a nice staff. But then I also considered staying in the high school to finish with the students who would be graduating. They were a great group of kids.

So I decided to pass on it; I wasn't that hungry for a principal position. I would just wait. Then I received a call from the associate superintendent of the middle school division and was asked to apply for this position. I thought what an honor, although the deadline had already passed. They said that it didn't matter and they wanted me to apply immediately, which I did.

I went through the interview process, which was very rigorous. Also, the interim principal was applying and wanted to stay there. It was a very sensitive interview process. In the end, I had a half hour with the superintendent who also knew me because of my work in the high school. About a month later they made the decision, and I was selected to be the principal.

Now because of the busing of the special education students, my middle school received students from 18 elementary schools. We had a large population coming from rather compromised areas, namely homeless children, African American children, Cambodian/Laotian/Vietnamese students. We had a large population of Filipino students from one area of the city, Chinatown. We had approximately 60% Pacific Rim students and a small population of Latino children. Basically, it broke down with these populations: Latino, Filipino, and African American. Of 570 students we had only about 70 African American.

Dubin:

What administrative staff did you have there?

Principal:

In a middle school, the district formula states that if your student population is less than 1,000 students, you get only one assistant principal. So the administrative team was the principal, an assistant principal and one head counselor.

Dubin:

That's a lot of work for three people.

Principal:

A lot.

Dubin:

As you began your school year, how did you look at priorities and the way you would address your faculty? How did that work?

Principal:

Well, the very first priority was to build trust into the administration, team building. I am a team builder. There was a lot of healing that had to go on. The last year with the former principal, the staff was very divided. You were either pro-administration or anti-administration. There were many cliques. There was disappointment for those who were pro-administration because they were not going to return. I walked in and I had to do my homework very quickly, that is, team building and looking at what services the school had, including community service.

I then started prioritizing. The very first thing I did was to write a letter, a month prior to school opening. In fact, all summer long I took the Title I information and the school site plan home and started reading everything about the school, on my own. I came to school the entire month of July just to familiarize myself with the school regarding these data.

The next thing I wanted to do was to meet the staff, one-on-one. I also wrote a letter to them introducing myself, my background, my experience and asked them for their resumes. I wanted a history about their experiences at the school; what committees they had served on, what their goals were for next year . . . what administrative support they expected. I told them that I would be in school beginning August 6 and for them to give me 15 minutes to one-half hour, to meet with them on a one-to-one basis so we could get to know one another. They could come in on their own or after school started. I had a one-to-one conversation with every staff member before the opening of school. That was a very eye-opening and wonderful experience.

Dubin:

What about the support staff? Did you arrange a time to meet with them?

Principal:

Yes, I met with the four secretarial staff and asked them to give me their job descriptions to review. We had a second meeting to tighten the responsibilities, that is, who did what, and so on. Then I met with the security staff and did the same thing. I met with everyone, teachers individually and all else, so I had a chance to explain to them what I was about. Then I asked that we take a look at the school vision and go with what we had this year. I suggested that the next year we would begin revising it, updating it, and making changes where we felt necessary. That's how I began the school year.

Dubin:

Yes, I see. The idea of going with what you had . . . Had you a strategy, not wanting to begin something new?

Principal:

Well, it wasn't that I wasn't introducing something new. I was reviewing everything. There were grants to review and many other things. Some people did not know how the grant worked so I consulted with two retired administrators . . . to revisit this grant and clear up any confusion people had regarding how the grant operated and supported what was already there. There was a reason why this middle school was receiving $250,000 worth of Title I money and $80,000 of ESL money. That's over $300,000. The first issue in this school was literacy. I wanted to examine how the money was being used, being spent, if it was being spent wisely. And so, it's not as though we were simply status quo, we were revisiting what was in place, how to shore it up, making sure that the teachers were being fully supported and whether the children were getting what they needed.

Dubin:

As you reflect back to that initial period, how did you spend your day, week, month, and so on? How would say you allocated time, that is, paperwork, managing the plant, instruction, safety, personnel, community relations, the various areas you need to be involved with?

Principal:

Any principal knows it's a 24/7 position. I'm a morning person and a people person. It was very important for me to be visible and accessible.

There is no question that there is an insurmountable amount of paperwork. I had to be at my desk from 6:30 to 7:45; I would come in and take care of all my paperwork. I would line up my priorities of the different tasks and reports that had to be done. I had one secretary who would come in at 7, one at 7:30, one at 8, and one at 9. In this way I had the clerical support if I needed it to complete reports, etc. From 7:45, I would make myself available for staff members, parent conferences, or meetings.

At 8:30 I always did yard duty. It was important for me to be there for the children, to be accessible. We only had two security guards, and you had to supervise a yard and cafeteria, so you had to be out there. Lunchtime, well, I always did lunch duty and after-school duty so the children always saw me. I always interacted with all the children.

I personally, well, I am blessed to have a memory for names and so, prior to the opening of school, I took the yearbook out and placed all the children's pictures on 3-by-5 cards. I knew at least 150 faces. I knew their names before the opening of school so that I could interact with them. I could go up to all the children and introduce myself. By the end of the school year I knew all the children by face and name. That also was very important to me.

It was important to me to be available to staff. After the bell rang I always cleared the halls and then said good morning to the third-floor classes or actually go into every classroom and say good morning. The next day it could be the second floor and the next perhaps the main floor. I was always clearing the halls and making sure I would say good morning to everybody, peeking in and out of the classroom to speak to the teachers. My personal goal was that by the end of the day, I would never go home without returning every message and opening up every piece of mail. I would do this every day as a routine, so I'd be accessible to staff, accessible to children and, on my own time, complete the paperwork.

Dubin:

You've covered a good deal of the ground. Based upon that response, how did you deal with burnout, overload? Was there any time that you felt that you needed something of a break, some distance?

Principal:

Perhaps that's why I retired. Someone asked me why I was retiring and I said that I was tired to be putting out 200% instead of 100%. I don't think I was burned-out. I was very fortunate to have known what the job was about before I took it on. Being a district resource teacher and a bilingual resource teacher for the entire district, I was a quasi-administrative for

8 years. I was running in and out of schools and I understood the role of the principal. I saw the job and what it entailed.

I personally said to myself that I would never become an administrator until my last child graduated from high school. It is a 10- to 12-hour job a day, easily. My husband was extremely supportive so I didn't have to rush home, pick up the children, and cook dinner. This relieved me of the time I had to be at work, avoided the burnout. I loved the school, and the staff was very good.

Nor am I a control freak. I viewed my assistant principal as my partner. We were truly partners. My theory was that if I ever went into a meeting or a conference or if I were sick, my assistant principal would be able to take over. The school was to go on. He knew every aspect and every report, area; I had no secrets. He was well aware of every situation that was going on in the school. He truly supported me, and we balanced each other. That is a blessing to have a partner where we were able to get along so well and balance each other out.

Dubin:

So you had your life in place and you also had the kind of experience where you didn't enter the position innocently or without an understanding of what the job would demand. You had your life and your professional sense of the job in order prior to accepting this position.

Principal:

Absolutely.

Dubin:

On another note, when we look at those considering administration, new administrators as well as veteran administrators, all of whom will be reading your comments, what would you say the major issues are facing leadership?

Principal:

The fact that the position is overwhelming. For the new people, it will be absolutely overwhelming. You must have a strong sense of who you are, what you are about, and what you believe in because you will be challenged. You will be screamed at. If you don't have a sense of why you made this decision or why it came to be, the thinking process, you're going to flounder.

All my decisions were always based on what is best for all children. I always used to say to the staff that I commended them. For example, I knew that when my PE teachers were yelling at me and fighting for their department or my music teachers wanted various things, I felt their passion. I commended their passion. But I was not allowed to have that tunnel vision. I had to have the total vision. I would share with them, listen to them so we would come to agreement as to what's best and how it affects all the children in the school. That's how decisions would be made in this school.

It is extremely important to be honest and available to the staff and include the staff wherever possible. Everyone throws out the terms, for example, decision-making and site-based management. Well, I shared with the staff how decisions were going to be made at our middle school. I said wherever possible I wanted their input. I would tell them that at times we would vote and make it a majority or other times I only wanted their input, after which I would make the decision. There would be times when I didn't even have the control because of the dictates from central office. I would simply state that this is what you have to do and why; simple as that. This would clear the air.

Dubin:

What about communication?

Principal:

Communication. Communication is so critical; you have to have people skills. It is critical to have people skills. You must know how to talk to people and listen. I always would say to the children and the staff, we learn to read; we know our ABC's, we learn to work with numbers. Another critical part of communication for a leader is reading body language. Your body is telling me this or that. Reading people is so important and somewhat instinctive. You do learn this over time.

You also need a communication support system, a colleague. There's nobody that understands the role of the principal except a principal. One day I could be mopping the floor and cleaning the toilet and the next day I could be making a presentation to the board of directors. The job is indescribable. You need to have a colleague and a friend who you could call up and cry, scream, and ask for help; someone to support you.

Another thing: Do your homework. Ask questions. Get to know who in your district can support and help you, who in central office or support staff or what is available. It is a never-ending job. That's what I say to those who are new or 2 or 3 years down the road. Know how to manage your time and balance yourself. And do have another life after school.

Dubin:

At 24/7 there seems to be a conflict.

Principal:

Yes, I know, but you do need it. Find it.

Dubin:

Yes. Let me follow-up with another question that you answered briefly. You mentioned your experience and support at home, your life situation as you entered the role. Is there anything else you've gained and understood you needed for the job?

Principal:

I would say the willingness to accept criticism, the willingness to ask for help, to do your homework in looking for new programs. In one situation, we were written up in a magazine: we met our API index. I said to my faculty that we had to keep pushing and never be satisfied. I felt that everything was a personal challenge. I always felt that we needed to look at the school to see how we could make it better.

For example, we went for a Title VII grant. I knew that I was not able to write a grant and I did not want to ask the teachers, so I hired a grant writer. We agreed that if he wrote and got the grant I'd pay him $8,000 as an evaluator. On another occasion, we went after a Healthy Start grant and got $250,000. By the end of the year we were bringing over $1 million to the school. We were working with over 18 community agencies, Sierra Club, Levi family, and professional development funds when I retired as principal from the middle school.

Those kinds of things will keep charging you, giving you the high, the energy to keep going. Those are the things that made me grow. As I mentioned, I realized my shortcomings, for example, that I couldn't write a grant. I found people who were the grant writers. I found people who could help us and improve the quality of the education. You need to reflect on your own weaknesses and strengths, where the area is I need help, and acknowledge it.

Dubin:

You mention these various agencies, constituents, and so on, outside influences. Do you find the principal position to be political?

Principal:

Well in this urban city, it is political. For example, how a person is selected for a position can be something of a political appointment. In my situation, I believe that for one of my administrators being Chinese was an important consideration in the selection. As my assistant principal was being selected, I wanted the best person for the job. This school was a gem, and I didn't want to lose it because the person was Chinese but not able to do the job. In some situations we want people of color in order for the children to have role models and for them to be placed in leadership positions. I understand that, but we must also stop and ask, "Who can do the job?"

Sometimes it's who you know on the board, so there's a lot of politicking. There's often much that goes on as to who is in the know; who you go to for help. That just happens.

Dubin:

Regarding politics and different constituents, how do you acknowledge staff or community and address the various needs in the community who want funds directed toward them and still balance all the different interests?

Principal:

Well, let me explain how I approached these many interest groups. In terms of grant writing, many business and companies wanted to give back to the school and community. Having a free and reduced lunch situation for our children helped garner their support; 60% of my school was second-language learners. All these things help get us support. We were a needy school. For example, junior achievement on Groundhog Day, I had 150 students going to 25 different companies, and it was a wonderful experience for them. We had so many buddies in the volunteer programs. These young people wanted to give back to the community.

When it was time to work with my parent groups, it was very difficult to bring them together as a group. Talk about evening meetings; you'd ask them what the best night would be or the best day, for example, it might be Friday nights . . . I'd think . . . you got to be kidding. . . . Nevertheless, twice a month, I'd give up my Friday nights and at 6:30 we'd have my Filipino parents come in and we'd talk about their needs and concerns. Then, I'd have a Chinese night. I'm lucky because theirs was a Saturday afternoon. And also my Latino parents. I had two parent liaisons: one Spanish and one Chinese to work with those parent groups to determine their needs and wants. The hardest group was getting my African American parents to come in. They'd come in, but it was hard. It was a personal goal to work with them, even though there were only 70 children. Luckily, through one of the grants, we were able to establish a hip-hop club and a young man's club. I did a basketball camp where they came from 7:30 to 8:30 in the morning, 3 days a week and played basketball. Two days of the week they had to do homework and academic studies. The girls wanted a hip-hop dance group.

Anything that I could say to the children that would convey to them that they were a member of the school. Even though there was only 70, and they looked out to the sea of Asian children, they were just as important as any of the other children. I always made sure that we had the African American assembly, Filipino assembly, and Chinese New Year assembly. We did International Day for everyone. I tried to be as inclusive as possible so everyone felt that they truly had a voice in the school.

Dubin:

Inclusive is the right word. You were able to accommodate all the factions, identify them from small to large, and balance all the politics, if you will, of your school.

Principal:

Yes. You had to know who your clients are. You have to know your community.

Dubin:

If you could think of a particular issue that you faced in your career that was particularly difficult, does any one come to mind? It could deal with a student, district, or parent. Is there anything that jumps off the page?

Principal:

Safety. Safety always comes up for the parents. They have to feel safe in the school. Our school's reputation was that we were in Chinatown and there were gangs. That was part of the very first thing when I started as principal was to change that perception. In this district the parents were able to select the schools, so one of my greatest challenges was safety. The parents did not want to come to school at night for meetings because they were concerned about safety. It wasn't so much at my end. Many of these parents came from neighborhoods where when they went home after the meetings; it might not be safe after 9 at night.

More specifically, there was a gang-related issue that happened at my school. Outsiders came in and attacked one of my students. He pulled out a machete, scared all the kids. One of my students put his arm up to block him, and he cut his arm. This amounted to retaliation time. I had to have the Chinatown task force, the mayor's task force, the transportation task force involved. I called a huge assembly and invited parents to come to the meeting so they could understand what was going on. I had to ensure the children's safety. During the assembly I said that I would do everything to protect them. I said that that was my job, to watch their back. Their job was to come to school to learn.

This went on for a month, and I had to keep assuring them that the school would be working in tandem with the police. Three weeks after the fight, the police were there every day after school when we loaded the buses. They rode on the buses with the kids to make sure the kids felt safe. This continued until the child involved went to court and was incarcerated for the duration of the school year. Throughout, everyone knew that we would be out there, at every bus; the police would be there; transportation riders on the bus so that the children felt safe. I called in the ringleaders; we had a professional facilitator and had a roundtable discussion, so everyone had a chance to talk and get it out.

That was one of the toughest situations and lasted 3 months dealing with this one incident.

Dubin:

How old were these kids?

Principal:

My children were eighth graders. These outsider kids were dropouts from high school. They were probably juniors or seniors had they stayed in school, but they hadn't. By the time I had worked with the neighborhood high schools to identify these kids, they had already dropped out school.

Dubin:

In several of the other interviews I've conducted, the problem of isolation has surfaced in many comments. What are your thoughts regarding the idea that the principal position is isolating?

Principal:

Perhaps because I am such an open person, I've never felt that. And maybe because I had a special relationship with my assistant principal. As I mentioned, we were partners. We were a team. I could share everything. He shared everything with me. I also created a very open climate with my staff. We had a leadership team. I had faculty meetings and had a faculty committee that worked with me: It was very open.

Another important factor, which made it wonderful at my school, was that, as a middle school "feeder" with other middle schools, the four administrators of the other feeder schools would meet once a month. We would talk about curriculum. We'd talk about summer school as our students moved up. The math teacher from the high school would come to us and support our math teacher. During my last year, the English department from the high school would work with our English teacher. Because the high school had a larger population and more money, we supported district workshops and involved consultants from the university. Our respective schools would provide funding for these workshops, that is, folders, pencils, treats, and would meet once a month. This was great and we did this for 5 years. The last year we even changed the venue to make it more relaxing and social. We had Diet Cokes and such. It really was collegial and supportive. Prior to this we were so dedicated and structured that at the end of that 5th year, we also found that a little unstructured downtime was a better approach.

So, in any case, I never felt that sense of isolation.

Dubin:

So it became a strong network of administrators supporting each other; professional development strategies with connections to the universities.

Principal:

Yes [joking]. We would say, "Who's got the agenda and who's got the gossip, the latest rumor." The format was really conducive to being honest, having fun, but being quite serious about our decisions. We would talk about students who might have discipline issues and their being transferred to our respective schools. Because we talked about summer school and moving our eighth graders up, it made for a smooth transition. We'd come together and discuss English language learners; what the beginning level would be and, for example, whether a particular student was ready to go to a regular program. We worked very closely with the assistant principal regarding eighth graders who had to go to summer school prior to being accepted to high school, and some of our students who had to be held back. That was very powerful and effective working with the high school.

Dubin:

You had a psychological support team with administrators with whom you could consult and a professional support team so that you could ask and question. You weren't dealing in a vacuum.

Principal:

It was so important. We looked forward to those meetings. At times, we'd say that we couldn't make the meeting, but we'd always simply have to meet. We'd find the time and were truly committed to making those monthly meetings.

Dubin:

Was this arranged by the group: group-initiated?

Principal:

Yes, group-initiated. We wanted to do it.

Dubin:

Last question . . . Is there anything else I haven't asked that you would like to add to your comments to those entering the profession and those actively involved? Is there anything I haven't asked?

Principal:

No, not really. Just remember who you are working for, the children. That will help you when the decisions are tough. It will help you when the day is tough. Also, find something that would help you de-stress your life. For me it was flowers. I love flowers. I would always have fresh flowers in my office. I would say that there are beautiful things in the world. When I had those angry parents yelling at me, I'd kind of hold the phone out there and look at my flowers. Yes, I was listening. That was my peace; that gave me peace.

Sometimes I'd have roses and other types of flowers. I'd buy unique types of flowers, and the children, urban children, asked if they were real. Many of these children didn't see flowers. It was important that I had something beautiful and something I enjoyed. If I was to be at my desk for 8 to 10 hours a day, that was something for me that gave me peace. But ultimately, you always looked out for the children.

Dubin:

And so, keep the children as your priority and keep that as your rationale for the decisions you are making. And secondly, equally as important, is to keep in perspective your priorities. For you it was the flowers that represented the greater picture, and for someone else it could be something else . . . to keep things in balance.

Principal:

Absolutely. Also, having a sense of humor!

Dubin:

That has come up before. Keeping things in perspective, not taking things too seriously. Not to minimize it but to always keep it in perspective, to come back the next day.

Thank you very much for your thoughts. You've obviously made a significant contribution to your school and the children. I know that they will never forget the work you've done.

Analysis

This very experienced and seasoned middle school principal assumed the position in the wake of a highly charged political environment. Her faculty and community population were anxious about the changes the school could undergo in the light of her administration. The school had been reasonably successful with regard to test scores although there were behavioral issues that needed to be addressed. She also wanted to implement a decision-making process that was consistent with her values and perspective about education. She had to build trust in her staff, provide legitimacy, and a supportive and meaningful environment for her students. Initially, she also had to balance the politics and involvement with the district in order to direct the school with autonomy and self-purpose but consistent with its policies. During the interview she addressed many of the general leadership areas involved in administration, for example, school goals and priorities, personnel, budgetary decisions, participatory management strategies, politics, ethics, personal goals, as well as a host of other leadership considerations specific to her educational philosophy.

Developing trust and strong and supportive relationships are central to any effective leader. How an administrator develops relationships can determine how effective she will be during her tenure as principal. When there is a true sense of trust among all the school personnel, the general climate of the school is greatly enhanced. Generally, such a climate will provide a school with an atmosphere marked by innovation, commitment, motivation, dedication, loyalty, and satisfaction. When a teacher's sense of satisfaction is directly linked to that of the organization, you have an ideal employer-employee relationship. In other words, if a teacher's sense of accomplishment and fulfillment is realized when she is responsive to a school need, the school benefits and the teacher benefits. The primary goal of the leader is achieved.

This principal wanted to develop that sense of trust as she planned for the fall semester. She acquainted herself with each faculty member and other significant school personnel and during the summer months even memorized the names of the students prior to the school opening. She did this in order to demonstrate commitment as well as develop relationships with her school community.

Discussion Questions

1. What are some of the key issues this administrator raised in this interview?

2. What is the tone of this interview?

3. What does she see as the role of parents in this community? How many parent groups does she identify in this interview and how does she accommodate them?

4. What was her perception regarding the district's reason to select her as principal?

5. Could you explain this principal's philosophy regarding curriculum?

6. What was her method of attaining trust, support, and feedback from her colleagues?

7. What changes would this administrator recommend that would significantly change the effectiveness of teachers?

8. Do you find her comments consistent with other schools and districts you've experienced?

9. If you were appointed principal in this school, what would some of your 1st year objectives be?

Student Activities

1. Write a letter to the superintendent explaining your school objectives for the 1st year.

2. Write a letter of introduction to the community indicating your philosophy, background, and goals for the upcoming school year.

3. Write a letter of introduction to the staff regarding your philosophy, background, and goals for the upcoming school year.

4. What agenda items would you include for your first faculty meeting at the beginning of the school year?

5. What funding sources did she pursue to support her school program?

Interview Question

What additional interview questions would you ask of this administrator?

Additional Assignments

Review a district's master plan and apply a timeline and task analysis for a specific project.

Assist in developing a school-level regulation that coordinates with district policy, for example, discipline.

Implement an SIP [school improvement plan].

Develop an action plan to meet a current school need (mission profile).

Simulations

Role-play the initial summer meeting the principal had with a veteran teacher. What types of questions would she ask? How would she approach the interview? With respect to the history of the school, how would she integrate that topic into the discussion? What would you expect her desired outcomes to be?

Role-play the first meeting with the president of the parent organization at the school. What information would the principal want to obtain from the parent? What information would the principal want to convey to this parent regarding her philosophy and direction for the school in the coming year?

This principal discussed the many types of decisions she had to make that affected the school. She spoke of decisions that could be shared, that would require a more consensual model, as well as those that she would make that would be more directive. She also mentioned that there would be times when decisions would be made at the district level and the school would not have a voice in those decisions. Role-play a faculty meeting where this information is conveyed.

Developing School Trust

Just what is trust? Is it illusory, implied only by a nod of the head, a pat on the back, gold stars in a student's notebook, or some other nuance suggesting acceptance, candor, and faith? As nebulous as the word itself is, without the understanding and development of this basic feeling, interpersonal relationships and exchange are guaranteed to be superficial at best. At the very worst, a school climate without trust can be destructive for everyone involved.

Trust is a balancing act between people. As a means of survival, we all attempt to achieve enough status to feel comfortable about ourselves. Often, byplay among individuals is aimed at developing or maintaining one's own sense of equilibrium within a situation. When a person's status or sense of balance is not threatened but is validated and reinforced, we have a trust scenario.

Principal Leadership Applications

1. How did the principal approach developing trust at the school?

2. Did she approach students differently from the way she approached teachers?

3. Why was she concerned about the prior administration and those who supported the previous principal?

4. Why did she feel her support system was so important? Consider this question in the context of trust.

5. Why would you consider trust to be cost efficient?

Questions Related to ISLLC Standards

See Appendix for ISLLC Standards.

1. How did this principal address Standard #1? Based upon the interview, cite at least one example that demonstrated that this standard was met.

2. How did this principal address Standard #4? Based upon the interview, cite at least one example that demonstrated that this standard was met.

3. How did this principal address Standard #5? Based upon the interview, cite at least one example that demonstrated that this standard was met.

4. Did you find that she also responded to other ISLLC standards? If so, which ones would you identify she addressed, and please cite specific examples.

Readings and Resources

Cummins, J. (1986). Empowering minority students: A framework for intervention. *Harvard Educational Review*, 56,(1), 18–36.
A critical, theoretical analysis of schools as to their institutional processes that operate to identify, perpetuate, and legitimate power.
Dubin, A. (1984, December). Developing a high-trust climate. *International Quarterly* (pp. 48–49).
A discussion focused on the role of administrators and leadership strategies to instill trust in the faculty, parents, and students.
Rothstein, S. (Ed.). (1993). *Handbook of schooling in urban America*. Westport, CT: Greenwood.
A collection of articles that focuses on topics such as urban education, political and organizational perspectives, minority perspectives, teacher-pupil relations, pedagogical problems and solutions.

7

Evaluation and the Political Arena: The Politician

An administrator must be able to negotiate a multitude of tasks to be an effective leader. While balancing the instructional program, personnel, budget, student needs, the school plant, and the community, to mention a few of his responsibilities, he must also be aware of and responsive to the demands and politics of the district. These demands focus on student achievement, which ties directly into his evaluation. As well, these pressures often result in high levels of stress, and so the need for him to balance priorities to reduce the likelihood of burnout is paramount. This principal discusses his leadership style and what factors were operating in his school during his tenure there.

Themes addressed in this chapter:

- Hiring and evaluation
- Administrative burnout
- Student support systems
- Administrative parent communication, expectations, and responsibilities
- Administrative decision-making team
- Administrator-teacher relationships
- Board member encroachment

Profile of the Politician

Principal: male

Ethnicity: Asian

Age: 49

Experience: 4 years as principal; 9 years as assistant principal; 7 years' teaching experience

School: middle; student population: 1,060

Well, no matter what we do, even when we do the outreach to the community, meet with the parents, we're still being held responsible for Black and White test scores for achievement. If we don't get the support at home, I don't see how we can do it. If the students do not respect their parents at home, I don't care what color they are. . . . We have the same problems with the Chinese kids coming from China. If the parents can't control them, and they don't respect their parents, what do you expect the administration to do? I don't know. And then if we start suspending too many kids, we get "inked" on that as though we're doing something wrong. . . .

I also questioned that the administration was going to be held more accountable in closing the achievement gap, particularly with certain low-performing groups, that is, the African American and Hispanic groups. I asked whether there was anything to hold the parents accountable.

Principalships are extremely political, particularly in this district. For example, they may indicate that they need an African American female in that school or a Chinese administrator in that school. You don't hear that you need a really strong person or competent person for that assignment. They look at race, gender, etc. I've not heard a discussion around what individual would be good for a particular school. It's not that. The decisions are based around affirmative action, for example, or that this particular individual is good but is on the superintendent's bad list so it's not going to happen. Or someone on the board wants someone to be at this school. It's not competency first, it's all politics.

There are teachers who are not very friendly, and I don't trust them. The principal needs to realize whom he can and cannot trust, conduct himself in a fashion that is accessible to everyone, and understand what and how much information he can share. There are some people where you must keep the information close to the vest, while with others you can relate as colleagues, even as friends. There are those you can go out to lunch and talk about everything but school. . . .

The things I could tell you!

School Context

Principals have the unending responsibility of providing effective leadership to their school constituents, while, at the same time, adhering to the district mandate for higher test scores. This is a very pressurized situation for any leader and requires the ability to balance these competing forces. On one hand, a leader must move deliberately and carefully so that he can make thoughtful, ethical, and effective decisions but, on the other hand, be immediately responsive to the political realities which will affect him and the ways in which the school is perceived. Our very experienced and politically astute principal in this middle school assumed the principalship with an understanding of these dual expectations.

The school was in the inner city where behavioral issues were a significant factor impacting the school. Test scores were also a very important consideration that drove many of the school initiatives. He had been the administrator for 4 years. His performance evaluation was largely determined by student test scores. Prior to this assignment, he had been an assistant principal for 9 years.

School Characteristics

The school consisted of approximately 1,000 students with significant Chinese and Latino populations. There was a small population of African American students.

School Climate

The administrator was well prepared to deal with the considerable needs of the school. He understood the ethos of the school, was very informed regarding curriculum, community politics, multiple funding sources, and downtown pressures. His assignment to the school had a politically charged backdrop.

School Organization

The school district had a student population formula that provided administrative support, for example, two assistant principals, a dean, and counseling support.

Interview

The following interview was conducted during the 1st week of the school year.

Dubin:

Could you tell me a little bit about your background, experience, and training to assume an administrative position?

Principal:

Of course. I earned my administrative credential and had been an assistant principal at a number of high schools for about 9 years. In my role as the assistant principal, I was involved in all aspects of administration, that is, curriculum, instruction, and pupil personnel. Based upon those experiences, I felt well prepared. I have also been involved in district in-services and professional development workshops on leadership training.

Dubin:

Prior to administration, how did you begin your career?

Principal:

Prior to administration, I was at a comprehensive high school as a teacher. I started as an ESL Chinese bilingual teacher at a high school and also did some coaching for the volleyball team. I was interested in moving up and was encouraged by my principal to consider administration.

Prior to being a teacher, I was a fireman in the city and prior to that I had been a paraprofessional at a middle school. I found that I enjoyed it and decided to become a teacher. I earned my teaching credential but, unfortunately, had trouble getting a teaching position at that time. Most of the positions I've held have dealt with human needs, people services, that kind of thing.

Dubin:

How many years had you taught before assuming an assistant principal position, which you had said you held for about 8 or 9 years?

Principal:

Well, I was a teacher for about 7 years, primarily Chinese bilingual.

Dubin:

And how long have you been principal at your current school?

Principal:

Four years.

Dubin:

Could you tell me about your school, that is, demographics, community, size, staffing, and so on?

Principal:

Well, we have 1,060 students, Grades 6 to 8. The enrollment hasn't been this high in 30 years. The test scores have continually increased over the past several years. In fact, last year our test scores were projected to go up approximately 4 points, yet we increased them by 9 points. The only area we fell short in was the test scores of the African American students; those scores did not go up. We got "dinged" there. Our school also has the strongest after-school program in the city. We have a very strong, diverse, and extended after-school learning program.

Dubin:

What's involved in the after-school program? Could you tell me a little more about that?

Principal:

Yes. We have tutoring, academics, and recreation. We have students who are here specifically to be tutored for math and reading and we also provide a place for them to do their homework. We have students who are learning to sail in the bay, learn music, drumming, traditional Chinese music, and Chinese dancing. We have martial arts disguised in dance. The YMCA is here and has a tutoring and recreational program. We have girls-only math and a focus-teacher group that works with other students after school on tutoring and on specific content areas.

Dubin:

You mentioned that your test scores had really improved, which is very impressive. What would you credit that to?

Principal:

Several factors actually. One factor dealt with the teachers. They have finally begun to buy into the fact that, whether they believe in it philosophically or not, the test scores are how we are being judged, graded, and being evaluated by the media, press, and the parents. That being said, as a school, teachers are being held totally accountable. Because of that they realize that if they don't prepare these kids for the tests, there will be consequences, so we've been adding different elements to support this effort. We've been strongly encouraging certain teachers to attend workshops on literacy. We've also encouraged outside consultants to come on-site to give us workshops.

In January of this year we were finally able to hire a second assistant principal who had strength in curriculum and instruction, a former English teacher. He had also been working with teachers, providing them with extra materials and support. For the past 2 years, all students who had scored below the 25th percentile were put into an extra reading class or a math program, which was an elective. It was very successful.

There were a few exceptions. Parents who preferred to keep their children in band, for example, because they were doing well, were permitted to do so. They indicated, in writing, that the school did attempt to provide the additional support but they did not wish to take advantage of it. I do, though, believe that the support we provided was a big help.

Dubin:

So you would say that it's a combination of things. Teachers buy-in that test scores are important and necessary. After-school programs provide extra support within the school itself for some students, rather than the electives, in order to focus on that area for reinforcement. So there are a number of things that you've done.

Principal:

Yes.

Dubin:

Tell me about your staff. How many teachers and other administrators are there? How does that configuration look in terms of the leadership and staffing the school?

Principal:

There is the principal and two assistant principals. We have a brand-new dean. The new dean is a very important figure, in that she is a female African American, strong background in counseling, and lives in the same neighborhood as most of our African American children. As you know, one of our main objectives this year is to raise test scores for all our children, particularly those who haven't done well. We are doing all we can to focus on the African American students, 126 students, because of their low scores. You see, when we started out the school year in 2001 to 2002, we had over 1,000 students. The rule of thumb was that any school that had over 1,000 students was given an additional assistant principal. Well, 4 years ago, when I first came to the school, there were 800-plus students, and the second year we had over 900-plus students, just below 1,000. We missed the additional administrative support by a few students. In 2001, we had the numbers, but it wasn't until January that we were able to bring that second assistant principal aboard. That makes a big difference.

Dubin:

I'm sure. How many staff do you have?

Principal:

Fifty-five teachers. As I was saying, the staff is different. It has changed. Many teachers have retired who needed to retire. It had been hard to bring them along. They wanted to continue to teach as they were teaching regardless of the methodologies. Test scores were not how they felt they should be judged, and if the district didn't like it, many teachers said, "I've got 30 years in. What could the district do to me?"

I felt that the issue didn't have anything to do with what could be done to them but rather what was being done to our students. Eventually they retired and were replaced with new blood, positive energy, and those more willing to accept new approaches.

Dubin:

In terms of administrative configuration, you have one principal, two assistant principals, one dean and 55 teachers. Do you have any counselors?

Principal:

We have two district-paid counselors. After shifting around some funds, this year we have a Title I counselor and a Title VII counselor. The Title I counselor deals with all the EDY (educationally disadvantaged youth) kids. That will help a lot. The Title VII counselor deals mainly with the Chinese dual-language program and the ESL kids; especially the Chinese-speaking ones. The district counselors split the load of Grades 6 to 8.

Dubin:

In other words, you have four counselors.

Principal:

Well, yes there are four counselors, but let me explain. Last year we began a new way of funding the school, with a weighted student formula. According to the formula, if you have 1,000 kids you were to have two counselors. I think that the following year this will be looked at again. You have more autonomy with the money; people might be looking at a counselor at each grade level.

Dubin:

That gives you the decision making at the school site as to what the school might need and allows you to take that site-level money and spend it accordingly.

Principal:

Yes, but it must go through the school site council.

Dubin:

Yes, but you have more decision making as opposed to the district determining that.

Principal:

Yes, but let me explain. Last year, without the weighted school formula, we would have had more money. The schools that really benefited and received more money were the under-performing schools. There was loads of money pouring into those low-performing schools. We're basically a bare-bones budget.

Dubin:

Let me ask you another question that you've answered in part. When you considered your priorities for this year, how did you determine them and then how did you communicate them to your staff and community?

Principal:

Basically, it has to do with the principal's evaluation. And let me answer truthfully and realistically. The principal's evaluation really spells out precisely what I need to improve on. The principal's evaluation is really black or white: either yes, you met the objective; or no, you did not meet the objective. This past year, I got a no in not meeting the objective dealing with raising the African American students' test scores, that is, closing the achievement gap. I got a no there. Another area where I received a no was meeting timelines, teacher-evaluation timelines. Both those areas became top priorities for me. The highest priority was raising the African American test scores. I drove that point home at the beginning of the school year, at the different faculty meetings and the department meetings. I let them know that that has got to be the focus. We were supposed to go up, expected to go up four points, and we went up nine points for all other groups.

Dubin:

Yes, that's pretty impressive.

Principal:

Yes. We're obviously doing something correct; however, we cannot forget the fact that African American students also need to go up. In this district, everything is by numbers. If I suspend too many students, I get dinged for that. Last year, I barely met my goal of lowering the suspension rate of African and Hispanic kids. I have to increase the attendance rate of the African and Hispanic kids. We met all those goals except for raising the test scores for African American students. We didn't meet that goal. For me, that's how the priorities are set.

Dubin:

I see. Is that communicated to your staff at the beginning of the year? Do you explain that there must be focus on test scores and reinforcement and so on and that many of the programs you've described earlier are created for that purpose?

Principal:

Correct.

Dubin:

Does that affect the way you spend most of your time or even relate to your staff? Would you say that a lot of it is focused on bureaucracy, personnel, instruction, safety, community, the various areas you are juggling every day? How would you say that you allocate your time?

Principal:

Every day is really different. I would say when it comes to bureaucracy you can't deal with paperwork until the end of the day. During the day you have people walking by the office or knocking on the door or appointments or the phone is ringing or what have you, the day-to-day stuff. It's hard to do the memos until after hours unless I am directed by my boss. If I were so directed, I would have to work on those memos.

Dubin:

With respect to memos, you mean reports from the district, grants that may need to be done?

Principal:

A good 30% of the day is spent on those things.

Dubin:

On another topic, what would you say the major issues are facing new administrators? And what do you think they should consider as they face a new leadership position? What would you say the issues are facing someone like you who is far more seasoned and a real veteran administrator?

Principal:

Let me be very honest with you. Last year, I and my administrative team killed ourselves and what did it get us? When I said we killed ourselves: I was working evenings and weekends. It got to the point where I was coming in on Sundays, Saturdays for sure, Sundays sometimes . . . evenings, I was with the family two evenings at the most. We were trying to do it all. What did we get for this? Zilch. We got zilch. This year when we started the school I told my two assistant principals, this year, no more evening work. When I leave and you're still here, I will physically take you out of the building. And some of the time I did that. They'd say that they need to crank this out and I'd say, no, we're going. That's it. And we don't come in on weekends. We needed to get to this point in order to save my career and my sanity.

What's challenging for them, new administrators coming into the field, is that the district oftentimes doesn't offer enough support to the administrators. Let me give you an example. If a parent doesn't get his or her way, they complain to the central office. Central office expects, after hearing a complaint dealing with racism, for example, or something volatile has happened, that it is the responsibility of the administrator to explain, justify, rectify, and/or appease the situation. That's going to be tough for the new administrator. It's tough now. But for someone new coming in, it will be easy for them to be intimidated.

I'm 49 years old. At this point in my career, I respond to parental pressure by saying, "Here's my card. If you need to, please go down to the district office and speak with my supervisor." If I know that I'm on firm ground, whether you are calling it racism, bias, unprofessiona. treatment, whatever, you need to get it off your chest and go on. My position with downtown is simple. In a straightforward way, I present the documentation, exactly what has happened. That is when and why the paperwork is so important. When the superintendent or board member gets to my boss, they want the paperwork immediately. It's always that the burden of proof is on us. That's where the pressure is. For new administrators coming into the position, they have to understand reality and be prepared.

Another thing deals with the students who aren't performing well, in my particular situation, the African American students. Nobody in the entire district ever said that we'd hold the parents accountable. That is not politically correct. In fact, there was a situation where I almost put my job in jeopardy.

When the superintendent first came on, she had a first lieutenant who advised her on a new plan, dealing with diversity and accountability. When all the administrators in the city first met in the beginning of her tenure, in that first meeting, they were talking about diversity and the need not to bus these kids all over the place, which was one major issue. With respect to diversity, I questioned how the busing was going to help these children and what impact would it have on the school, the parents. How will they all benefit? My direct questioning was not well received.

The second issue dealt with accountability. I also questioned that the administration was going to be held more accountable in closing the achievement gap, particularly with certain low-performing groups, that is, the African American and Hispanic groups. I asked whether there was anything to hold the parents accountable. Well, she snapped at me in public.

You see, we don't have to hold the parents accountable. That was the answer. How does this translate? Well, no matter what we do, even when we do outreach to the community, meet with the parents, we're still being held responsible for Black and White test scores for achievement. If we don't get the support at home, I don't see how we can do it. If the students do not respect their parents at home, I don't care what color they are. We have the same problems with the Chinese kids coming from China. If the parents can't control them, and they don't respect their parents, what do you expect the administration to do? I don't know. And then, if we start suspending too many kids, we get "inked" on that as though we're doing something wrong.

We're supposed to take a proactive approach. Well, I used to have something called an opportunity program which was an in-house suspension program. If a child was in trouble, they were suspended but they didn't go home. The child would come to school, be assigned to a particular room, eat lunch, but be away from their normal schedule in order to do work. Since going to a different spending formula, we no longer have the funds for this program. And we recently got dinged because we were the only school that suspended eight students, and most of the students were African Americans. Our dean is African American, and she did the suspensions. Those are some of the challenges that I think these new people will face.

Dubin:

And these are the issues that seasoned administrators must also face. How do you deal with these issues when you know it's actually in the best interest of the students and the school and it's reasonable for you to take that action, and yet there appears to be a political front that says you can't do that? How do you deal with that and the level of stress and frustration?

Principal:

Well, in this case, I've told the dean that we'll take a different approach that would involve an after-school detention program. She responded that the teachers wouldn't volunteer to do it; although they wanted it; they wouldn't volunteer. I then explained that, by law, you could have a classified personnel watch the detention program; in other words, have security do it. It's not a normal class. There's no attendance sheet, there's no roll. All you're asking is to have the security aide supervise the students. That would be our after-school detention program. You have to be creative.

What you would need to do is work with the teachers and find out what classrooms are available to hold the detention. Right now, we're filled to capacity. I'm telling you, every nook and cranny of our school is being used. And so, I gave the responsibility to the dean of finding a classroom that is not being used by after-school programs. And this was an attempt to put the detention program in place. That's one intervention approach.

But how to deal with the stress? Well, I've trained myself not to take things too personally.

Dubin:

Keeping things in perspective.

Principal:

[Laughs]

Dubin:

Well, you're not the first one to respond that way, and I've had many comments as to how to deal with stress. Some principals have had trouble dealing with it; physically feeling the effects of the pressure they undergo since you are that number one person at the school.

Principal:

I've had friends who gave it up. They didn't want to deal with it, and many very quickly.

Dubin:

Let me ask you another type of question, particularly in the context of some of the things we've already talked about. Do you think that the principalship is a political position and in what way?

Principal:

Yes. Very political, extremely political. One of the reasons why the enrollment at my school has gone up consistently over the years is because I am Chinese, male, and I speak Cantonese. The majority of the children here are Chinese and their parents, well most of them, speak Cantonese. When they're able to come to the school in order to resolve some issues and speak with the principal, that really helps. Also, my own daughter, son, and now youngest son are at this school. For a principal to place his own children in the school where he works, it must be a good school. That's one way I sell the school. I get credit for pushing the school in that way.

Principalships are extremely political, particularly in this district. For example. They may indicate that they need an African American female in that school or a Chinese administrator in that school. You don't hear that you need a really strong person or competent person for that assignment. They look at race, gender, etc. I've not heard a discussion around what individual would be good for a particular school. It's not that. The decisions are based around affirmative action, for example, or that this particular individual is good but is on the superintendent's bad list and so it's not going to happen. Or someone on the board wants someone to be at this school. It's not competency first; it's all politics.

Dubin:

Again, this is not the first time someone has responded that way.

Principal:

The things I could tell you!

Dubin:

With respect to your career, if you could think of an issue that you have faced, a tough decision, for example, students, parents, teachers, district issue, either as a principal and even assistant principal, that comes to mind, what would it be?

Principal:

Well, let me share this with you regarding the board involvement. This happened several years ago, when I was assistant principal of a high school. Of course, prior to my being assistant principal, I was a teacher. At that time there was a particular board member who was quite active. Well, we had a situation where a Chinese kid, a kind of punk kid, was angry and looking for a Hispanic kid who was harassing him. The Chinese kid approached the Hispanic kid and brandished a pellet gun. I personally found the Chinese kid, brought him into my office, and took the gun. The Chinese kid was obviously wrong, and so the child was expelled, the whole nine yards. Well, when this was brought to the attention of the board, we were informed that the board member responded by saying that we got the kid, but what was done to this Chinese kid before it even got to this point? That was his response.

The second political incident involved a Chinese 18-year-old girl who got into an argument about a grade with a teacher in the hallway. She continued to argue until she saw another teacher coming down the hallway who saw them arguing. The girl told the newly arrived teacher that the teacher had just slapped her. There were no witnesses. No one saw the slap. They all then came down to my office.

By law I had to make the report, and so I called the child protective services. They told me that because she was 18, I had to call the police, which I did. This girl happened to also work as a file clerk in an office that was involved with the board. The board member I'd spoken of earlier contacted my principal and talked about how the Chinese students were not being treated fairly. Keep in mind that I didn't even know the board member but I decided to call him up directly and try to talk to him. We decided to meet at a coffee shop where I explained about situations like this with students, and everything that we had done. He related his understandings of the Chinese gangs and other gangs and his perceptions of what was going on. I tried to clarify what was really happening and told him that these really weren't gangs but rather guys who were acting tough; they really weren't gangs. Again, I explained everything and suggested that if he had any future questions about this high school and the Chinese kids for him to give me a call. He said that if he had any questions he would call the superintendent personally; he wouldn't have to call me. That's how the game was played.

Then I found out that, as other things were coming up, this board member was bad-mouthing me. Suddenly, I got moved from my assistant principalship at my high school to a dean's position at another high school. At that point, I finished at my new high school and turned my keys in and said, "That's it, I don't want to do this anymore." Soon after, I got a call from an assistant superintendent who asked me to come to the district and speak with him. He told me that there was an assistant principal position opening at another school, and the principal there wanted me to be his assistant principal. Prior to that, I had heard that the board member was stating I hadn't done enough for my community, of which he was a part. At that time, coincidentally, he was interacting with someone dealing with a special commission, who knew me and was supportive of my work in the community and felt that I tried to be fair.

At that point, he seemed to change his mind about me and said he would try to help me. When I met with the assistant superintendent, I told him that I really wanted to accept the assistant principal position, but if this board member had anything to do with this promotion, I didn't want it. I did not want to be beholden to him or anyone. If I got the promotion, I wanted to get it on my own merit not through any political connection. The assistant superintendent assured me that the board member had nothing to do with this, and they hadn't talked to him. I had been requested by the principal of the school. That's what I was told.

I did find out that this board member indeed had felt that I had not been supportive of the community and was behind my being an assistant principal for 9 years and not advancing. That's why it's taken me so long for a promotion before this new situation happened. He perceived me as not supporting the Chinese. That's why I say that the position is political and can be very tough. I'm also quite outspoken about it.

Another example of politics involved several Chinese associations, which included administrators, teachers, and bilingual educators. The topic focused on recruiting teachers, college graduates from China, to teach Title I students in our schools. During the association meeting, I stated that while I only represented my school, my approach was if, after interviewing prospective teachers, I found that the only experience they had was teaching Chinese kids, that is, they had no classroom-management skills, no teaching experience to a more diverse student population, and even I had difficulty understanding their English, I was not going to hire them. I didn't care if they came from the same province as my father in China.

You see, if they were to come over here to teach and they had problems in the classroom, I was going to end up cleaning their mess. I'd experienced that before. I was tired and I was not going to do it. Well, all hell broke loose at the meeting. The board member whom I mentioned in the earlier situation was there and, after my comment, related that if it weren't for the fact that

I was Chinese, he would have kicked me out of the meeting. I challenged the board member to try. People thought I was anti-Chinese, antibilingual.

You see, from an administrative point of view, I don't care what color or background you are. I know that we would have significant problems with classroom management and I, or other administrators, would need to go into the classroom to work things out. The parents would complain, and I'd have to deal with that. They don't see that; they just see the politics.

All these issues are tough on me. But you know what? I'm glad I didn't move up in that way because at this point I can honestly say that nobody owns me. Nobody can say that I got to this position because of someone else. Nobody can say that. That's something I'm very proud of.

Dubin:

Yes, of course. You've got a clear conscience. You're not indebted to anybody for favors, and that's what politics is all about and, apparently in your experience, very much a reality in this district.

This brings me to another question about that. In light of your having to deal with what you think is really important to the school without compromising yourself, do you think the position leads to one of isolation, that you are really all alone? What do you think of this idea of isolation?

Principal:

I don't think so. At least right now, I have a very strong leadership team. If you can build a good team, if you're fortunate to have a good team, you're never alone. Even when I do something very individual, like writing school manuals, I always share it with my administrative team and I ask them what they think. When they write memos, they do the same with me. It's not because of writing skills. We simply help each other, whether it's the wording, grammar, or tone or whatever. I think new administrators need to remember these basic things.

For example, what I tell new teachers is that they're not here to be liked by the kids but rather to earn their respect. If they respect you then they'll probably like you, but respect is extremely important. As a principal it's similar. There are teachers who may not like me, but they respect me, they respect the position.

There are teachers who are not very friendly, and I don't trust them. The principal needs to realize who he can and cannot trust, conduct himself in a fashion that is accessible to everyone, and understand what and how much information he can share. There are some people where you must keep the information close to the vest, while with others you can relate as colleagues, even as friends. There are those you can go out to lunch and talk about everything but school. . . .

Dubin:

So then, you would say that the idea of isolation can be offset by having a strong leadership team: people you can trust and help you make a shared kind of decision.

Principal:

It's important to surround yourself with good people.

Dubin:

Someone who has your range of experience and a good supportive administrative team can function in a healthy way without the feeling of isolation. Interviews I've had with younger, less-experienced administrators have expressed isolation because they don't have the necessary information, they don't know whom to contact and they are operating by themselves. In some cases, they are desperate.

Principal:

Well, for 1st-year principals, the district does supply them with additional support. So perhaps they're overwhelmed or not internalizing the information. They are just a phone call away. They should get support, even by calling other principals.

Dubin:

Some do try to do that. Other times, when they need to make contact with the district, they are seen as an unknown commodity. They don't know who to contact, what to say. They're insecure about essentially communicating that they're not in control. They have lots of issues as a young administrator.

Principal:

I know that at the high school level, the principals do have problems feeling unsupported. But at the elementary school level, perhaps they're not used to that position.

Dubin:

Is there anything else you'd like to add to those new to the position and those who have been around for a while and would benefit from your wisdom and experience? Is there anything you'd like to add?

Principal:

Well, hopefully for the young people, they need to have a network, a support system, and they need to know that before going in. I don't care if you're a beginner or seasoned, if you make a mistake, admit the mistake, learn from it, and move on, don't dwell on it. Don't take things personally. Make sure you know how to take care of yourself physically, mentally, emotionally, and you should be fine. Always remember that what it is you're doing is going to benefit the children. You need to look at yourself in the mirror every day!

Dubin:

Thank you again, and I appreciate the time you've taken.

Analysis

This very experienced, field-tested, politically experienced middle school principal assumed the principal position after a considerable amount of time as a vice principal. The school had been successful with regard to test scores, although there was a student population whose test scores were not high enough for the No Child Left Behind mandate. While on one hand he wanted to provide a supportive and effective educational environment for his students, he felt the district pressure to improve test scores for certain student populations was considerable. He was also aware, albeit it was very difficult, that he had to maintain a cordial relationship with downtown without compromising the decision-making process at the school site. He also conveyed political issues and situations in this district that affected him personally and professionally throughout his years as an educator.

He also talked about how the principalship required a balanced perspective and that it was important not to over extend and burn out. During the interview he addressed many of the general leadership areas involved in administration, for example, school goals and priorities, personnel, budgetary decisions, participatory management strategies, politics, ethics, personal goals, as well as a host of other leadership considerations specific to his educational philosophy.

To understand burnout, an administrator must understand how complex this feeling is. While it involves an overextension and an unrealistic work commitment on the part of the administrator, it impacts everyone around him. Therefore, the ramifications increase exponentially. He is overwhelmed, which adversely affects his job performance, his relationship with his colleagues and teachers is affected, and the school environment, which forms the basis for instruction, becomes compromised. This syndrome, if you will, generally develops if the administrator assumes more than he is able to do, the job expectations exceed his expertise or, in some manner, his physical ability to do them.

In the event that conditions such as these exist for the administrator, it is extremely important to create a working environment that identifies the more significant stressors and design a work schedule that reduces them. It could be a schedule limiting the number of conferences an administrator may schedule; delegating responsibilities to other capable members of the school, be it teachers or others with assigned time; utilizing time to focus on less frequent people-contact, should that produce tension, or, alternatively, more time with personal contact and less time dealing with bureaucracy and paperwork. The point is to change conditions that create burnout and develop strategies to ameliorate these conditions. In the end the administrator will be far more effective and contribute in a more meaningful way to his school and community.

Discussion Questions

1. What are some of the key issues this administrator raises in this interview?

2. What is the tone of this interview?

3. Did he identify or stress the role of parents in this community?

4. What is the pressure he articulated regarding the role of the district's educational philosophy, and what drove that perception?

5. Could you explain this principal's philosophy regarding curriculum?

6. What was his political view of the principalship?

7. What test-score mandates was the school experiencing that significantly changed the ethos of the school environment?

8. Do you find his comments consistent with other school leaders you've experienced?

9. If you were appointed principal in this school, what would some of your 1st-year objectives be?

Student Activities

1. Write a letter to the superintendent requesting additional administrative support.

2. Write a letter of introduction to the community indicating your philosophy, background, and goals for the upcoming school year.

3. Write a letter of introduction to the staff regarding your philosophy, background, and goals for the upcoming school year.

4. What agenda items would you include for your first faculty meeting at the beginning of the school year?

5. What funding sources would you pursue to support your school program?

Interview Question

What additional interview questions would you direct to this administrator?

Simulations

Role-play the conversation you would have with your administrative team regarding burnout and the need for them not to work during the weekends.

Role-play the discussion you would have with another board member regarding the issue the principal discussed about the problem board member.

Role-play the board member who challenged this principal. What attitude or perspective would he bring into this situation?

Creating a Manageable Work Environment

The principal explained several situations regarding the work schedule for himself and his administrators (assistant principals, counselors, and so on) that would help provide relief from the added stress and excessive time spent on their work responsibilities. Consider the following:

How do you define the workload to your administrators in a way that acknowledges their job assignments but with an eye on burnout?

What formal and informal mechanisms could you employ to ensure that they were working effectively?

Do you think that it is the principal's responsibility to manage their work output or should they assume responsibility for this?

Principal Leadership Applications

There were several anecdotes the principal mentioned regarding the need to raise test scores. He mentioned that his evaluation was based upon these scores and that he wanted his teachers to understand that.

Do you feel he felt too pressured by the need to raise scores?

Should he have conveyed this to his faculty?

How do you feel the faculty would react to this level of honesty?

Role-play a conversation you would have with the district supervisor regarding the importance of test scores. What would you ask the supervisor about the importance test scores play in determining principal effectiveness? What other evaluative criteria do you think are important in determining a principal's job performance?

The principal mentioned his frustration dealing with teacher preparation. How do you feel about his attitude about teachers? Do you think he was justified? If you have been on hiring committees for teachers, what have you experienced?

Simulate a hiring committee interviewing teacher candidates. What questions would you ask? What type of teacher would you be looking for? What criteria and evaluative instrument would you use in your interview? What legal guidelines must you follow?

Questions Related to ISLLC Standards

See Appendix for ISLLC Standards.

1. How did this principal address Standard #3? Based upon the interview, cite at least one example that demonstrated that this standard was met.

2. How did this principal address Standard #6? Based upon the interview, cite at least one example that demonstrated that this standard was met.

3. Did you find that he also responded to other ISLLC standards? If so, which ones would you identify he addressed, and please cite specific examples.

Readings and Resources

Snowden, P. E. & Gorton, R. A. (2002). *School leadership and administration: Important concepts, case studies, & simulations.* New York: McGraw-Hill.
A cross section of various administrative practices and concepts which addresses leadership issues. Some of the topics covered are leadership behavior, relationships, community relations, change processes, race, and drug issues.

8

Students in Transition:
The Wise Veteran

S chools must provide an atmosphere that is responsive to change while maintaining a stable and balanced structure. Within the middle school environment, a school principal must be particularly vigilant in acknowledging this basic leadership strategy but unusually proactive in understanding and accommodating students, middle school being a developmentally dynamic time in a young person's life. How can a principal balance the school structure necessary to direct, guide, supervise, and control a student's academic, social, and physical life while providing opportunity for them to develop decision-making skills and integrating them into the extremely important social fabric of the school? The middle school principal profiled in this interview focuses on that perspective and the administrative process he has found effective.

Themes addressed in this chapter:

- Tri-level developmental and academic balance: elementary, middle, high school integration
- Participatory decision making
- Structure and flexibility
- Short- and long-term planning
- Maintaining personal balance and perspective

Profile of the Wise Veteran

Principal: male

Age: 50+

Ethnicity: Asian

Experience: 7 years as principal; related administrative experience

School: middle; student population: 1,179

The middle school is when they are really changing and their growth is remarkable. Within 3 years, they come in as little former fifth graders and within 2 years puberty begins and the growth physically, emotionally, socially is amazing. They grow up to be preteens to almost teenagers. At the high school level, they're thinking about college and the future. . . . And at the middle school, I certainly take pride in preparing the middle school children for high school in order to take on more challenges. It's challenging enough in the middle school, to survive at this level. It's important to have the necessary tools physically, socially, emotionally, and academically to handle high school.

Personally, you must look inside yourself to see if you have the passion to do this kind of work. First of all, do you like working with children and with adults? Do you like working with people with different points of view and different agendas? Do you have good organizational and communication skills? Do you have good people skills, patience, integrity, and respect? It's really all -encompassing. It's also something you have to work on. Do you have that sense of doing the right thing and what's best for the children. That's why people generally come into education in the first place. They enter as teachers, as humanitarians. We come in because we want to make some changes. One thing about being an administrator: if you want to make changes, the change process takes a long time and requires a lot of work. You need patience and you must learn from your mistakes and, again, challenge the process.

I would say that anyone contemplating administration . . . keep an open mind, see everything as a learning situation. The principalship is something where you should not feel that you are only the boss, always in control. Part of being an effective principal is learning to let go and let people whose strengths and skills are better in certain circumstances make decisions. Enable them to shine and keep in mind what the focus of your school is all about. That is the bottom line. At this time in schooling, we are under the gun to bring up test scores. It is important to keep in mind the learning process and the entire curriculum. Don't let the test scores be the only target. You must consider the culture of the school. What are we all about? How are we all defined? We are all in this together. You will find then that the test scores will go up.

In leadership theory they speak of the four core agreements: to be impeccable with your word; don't take anything personally; don't make assumptions; and always do your best.

School Context

Middle school principals have the unique responsibility of providing effective leadership to a student population some consider to be the most developmentally challenging. The students are changing in very dramatic ways academically, physically, and emotionally. The teachers they supervise must be cognizant of, and responsive to, these changes in order for students to succeed. This is a very complex environment for any leader and requires the ability to manage his school with sensitivity and clarity. Our very centered and experienced principal in this middle school assumed the principalship with an understanding of these expectations.

The school was located in the inner city where behavioral issues were not a significant factor. Test scores, which were high, were a very important factor that drove many of the school initiatives. He had been the administrator there for 7 years. The parents had a very strong influence on the direction of the school and were involved in the decision-making process. Prior to this assignment, he had had administrative experience as an assistant principal for 3 years.

School Characteristics

The school consisted of approximately 1,100 students with significant Chinese, Caucasian, and Latino populations. There was a small population of African American students.

School Climate

The administrator was very comfortable and experienced in dealing with the academic and developmental needs of the students. He understood the ethos of the school, an appropriate and relevant curriculum, community politics, and downtown pressures.

School Organization

The school district had a student population formula that provided administrative support, for example, two assistant principals, a dean, and three counselors.

Interview

The interview was conducted during the 1st few months of the school year.

Dubin:

Please tell me about your administrative experience, training, and educational background.

Principal:

Of course. I started as an elementary school teacher. I really wanted to be a high school social studies teacher, but I ended up in elementary education because in the mid-seventies that's where the jobs were. I began as an ESL (English as a second language) "pull-out" teacher and then taught Grades 1 through 5. I left teaching for a year after the strike of 1979. I was a limited contract teacher for several years. I went to work at Bank of America and then, after a year, I came back to the district as a middle school teacher, counselor, assistant principal, and now as principal.

Dubin:

How long were you an assistant principal?

Principal:

I was an assistant principal for 3 years, and then I became principal.

Dubin:

Could you tell me a little bit about your school?

Principal:

Certainly. We are a large, comprehensive middle school consisting of 1,179 kids. It is a high-performing school in this city. I have a lot of parent involvement, good students, good staff. It is a large middle school that has something to offer everybody.

Dubin:

Tell me about the demographic composition of the school, that is, students, staff, and your administrative support and counselors.

Principal:

We have a large staff of approximately 57 to 58 teachers and we've always had two counselors and one head counselor as well as two assistant principals. This year I've brought aboard an additional counselor so we have one counselor for each grade. As far as student demographics, we have 50% Chinese, 5% African American, 6% Latino, 22% to 23% White, and then other nonwhite.

Dubin:

How was it that you were able to bring aboard the additional counselor? How did that happen?

Principal:

How did that happen? Well you have to challenge the process, create; you had to find the opening. This year because of a specific funding formula, we were budgeted for fewer students but because we had additional students, I was able to hire an additional counselor and a teacher for math and science, seventh grade.

Dubin:

That must have been greatly appreciated by your other counselors, that much-needed relief.

Principal:

Oh, absolutely. From a student ratio of 600 to 1 reduced to 400 to 1 gave them a considerable amount of relief.

Dubin:

That's a big change. Let me ask you. You've been an administrator and in the leadership position in your school for some time now. . . .

Principal:

Oh, yes. This has been my 8th year in this middle school.

Dubin:

Well then, you are what I would consider to be a veteran.

Principal:

Yes, indeed. [laughs]

Dubin:

When you look at the school year and begin to establish your school priorities, what process do you go through? How do you communicate to the staff? How do you address that?

Principal:

I work with my PTSA, my counselors, my staff, just about everybody in the community. We look at the needs of the school for the next 5 years. For example, we definitely know that we have to upgrade our technology. We know our scores are high, but there are certain areas where our kids are not doing well. We still have some kids in the bottom percentile in reading and math. Generally our reading scores are in the 70th percentile and math scores in the 80th, but there are still 15% to 20% of our kids who are not achieving in math. We have about 30% who are not reading on grade level. We have to look at where the needs are, although we are ineligible for Title I money and for any other extra federal money. We use general-fund money and school improvement program monies to deal with these needs.

We have some children who do not take electives because they need to take the extra reading courses. In fact, we established that program 3 years ago. We have a teacher who was a former special education teacher using a direct method of instruction as to how to read and develop basic reading skills. We have also established a class for those who are in the second percentile who normally would be funded with Title I money. Although we do not have that money, we started the class for eighth graders, in particular. We feel that it would be very hard for those students to catch up when they go to the high school.

Dubin:

You said that you involved everyone, and that was clear from your response regarding the yearly plans and priorities. After the summer is over and you are beginning to think about these priorities, do you develop an outline or plan? As principal, do you get a sense of where you want to head before you meet with everyone?

Principal:

Oh yes, in fact I meet with them in the spring to plan for the fall, that is, March, April, May. We plan, of course, and revise for our new sixth graders. We're currently in November and we are going through our revisions right now for those things we didn't take into account last spring. One thing about this school: We have a very active school site council, which consists of parents, teachers, students, administrators, and other classified staff.

Dubin:

I've been interviewing other administrators in elementary, middle, and high school levels, and one of the questions I've not asked of the administrators is to differentiate elementary, middle, and high school kids. Let me ask this question of you since you've had a range of administrative experiences at the different school levels.

Principal:

Well, the elementary schoolchildren require a great deal of nurturing, TLC, and opportunities for them to succeed; they need to learn so much of the basics. The whole world is before them, and they're like jelly in your hands. The middle school is when they are really changing, and their growth is remarkable. Within 3 years they come in as little former fifth graders and within 2 years, puberty begins and the growth physically, emotionally, socially is amazing. They grow up to be preteens to almost teenagers. At the high school level, they're thinking about college and the future. While I don't have that much experience at that level, at the middle school level I certainly take pride in preparing the middle school children for high school in order to take on more challenges. It's challenging enough in the middle school to survive this level. It's important for them to ultimately have the necessary tools physically, socially, emotionally, and academically to handle high school.

Dubin:

So the document produced by the state several years ago, *Caught in the Middle*, which emphasized developing a different kind of school environment, was very insightful and relevant. While it did identify the need in preparing children for high school, it also acknowledged this special kind of youngster at that point in their lives. Nurturing, for example, which you mentioned before, was a very important aspect to the environment that needed to be present.

Principal:

Yes. They need to work in groups, similar to elementary school, and develop relationships with students, but they also need to let go, to take initiative themselves. The challenges ahead won't be easy in high school. They must have the affective piece as a part of the culture in addition to the academic piece.

Dubin:

Yes. In the past, prior to this movement, there was a very strong focus on the junior high school approach of compartmentalizing the curriculum, as opposed to what you were saying, the more nurturing, social-group orientation to develop the foundation for them.

Principal:

It is physically taking the child where they are at that moment, as a middle school child, just as the document states. You're really caught in the middle. You're no longer dealing with an elementary school kid and you're not in the high school. Some kids are early bloomers and some are late bloomers.

Dubin:

On another note, when you think of your daily, weekly, monthly, yearly expenditure of time, how do you spend it? By that I mean in terms of bureaucracy, plant management, personnel, safety, instruction, community: There are so many different areas. How would you say you allocate your time?

Principal:

You need to look at your calendar for the week. For example, this week I have a parent conference week. I have grade-level meetings. I plan to spend a good deal of time with the parents; they're here for the formal teacher-parent conferences. At this middle school we parent-teacher conference every day. We have parents here all the time, either a concern about their child's education, placement, or anything they consider important. On top of that, I deal with the daily operational needs. For example, today is Friday, and we have a lot of teachers out sick. We have a lot of classified personnel out today and also a security person. So today I was part security. We have substitutes who were late due to traffic and we needed to apply coverage. On a day-to-day basis, personnel management is very important.

Then there's the enormity of paperwork, as I literally see before me. I have paperwork that focuses on human resources. I have assistant superintendent reminders for next week. I have formal and informal observations with a curriculum piece dealing with differentiated instruction. Next week we have department meetings working on samples and examples regarding teacher differentiation of instruction, schoolwide, across the curriculum from PE to language arts.

Dubin:

Lots to do and very multifaceted.

Principal:

Like I said, multitasking. Everything is done at that moment and then move on to something totally different and unconnected to what you just did.

Dubin:

So you would certainly say that a skill for an administrator is the ability to make a variety of decisions and in different areas quickly.

Principal:

That is correct. But this is not done unilaterally. I do make certain decisions unilaterally, but I approach these decisions in a collaborative way, making sure that decisions are made with people who know what that situation is about. For example, a decision about a student should be directed to a counselor, teachers, or someone who knows the student. They provide input to you so you can make a decision, that correct decision.

Dubin:

An informed decision.

Principal:

Exactly, an informed decision. Teamwork is really important in any school situation.

Dubin:

What do you think the issues will be that new administrators face as they consider moving into a leadership role? By the same token, what would your comments be for those already an administrator, like yourself, an audience of experienced administrators?

Principal:

Well, I would have to go back to the leadership process: how to inspire and have a vision, to model the way; encourage the heart, enable those around you to act because you can't do it alone. There are also times when you need to challenge the process. You have to find creative ways to solve problems. It should be done in a way where it's clear, that it's the right thing to do at that time, at that moment, on that day. And ultimately it must be what's best for the child, the program, and the school.

Dubin:

Do you think that everyone can be an effective administrator? For someone contemplating becoming an administrator, what would you advise?

Principal:

No. Personally, you must look inside yourself to see if you have the passion to do this kind of work. First of all, do you like working with children and with adults? Do you like working with people with different points of view and different agendas? Do you have good organizational and communication skills? Do you have good people skills, patience, integrity, and respect? It's really all-encompassing. It's also something you have to work on. Do you have that sense of doing the right thing and what's best for the children? That's why people generally come into education in the first place. They enter as teachers, as humanitarians. We come in because we want to make some changes. One thing about being an administrator: If you want to make changes, the change process takes a long time and requires a lot of work. You need a lot of patience and you must learn from your mistakes and, again, challenge the process.

Dubin:

You raise many important points. One in particular, which brings me to my next question. When you say challenge the process, being creative, learn from your mistakes, taking risks, those kinds of things, what do you mean?

Principal:

You must have focus. If you want to challenge the process, that is, the policies or procedures, you must know what your focus is and what your priorities are. You must determine what the specific process is for your school. One size does not fit all. You must creatively come up and rationalize what will work for my program, my school, my group of kids, and then you go from there.

Dubin:

In hearing your response here, would you say that the principal position is a political one, since you talk about challenging the process?

Principal:

Well, it's political in that you must know your community; you must know who your constituencies are. You need to know your parents, their values about education. What are their attitudes about the school programs? It's important to know that and very important to know your philosophy of education. Can you really work with these groups, [with] the standards we're teaching and using?

Dubin:

So there must be a balance between these constituencies. And you're in the middle of it to make it work.

Principal:

Yes, that's right. And as the educational leader you also have to come out and identify the effective research and present all sides in order to meet the needs of your particular school and student population.

Dubin:

Thus, the idea of being patient and being clear about what your vision really is.

Principal:

Yes, and a sense of humor really helps . . . also being human. You must be your own person, yet in many ways you must also think like a politician. It's something you may not have intended to get into, but you will find that you are involved in that. But you still must be yourself.

Dubin:

In other interviews it has been said that the position of principal is one of isolation. How would you respond to that perspective?

Principal:

I really don't see it as isolation. I keep my doors open and I am very much a hands-on person. I don't get into everything all the time but I do try to keep on the pulse of what's going on in the classroom, in the yard, the office, my key department chairs, my teachers, counselors, my assistant principals, my custodial staff, and my secretaries. So I don't feel the isolation because if you do, you're doing it to yourself. You'd be putting up a wall. I always think of we, we, not me, me.

Dubin:

So then to a large extent, making sure that you're involved and having people involved in the decision making tends to lessen your sense of isolation and being apart from everyone else.

Principal:

Exactly. One example would be the union-building committee (UBC). Their function is to ensure that the contract is being followed. If you develop a collaborative approach and trust, there's no isolation. Yes, the job does involve making the tough decisions; you feel that you're it. Right now I'm in my office myself, alone, discussing this with you, but I don't feel isolated. I'm looking at pictures of my outdoor education program and I'm also looking outside my door watching that the kids are being dismissed. I don't feel isolated.

Dubin:

Yes, but you raised the other part of that question. You certainly answered the first part completely, but what about that aspect of loneliness? You are the principal and the critical decision maker. The buck stops at your desk. Is there any feeling of isolation in that role?

Principal:

Oh yes. It is my job to make this decision. It is my job to make this call. In fact, yesterday when we were going to talk, I wasn't able to because I had to call for an ambulance regarding an emergency medical situation. The mother had problems communicating with my secretary, and I didn't know if the mother was coming to school or not, so I had to make the call to send the child to the hospital. I had to make the decision.

Dubin:

Yes, exactly. And you feel secure at this point in your career to make that decision. Yet, I've spoken to others who aren't secure even though they have several years under their belts. Having that security is very important.

Principal:

Yes, taking the risk.

Dubin:

Right. You mentioned just a moment ago about secretaries. How important are they in the context of the school?

Principal:

They are very important, particularly in an elementary school. They run the school. They serve like an assistant principal. They help keep everything going, the normal day-to-day operation, for example, the handouts that need to go out, all the little things, like a well-oiled machine. They are human beings also, and they have their days, but they do so many important things on the front lines.

Dubin:

In the light of the incredible amount of work, sacrifice, and commitment that principals clearly exercise in taking on that role, how do you deal with burnout and stress and those kinds of issues?

Principal:

Well, as a matter of fact, this year I've developed an ulcer. I saw a doctor last month and was told that I had the symptoms of an ulcer. I just recall that this past September when things were getting hectic, I went days, weeks without eating lunch until late in the afternoon. It has gotten much better now, and in fact I just finished my lunch just before talking with you.

Dubin:

Good! What advice would you offer new administrators in this respect? What would you tell them?

Principal:

I would tell them to slow down. For the first 3 or 4 years, you must decide what the most important things are that you need to do during that time.

Dubin:

That's the wisdom of experience. On one hand, for young administrators, they are so anxious and want to do well. For the seasoned administrators, they know that it's important to keep things in perspective and slow down. Change and effective decisions require time.

Principal:

In leadership theory they speak of the four core agreements: to be impeccable with your word; don't take anything personally; don't make assumptions; and always do your best.

Dubin:

Yes. That's good, if you could live by that and certainly keep it in mind. It's important to have a plan.

Principal:

Yes, and of course, plans are subject to change. You need flexibility!

I would also say that anyone contemplating administration [should] keep an open mind, see everything as a learning situation. The principalship is something where you should not feel you are only the boss, always in control. Part of being an effective principal is learning to let go and let people whose strengths and skills are better in certain circumstances make decisions. Enable them to shine and keep in mind the focus of what your school is all about. That is the bottom line.

At this time in schooling, we are under the gun to bring up test scores. It is important to keep in mind the learning process and the entire curriculum. Don't let the test scores be the only target. You must consider the culture of the school. What are we all about? How are we all defined? We are all in this together. You will find then that the test scores will go up.

Dubin:

That's how you balance it all. You stated in your last response the need to deal with the pressure of having high test scores but, on the other hand, understand the value of teaching outside of that, which escapes test scores.

Principal:

Yes, that's correct. You must have a complete and accurate view of your school in order to be effective.

Dubin:

Thank you very much for your comments. They have been very informative.

Analysis

This very experienced and focused principal was responsible for overseeing and maintaining the activities of a high-achieving middle school. He was clear about his mission and philosophically anchored to the middle school child. He had a very strong understanding of his school and of the need for him to apply a collaborative decision-making style. While being comfortable with himself, he still felt the pressure of the position, as evidenced in his comments about his physical health and about overextending in order to help and support the school.

During the interview he addressed many of the general leadership areas involved in his administration, for example, school goals and priorities, committee work, personnel, budgetary decisions, participatory management strategies, politics, ethics, personal goals as well as a host of other leadership considerations specific to his educational philosophy within the middle school context.

Creating a school environment that is philosophically and programmatically driven by student developmental issues is very important, particularly at the middle school level. The family systems paradigm is the conceptual underpinning for this principal's approach to managing and directing the activities of his school. While families have to adapt to changing circumstances, so do schools, particularly with middle school-aged children. A healthy school must be resilient and have the capacity to change procedures and processes to accommodate the needs of its students and community. A dysfunctional school cannot discern the need for such adaptation and, when it does recognize the need for adjustment, it is not capable of following through. Adaptation is one of the pillars of the family systems paradigm.

Another component of the family systems model that relates directly to this principal's approach is the basic integrative application, that is, the attempt to address individual needs within the context of the environment: school or family. For many decades now, our schools have been called upon to replace or augment the societal and family elements that have been compromised through our macro-capitalist system and to direct those interactions and activities to the school. Those elements now are more definitely assumed by the school and reflect sensitivity, compassion, and trust, underscoring the family structure, and with a view of children—individuals— growing and evolving in an organic way.

As the principal frequently indicated in the interview, the need to focus his leadership decisions based upon the interests and needs of the child is paramount. This is not to say that there would be a reduction or absence of the mandates of the school system regarding curriculum, codes of conduct, academic performance, and so on, but that the school would provide the flexibility to make adjustments to accommodate the needs of the evolving individual, as in a family, in concert with the expectations of the school system.

Another important aspect to the family system model, as it relates to this principal's approach, focuses on history. The historical context appreciated by family members, when they consider their heritage, tradition, background, and so on, is also transferred to the school. Traditions and the ethos of the school are also assumed and learned by the students as they discover the school culture. This is quite powerful and creates the connection between their goals and expectations with those of the school. This suggests the continuum we see functioning within a healthy family environment.

Still another important element focuses on decentralized decision making. In this school, the opportunity for students to be involved in the decision-making process not only prepares them to be individual thinkers but reflects the healthy family environment, where individual input and participation is not only present but encouraged.

Discussion Questions

1. What are some of the key issues this administrator raises in this interview?
2. What is the tone of this interview?
3. Does he identify the role of parents in this community?
4. What is his perception of the district's educational philosophy and what drives that perception?
5. Could you explain this principal's philosophy regarding curriculum and education in general?

6. What is his political view of the principalship?

7. What understandings about this student population did this administrator reflect upon that were extremely important to him?

8. Do you find his comments consistent with other schools and districts you've experienced?

9. If you were appointed principal in this school, what would some of your 1st-year objectives be?

Student Activities

1. Write a letter to the superintendent requesting additional administrative support.

2. Write a letter of introduction to the community indicating your philosophy, background, and goals for the upcoming school year.

3. Write a letter to the staff regarding your philosophy, background, and goals for the upcoming school year.

4. What agenda items would include for your first faculty meeting at the beginning of the school year?

5. What funding sources would you pursue to support your school program?

6. What type of letter would you expect this principal to write to his community as the new school year begins?

Interview Question

What additional interview questions would you direct to this administrator?

Simulations

Role-play the principal welcoming the new class of students just entering the middle school from the elementary school. What would you convey to them to make them feel comfortable yet relate certain behavioral and academic expectations?

Role-play the principal giving a tour of the middle school to interested parents and students during the early fall period when families are deciding which schools their children will attend for the following year. What would you say to the entire group to interest them in your school? What types of questions do you think the parents or students would ask? How would you distinguish your school from another middle school?

Role-play the principal orienting new teachers to the developmental issues they will experience in working with the middle school students. How would you distinguish the middle school student from the elementary or high school student?

As principal, role-play a conversation you would have with a high school or elementary teacher recently assigned to your middle school. What would you say to orient them to the differences between the high school or elementary school student and the middle school student? What insights would you give them? What problems could you anticipate they might experience?

Developing an Organizational Awareness of the Changing Middle School Child

How would the principal interviewed deal with testing and assessment with his particular school population?

Which strategies would he consider in order to recruit highly qualified and sensitive teachers?

What strategies would he use in order to address his limited English-proficient students?

What additional strategies could he use in order to develop stronger connections to the high schools in which his students enroll after they graduate from his middle school?

What curriculum strategies would he develop to maintain high academic standards with his students?

Principal Leadership Applications

At one point in the interview, the principal discussed the important role the secretary plays, particularly on the elementary school level.

1. As a new principal, how do you balance your authority with the understanding that the secretary can be such an informal power?

2. Do you explain that job definition in your first meeting with the secretary?

3. Would you let the process flow naturally?

4. Would you give her the range of authority she was used to?

5. The principal stated his code of leadership behavior; don't take anything personally, don't make assumptions, and always do your best. How do you respond to these suggestions?

6. Do you have any codes of behavior or philosophy you follow?

7. The principal mentioned that his health was suffering due to the demands of the position. How would you be proactive regarding your health?

8. How would you work with your administrative team and teachers regarding burnout?

9. Do you think a school should provide an environment similar to the home, as suggested by the Analysis section focusing on the family systems model?

10. Where do you think the school should draw the line between the responsibilities of the family and that of the schools?

11. Do you think schools should teach values, that is, sex education, ethics, politics, and so on?

Questions Related to ISLLC Standards

See Appendix for ISLLC Standards.

1. How did this principal address Standard #1? Based upon the interview, cite at least one example that demonstrated that this standard was met.

2. How did this principal address Standard #2? Based upon the interview, cite at least one example that demonstrated that this standard was met.

3. How did this principal address Standard #3? Based upon the interview, cite at least one example that demonstrated that this standard was met.

4. Did you find that he also responded to other ISLLC standards? If so, which ones would you identify he addressed, and please cite specific examples.

Readings and Resources

Dubin, A. E. (1995). Emerging educational structures. In S. Rothstein (Ed.), *Class, culture, and race in American schools: A handbook.* Westport, CT: Greenwood.
A compilation focusing on issues in education: racism, special education, urban development, multiculturalism, women's issues, and so on.

PART III

High School

9

Perceptions and Assumptions: The Multitasker

The perceptions and assumptions held by the leadership of a school dramatically affect the school climate and have a direct bearing on the willingness of faculty to participate in school functions and activities. How the leader of the school feels about her faculty determines the working environment. What decisions can she make that inspire volunteerism, improve attendance, motivate and develop teacher professionalism, and heighten faculty morale in order for them to go the extra mile on behalf of the school?

Themes addressed in this chapter:

- Assumptions and attitudes about faculty and students
- Gradual changes in school decision making
- Structural support for students and faculty
- Short- and long-term planning
- School and community interaction

Profile of the Multitasker

Principal: female

Age: 50

Ethnicity: Caucasian

Experience: 3 years as principal; 6 years as assistant principal; 3 years related administrative experience

School: continuation high school; student population: 200–250

You go through this incredible interview and then you're hired, you're anointed, and you're the principal. Then, there you are, alone. You are the leader: the curriculum leader, the visionary, the person who is going to make decisions about people's lives. The buck stops with you on everything. You're supposed to have the time and knowledge to know how to solve all of this and you don't. . . . It's OK to be a learner in this struggle and just admit it. Then work to make it different.

I think that there are only a few decisions that you have to make on the turn of the dime. Because someone comes into your office and lays a problem down does not mean that you have to give an answer. There's always the feeling that you have to fix it. And your tendency is to say, OK, we'll do this, because that's the position you've been put in. What I've learned is that I rarely respond by saying, Let's do this. Now I say, what would you like from me? What do you think we should do? Often they already know. They have a better feel for the problem and the solution than you do.

In a way I see that I do a considerable amount of personnel management, and listening to everyone's moans and groans, keeping people calm and centered, if you will . . . getting rid of things that get in their way in order for them to continue focused. Sometimes I feel as though I'm more of a therapist than a principal. I spend a lot of time doing that. I don't think that that's bad; that's why it moves.

School Context

Principals of continuation schools have a different mandate as they assume leadership roles. They are working with a population of students who have not been successful in traditional school environments. They have not demonstrated an ability to perform effectively in the mainstream, academically or behaviorally. For this reason, continuation high school principals have to provide a different and more structured type of leadership. The continuation school selected for this interview had a student enrollment of approximately 200. Because the students had unusual backgrounds, the principal approached her position by balancing the academic expectations of the high school, that is, district and state goals and objectives, with a nurturing yet structured support system. She also had a strong background in the field, having been a teacher and high school assistant principal prior to assuming the principalship of this school.

The school was in a suburban neighborhood. While test scores were quite low, as one might expect with students who have had histories of significant school issues, emphasis was still placed on achievement. It was a very important factor that drove many of the school initiatives.

School Characteristics

The school consisted of approximately 200 students with significant proportions of Caucasian, Latino, and African American students. This principal was also responsible for two additional programs: one focused on students with more threatening and documented behavioral problems; the other dealt with students who had more issues concerning fitting-in to normal high school settings.

School Climate

The administrator was well prepared to deal with the considerable needs of the school. She understood the ethos of the school, appropriate and relevant curriculum, parent needs, and district pressures. Her school was a focal point of the district, since she focused on lower-performing students who had very problematic behavioral histories.

School Organization

The school was provided administrative support, for example, one dean who served the function of an assistant principal, and a full-time guidance/academic counselor. The counselor had her PPS (pupil personnel services) credential and an MFCC (marriage, family, and child counselor) credential. This academic background served her extremely well in providing both academic and psychological support to the students.

Interview

The following interview was conducted during the 1st months of the school year.

Dubin:

Could you please tell me a little about your administrative background and training? In this way I can get a sense of your experience and schools in which you've worked.

Principal:

I was initially a speech and language pathologist in hospitals. I moved from that to itinerant positions in schools. From there I went into special day classes and did that for many years and on several different levels. I worked with babies, as well as on the elementary, junior high, and high school levels. I have been involved with public school districts and the county as an SDL (severe disorders of language) teacher. I found that when the county started drifting apart and the quality of services they offered declined, I decided to leave it. . . .

I began working in special education in the high school and decided I didn't want to do that anymore. I wanted to move into the regular population, if you will. I took a position as a dean and did that for a number of years. I saw that position as a stepping-stone. I realized that I didn't want to do that forever, so I pursued my administrative credential and from there I moved into AP positions on the high school level, that is, two comprehensive high schools, although I knew I didn't want to stay in the comprehensive high school.

Dubin:

How large were the comprehensive high schools?

Principal:

They were approximately 1,100 students.

Dubin:

How long did you stay there?

Principal:

I was there for 4 years and then I came here.

Dubin:

Tell me about this school.

Principal:

This is a continuation high school. We take students from six compre-hensive high schools in the district. We take students every six weeks. These students are academically at risk and emotionally and physically, in some cases, at risk of getting an education. Moreover, more serious than that is finding out who they are and how (they can) live safely and well. For me, the goal here is not only for them to get a diploma but to help kids deal with the baggage they have. I want them to attain this at this point in their lives.

Dubin:

How large is the school?

Principal:

On paper they say you can take 250 students, although we have approx-imately 210 to 220 kids.

Dubin:

What would you say your priorities are for this school year? As the leader of the school what is your vision for this school year?

Principal:

The vision is the continuation of what we had defined and begun last year. The district is moving on equity; educational opportunity. We have done a good deal of data analysis, and what we found here in this school is that there are no equity issues. No one here is doing well, and so it doesn't matter what color you are or what sex you are; the kids are not performing well. We looked at some of the other factors and what surfaced was that the students were not good readers, and if you can't read you are not going to be successful. If you're not successful academically, where else are you going to be . . . just how that all filters down. We looked at last year's reading data as something to investigate.

Dubin:

How did the district respond to these data and your strategy?

Principal:

We got a lot of support from the district to bring in reading specialists and a reading program that, in fact, had not been utilized at this school but had been instituted at all the other comprehensive school sites. They were very generous in providing money, books, setting up classrooms, consultants, for us to get on board. We tested every student in the school and got a baseline to place the kids in the appropriate reading classes. We identified a teacher with a reading specialist credential. Our teachers really rose to the occasion as to how to teach reading across the curriculum and how they could teach reading in their classrooms. A couple of dynamic teacher-leaders grabbed onto this and ran with it, which was really important.

What I've recognized is that I can't do it all. I do need to have people who I trust and are on the same mission and have the same sense of integrity and dedication. And they actually appeared.

Dubin:

How did you go about this?

Principal:

We did in-services throughout the year. A big concern with the teachers was that they didn't want to get a one-hit in-service, and then the administration says, OK, now go back to your classrooms and do it. So we really pledged to the faculty that this would not happen . . . we would go slowly and we would provide a lot of support. We had the specialist who came in and went into the classrooms and met with teachers individually in addition to giving presentations to the faculty as a whole. The teacher-leaders ran with it and had teachers volunteer and present lessons that they had done. It was incredible . . . to the point where on the last day of school in June, I had two teachers come up to me and say that they knew it was the last day of school but they were concerned because they had some great ideas about how they were going to institute this and make it continue in September.

Dubin:

How did you react to this overture?

Principal:

Well. I was really blown away. Generally, my experience had been [that] at the end of the year, most teachers say, "See ya," and they're out of there. In addition, they presented me with an outline for the entire year . . . a rough draft as to how they saw the in-services working throughout the year. If that wasn't good enough, they knew we had a faculty meeting every week and so they would build in what we could be covering in the faculty meetings and how we could readjust it and provide more time, collaboratively, not only using the faculty time but using the six-period prep. So to get back to my goals for the year: It is to have this actualized.

Dubin:

Have you had an opportunity to discuss this with your superintendent?

Principal:

Yes. I've also consulted with him. In fact, he asked me to give a presentation about this. He was extremely impressed and said that we were ahead of every comprehensive school in the district regarding the institution of this reading plan. Now granted, my school is a smaller learning community, and it's much easier to move us, in that sense. I do not have as many factors in my face, you know. It's very clear what our issue is. Regardless of how easy it was to identify this, he was thrilled. He felt that we needed to figure out what we really wanted for the rest of year . . . how I was going to do it . . . what I needed from him. Did I need someone who could collect data? He wanted data, data, and more data so we could present this and use this as a model as to how to move a school in the area of equity. So my goal is to have that happen and provide these data . . . to have kids leave us more prepared to handle what's out there as better readers, better consumers . . . and the kids aren't going to have missed opportunities and be taken advantage of because they can't read.

Dubin:

Getting back to what you had said regarding the response of the teachers. If you were going to look at what happened to get that reaction, what do you think caused this reaction from the teachers?

Principal:

It was not shoved down their throat . . . information was put out to them. Clearly, it was presented as what this committee sees; in fact, it was two committees, which meant it was almost 50% of the staff that looked at these data before it was put out to the rest of the faculty. They saw these data, and there was a recommendation, which essentially said that this is what we see and asked, "What do you see?"

It was clear that anybody could identify the need . . . and then it was a conversation, directed, but not shoved down anyone's throat. It was participatory, their concerns about it . . . how to do it . . . was all taken into consideration. Behind closed doors, the teacher leaders who were planning it, hearing this from teachers and knowing that some will drag their feet and say they can't do it and buck it. Well how do you get them on board and not let them damage the energy?

A piece of that was really feeding what the teachers wanted, which was individualized, slow instruction. "Don't load me down with this, I still have my curriculum to teach," was a common concern. We took strategies that, in fact, they were already doing in their classrooms. We took some of the fear out of adding something new for them to do. How was a math teacher going to teach reading? My goodness. Well, if you showed them that this reading strategy was one they actually used and was nothing new but the terminology, it relieved them. We could help them do this even more. We'd say that you'll find that you'll be teaching math and reading and become even a better teacher than you think you are. So, I think listening and guiding teachers and avoiding giving them more information and ideas which they found burdensome. This way I let them own it by their stepping up to the plate and defining their needs, and then responding to whatever fears that might surface that would inhibit them from getting on board.

Dubin:

Let me see if I can identify some areas in your response that speak to the strategies you used. It would generate from them, after the research identified this obvious need as to how it would work best, the "buy-in," although it was directed by you and the teacher-leaders, giving them resources in time and supplies, done in intervals over time so that it would not impinge on their time.

Principal:

Yes. It really reduced their stress and the threat of taking too much of their time. I can't tell you that in my experience over the years in watching in-services and [having] been affected by it as a teacher, the problem with staff development always, in my mind, has been that a teacher is given a day of this professional development. You throw something at them and then you leave them . . . there is no ownership. This is not what they wanted, their opinion was not asked, and they were not given any support. Well, we did not do this. We showed them . . . they asked for it . . . they told us their fears and what they needed, and we accommodated them. Every time, we responded to the opportunity to give them some feedback.

Whether it was data feedback or just commentary of different things that had happened. Kids reported about how they felt about it. This kid said this to one teacher, and it wasn't just me providing the feedback, it was the teachers sharing that . . . this happened in one classroom and other examples . . . it served to reinforce the feeling that this was working and it was a good thing. It energized us even more. You know what we're doing is paying back and is working.

Dubin:

Let me touch upon something you mentioned earlier on. You said that in your staff there is a range of teacher reactions. You had those who immediately came aboard and also those who were more resistant. How did you deal with those who were not team players, who did not respond to this success that the kids were, indeed, getting something out of this?

Principal:

I'll tell you. The couple of teachers that were initially resistant, well one of them retired, and, frankly, he was never going to get on board; he was going to drag his heels for anything and everything. In fact, there are still a few teachers who still are not on board. The ones I'm concerned about who are not supportive and could move and influence the faculty, those people who were pivotal in my mind, I listened very sincerely to their demands when it was first presented, what they would need in order to buy in. Then I made darn sure that I met those needs and these people were groomed, if you will. Those that I knew wouldn't be responsive I essentially ignored. I didn't give [them] any attention at all. I moved with the positive stuff. There are still one or two this year, but we're on a roll, so I don't think it matters at this point.

Dubin:

It seems that your strategy is working extremely well. And incidentally, the size of the school is far less important than your thinking and approach in working with your staff. Don't minimize your success. Your approach would work anywhere and, without that staff support, will fail anywhere. Give yourself credit.

Principal:

I appreciate that feedback.

Dubin:

On another leadership area, how would you say you spend most of your time? For example, issues that deal with bureaucracy: documentation, accreditation reports, and so on; or personnel issues, that is, due process matters, or teacher class scheduling, room allocation, lesson plan design, and so on; or community relations/outside groups; or instructional material, that is, textbook adoption, supplementary material; or school budget or funding from the district. Considering this array of possibilities, how would you say you allocate your time?

Principal:

Well, I can tell where it is and also tell you where I wish it was. I spend an incredible amount of time on management issues, just managing the school. Incidentally, this is not just my only job in the district and that affects how I allocate my time. I am not only the principal of this school. I also have to work with the development of the community day school and where I want that to be going. Middle college, another district program, is also under my supervision, so I need to continually work on those two programs.

Dubin:

Could you briefly tell me a little bit about those programs?

Principal:

Yes. Community day school is the district's expulsion school. The district has a very hard line on expulsion. Those kids come to us for a variety of reasons and time, from a semester to a year. I have two teachers in there; I have an aide that also does the state reporting. For a number of years now it has been for us, a school of consequence . . . you were bad and now you were to go up the hill . . . you're not going to see anyone, touch anyone . . . you're going to be in a self-contained classroom. It is a punishment.

Dubin:

How do you see the school?

Principal:

I don't want that school to be a punishment. It has taken me 2 years to change a particular personality there who was keeping it from becoming an intervention as opposed to a negative consequence. After 2 years of working with personnel and looking for more personnel and working with downtown, I've let them know how I saw this school going. I believe that I finally have the personnel I want there, but I spend a great deal of time with them, getting them to identify what the school can become for these kids and how we're going to get there. And so, I'm running with that while I'm still running here.

In the middle college I have a principal who I supervise but who basically runs the program. Again, we take kids who are not making it in a comprehensive site, but who are not necessarily credit deficient. These kids need another environment to be successful. They have dropped out of the normal situation but can take college courses while continuing to take their core courses for high school graduation but on a junior college campus. That program . . . expansion . . . open houses, meeting parents . . . ensuring that the students are placed there correctly, takes a good deal of my time.

I'm also on the district committee for reviewing kids going to adult school. So you see that this school is not my only piece of obligation. In a way, I do a considerable amount of personnel management and listening to everyone's moans and groans, keeping people calm and centered, if you will . . . getting rid of things that get in their way in order for them to continue focused. Sometimes I feel as though I'm more of a therapist than a principal. I spend a lot of time doing that. I don't think that that's bad; that's why it moves.

I know in my heart that I want to spend more time with kids. I feel that I'm moving away from knowing the kids and their histories. I also feel that I'm not spending enough time in the classrooms . . . curriculum . . . what the teachers are teaching! I just don't get there enough. I pledge every year that I'm going to do more of that. Perhaps this year I've gotten better at identifying teacher-leaders to run some of it for me—reading across the curriculum, for example—and then for them to come back to me and say what they've put together to let me know what I think. This would be different from me saying what I think we should do and trying to sell it. This would free me up a little bit. Hopefully, I would be able to spend more time in the classroom.

Dubin:

For clarification, the middle college students, how old are they?

Principal:

Oh yes. They are juniors and seniors.

Dubin:

And the community day school?

Principal:

They can be freshmen up to seniors.

Dubin:

This is a different entity from the continuation school. How do they become identified and siphoned off to one of these schools?

Principal:

They get siphoned off to the community day school because they are responsible for an egregious act. They have violated one of the tenets of a comprehensive high school (or of a continuation school) here. For example, if you've been in a serious fight and almost killed somebody and spend time in jail, the district might say that you are a danger. We're going to isolate you for a while and place you in the community day school. It is always a consequence of a behavioral violation that is severe enough for the principal to say you are a danger to the rest of us on this campus. Maybe you had a weapon or several documented incidences or a drug violation . . . it is a disciplinary issue and a violation of the education code.

Dubin:

And that is a more serious violation, to be placed in the community day school. And they could get there from any school.

Principal:

Yes.

Dubin:

Is there another assessment made so that they can move out from the community day school?

Principal:

No. There are no further assessments. Previously, their case was reviewed by the school board. Now there are stipulated expulsions where you admit guilt and that defines the length of time, for example, 6 months or a year. The board never hears it. But basically, you have the right to present your case, that is, due process and have it heard by the board, and a consequence is assigned, hopefully that is appropriate to the offense. In addition to serving this time in CDS, there is a counseling component attached to this. In the past, it has been that you've needed four counseling sessions, and your parents have to be there and you can go to any of these agents. This is a piece of what I've been trying to tailor because I think that this is ridiculous. If you know this kid and you know he or she is a substance abuser, the counseling should be for substance abuse, not something else. Often the counseling does not relate to the specific problems. Really, we should get more organized about this. That's not an easy thing to do. . . .

Dubin:

What about middle college?

Principal:

To get to middle college, a referral from the counselor from the site indicating that a student has potential . . . there are no drug problems, no discipline issues . . . it seems that the student is simply not fitting in. The student is not doing his or her best, not fitting into the comprehensive high school scene . . . a computer nerd type of student, or very, very bright student, and things seem to be too slow for them.

So middle college is an alternative, not disciplinary, not related to credit deficiency, although sometimes that is a piece of it, but certainly not in the same category as if they were placed here in the continuation school.

Dubin:

You mentioned that there are approximately 200 to 220 "live bodies" here in the continuation school. How many students would you say are in the community day school?

Principal:

Right now I would say that they're starting the school year with approximately 18 students.

Dubin:

And what could it go up to?

Principal:

Well, it could go up to 30, and that is a major issue, which is another story, and will take up much of my time to negotiate that and see how that will work out. Clearly, these are management issues. For example, if you have one classroom, two teachers, and there are 30 students in that classroom: issues about two classrooms, team teaching within one classroom with all the students . . . these are the issues. What was promised initially to the teachers . . . the attitudes and now how it's developed . . . all this deals with the management of the program and personnel.

Dubin:

And you oversee the hiring, management of all of that?

Principal:

Yes.

Dubin:

And what about the middle college? How many students are there in that program?

Principal:

About 20 to 25 students. There is a principal or actually an assistant principal who actually runs it and two teachers and a counselor.

Dubin:

You oversee all of this. You are responsible. They all report to you.

Principal:

Yes. The buck stops here.

Dubin:

That is a lot! So, you manage three different sites. But through it all, your regret is that you don't deal with the kids directly as you would wish, nor do you have the opportunity to deal with direct instruction, since so much time is committed to the management of these programs. As a result, your focus this year will be on delegation with teacher-leaders who can represent your philosophy since your time is so limited.

Principal:

Also, there is a summer school program for the district that I oversee as director. This program has approximately 1,200 students and two sites. I do all the hiring. My secretary and I put that program together in February and March, that is, setting up the sites, placing students in classes. This also means that after the summer school, all the problems that have happened during the summer, for example, parents calling regarding grades of their kids, calls for me to serve as liaison between the parents and school. I spend September and October dealing with those issues and problems from summer school.

Dubin:

With respect to these different programs, are the parents involved? Since we are dealing with very interesting student populations and on many different levels, do you find that they are involved. . . . Is it difficult to get them involved?

Principal:

It is difficult to get them involved, but they are not cantankerous; no moaning and groaning. They are thankful that someone finally cares about their kid; no one is trashing their kid, saying that he's a loser. Because of the work that's done here, the kids start to feel it, that someone knows who they are. It's very rewarding. It would be great to have more involvement, but I haven't got the time to make it happen. We try to have parent meetings once a month and we get 8 to 10 parents, so we don't have a large turnout. But look, they're working two jobs. The majority of parents don't have the time. They get involved with their kids when they're in trouble. Some, though, are very educated and involved and balanced.

Dubin:

But generally you find them receptive.

Principal:

Yes, they are great. When they come in here . . . I interview every student with their parent. I love that piece of my work. That's probably the best piece I have with them. They are grateful. I don't look at their kid and say you're a bad kid. I don't say that. I do say that you've made some rough choices, and I'm not here to judge you, but I'm definitely here to tell you that this is what we have to do to get out of this mess. Your integrity must now step up to the plate if you're going to be successful. There is no more time for playing . . . me against you . . . or against the system. I have to be straight with you, and you have to be straight about this with me.

Dubin:

Do you find that they respond to this?

Principal:

Oh, yes. Most of them do. Most of them do. I made some bad calls. I take some kids that I shouldn't; really truant kids, for example. There are some kids that I should pass on, I should say no, but I try to give them one more opportunity, one more semester. At times it's hard not to. It's why we're here.

Dubin:

Regarding entry-level leaders pursuing this career, what would you say are the issues facing a new administrator. . . . What you think they should consider as they face their new leadership position. By the same token, what would you say the issues are for a more experienced administrator?

Principal:

If I were to tell you what new administrators need, I would say they need a coach. They need an administrator coach. The administrative programs do not address the day-in and day-out; how a school works. I mean that in paperwork, budget, mechanics of knowing issues of personnel, strategies of motivating your faculty . . . data, what is available. They need a coach. You go through this incredible interview and then you're hired, you're anointed, you're the principal. Then there you are, alone. You are the leader; the curriculum leader, the visionary, the person who is going to make decisions about people's lives. The buck stops with you on everything. You're supposed to have the time and knowledge to know how to solve all of this, and you don't. You also don't have someone whom you can call and say, "You know what just happened to me?" Where do I get this money from . . . I have all these piles of money. . . . There's no booklet you can refer to that says you can take from here, but not from here . . . this is for personnel . . . this is for food. . . . And, should you take it from the wrong place, this becomes a problem. There's no coach.

I was told by a former principal that you learn to fly on your own once you're here . . . no one teaches you this job. He said it was OK to call him on the phone if I had a question. I had no idea what FTE were. How do you do your staffing? When everyone was telling me that I was over my FTE limit, I didn't know what to do or what that meant. I never had a course that told me about FTE . . . how to figure staff and student ratio. I still don't have it clear . . . numbers are always a very confusing area. I was fortunate that I was able to go to someone who gave me feedback and clarified things for me.

And you can't tell everyone that you don't know. You don't want to admit that. My, you've just been anointed king of the palace. I think that this is a common problem. . . . And so, to sum up, none us knew when you get the position, and that's OK. If the districts really want to support their new administrators, they should have a coach-principal who had the time who could meet with me once a week, behind closed doors, where I could say that I'm overloaded. . . . You're just not taught everything.

Dubin:

As for a colleague who has had similar experiences, what would you share as to what you've gained, learned that makes you a more effective leader?

Principal:

I've learned that I can't do it all. I've learned to delegate. I've learned to be comfortable with myself as a 3rd-year principal at this site. Get to know your faculty.

Dubin:

Tell me about delegation and working in a shared decision-making format. Could you tell me a little more about your thinking in this regard?

Principal:

Yes. I've learned how to prioritize. I don't have to fight every battle and I'm not going to win every battle. That is a recognition for me, an epiphany. You want to do it all. You can't have it all. You have to compromise because you're a part of a larger picture. I think I've worked very hard to keep that in mind, considering what piece I play with respect to the district perspective . . . where I can get my support. I've learned to negotiate a little bit more . . . build relationships not only on the site but with other principals and the powers that be. And as time goes by, I think that, yes, I can do this. I may be a little bit crazy, but I can do this.

Dubin:

With respect to the powers that be that you mentioned, I infer from this that this refers to the position as being political. If this is so, In what way is this a political position?

Principal:

Well. I think that being a principal in a district is clearly a political position. You're a member of a team, part of a bigger body. You're a piece of a machine. You need to know how to listen, where you fit, what you can give and what you can receive, to not always be selfish. Sometimes you have to give up something for the good of all, which, ultimately, gains you respect. You get something back from that because you're a team player. It is political because you recognize that you are not the only wheel on the wagon. Everyone must work together to move the wagon. If you don't move for the benefit of the wagon your little wheel is not going to go anywhere. So that is political to me.

Dubin:

In other words, compromise. . . .

Principal:

Exactly.

Dubin:

If you were to think about a particular issue that you have faced in your career . . . one tough issue; for example, a student, a district issue, parent, and so on. Does one come to mind you could address?

Principal:

Well, let me respond in this way. A general theme that I've learned over the years regards staffing. And remember, teachers affect kids' lives. I've learned to separate the fact that I like you . . . that you're a nice person or even that I feel badly for you. I hate to say that, but I need to compartmentalize, which may seem contradictory. People may think that because I really like them I wouldn't make a decision that could affect their livelihood, their income, to live. Well, it may be necessary to cut someone, two periods, for example, and it has nothing to do with whether or not I like them. It has to do with the fact that I may not have the money, or perhaps I can find somebody who could do better.

And it applies when we're dealing with kids. I may like them, but I'm going to do the right thing. I'm going to do what is morally and legally the right thing. I'm not saying that I won't exercise my right to compromise at times, but when it comes to a certain moment. . . . I remember kids crying with the threat that they might go to jail. Truly, it is a very difficult time and it may appear cold but, bottom line, my responsibility, my integrity is on the line. And, there is an expectation from the superintendent, media, school board. They are not going to understand that I didn't tell the truth or do the right thing, legally, or otherwise because I felt bad. . . . They would legitimately ask, where is my common sense? They hired me to do the job, not to have to have confusions about emotions. The decision has to be determined by what is in the best interests of the students. It is not always an easy decision. I've learned that over the years through a variety of tough decisions, whether it was about students, parents, or personnel.

Dubin:

Another point worth mentioning that I gather from your comments is that it is a job of isolation. You're really alone and you don't know it or appreciate it until you are behind that desk. You become all things to all people, that is, therapist, curriculum, manager of the budget. . . .

Principal:

Yes. All-knowing guru and wise one. To ask the questions that need to be asked more than once. In my 1st year I felt that I could ask questions because I was new. Why should I know this particular thing? People would say to me, "You mean you don't know that?" This would generate a defensive reaction in me. But I started responding to that by asking, "Why should I know that?" as opposed to formulating some excuse. "Where do you think I should have gotten that information from?"

Dubin:

Another point is dealing with the information that you receive at different points in your career. What you hear today will be understood very differently a year from now because you'll have grown.

Principal:

That is very true. And something else I've found, and perhaps it is the leaders with whom I've worked with downtown, I never have been made to feel bad, and that is to their credit. They haven't ever made me feel insecure. That has kept me going. I'm certain there are other district leaders who do not know how to keep their administrators going . . . how to nourish them.

Dubin:

That's a really important and insightful response, and one that should be directed to leadership on the district level who are either distanced from the job or insensitive to leaders in the field.

Is there anything else you'd like to add?

Principal:

I think that there are only a few decisions that you have to make on the turn of the dime. Because someone comes into your office and lays a problem down does not mean that you have to give an answer. There's always the feeling that you have to fix it. And your tendency is to say, OK, we'll do this, because that's the position you've been put in. What I've learned is that

I rarely respond by saying, Let's do this. Now I say, what would you like from me? What do you think we should do? Often, they already know. They have a better feel for the problem and the solution than you do. And so, you listen. . . .

You don't have to make a decision right then . . . you could say that you'll get back to them tomorrow . . . you don't have to commit. That was a real realization for me. I don't have to have the answer. I could say, "What do you think the answer is?" The other important thing for new administrators is to admit if you're wrong . . . not even a mistake but the wrong decision. Don't rationalize. Don't defend it. Say, "Yes, I did that, but now I'm going to make it better." I cannot accept the blaming stuff . . . it's not my fault that I did that. No one makes a poor decision because they're trying to do a poor job. It's OK to be a learner in this struggle and just admit it. Then work to make it different.

Dubin:

Thank you, and a wonderful response to end our interview.

Analysis

This very experienced and seasoned principal was responsible for directing the activities of a specialized under-performing school. She needed to utilize a structured alternative leadership style that would speak to the needs of her student and teacher population. She had to provide legitimacy, consistency, and a supportive and meaningful environment for her students. She also provided the leadership for two other schools and a summer school program, further expanding her role and specialization with this special needs population.

During the interview she addressed many of the general leadership areas involved in administration, for example, school goals and priorities, personnel, budgetary decisions, participatory management strategies, politics, ethics, personal goals, as well as a host of other leadership considerations specific to her educational philosophy.

Understanding your attitudes and expectations regarding the members of your school community is critical. In order to apply an appropriate leadership style you must be aware of your own personal perspectives and assumptions about people in order to determine the appropriate professional approach in working with your school community. If you believe that the faculty requires consistent and constant monitoring, it is highly likely that you will implement a policy and create an environment that will reflect these beliefs. Alternatively, if you feel that a more open-ended and laissez-faire leadership approach is more conducive to creating a more effective and efficient workplace, you will likely create that type of structured environment. This theoretical underpinning, was known as Theory X and Theory Y in the work of Douglas McGregor in "The Human Side of Enterprise," his classic contribution to the organizational literature. In essence, McGregor felt that all leaders held certain assumptions about workers. The belief that people were capable of making independent decisions, were creative and able to be autonomous he labeled Theory Y. On the other hand, the belief that people required close monitoring and supervision, were innately lazy and dependent he labeled Theory X. He believed that life conditions created the mindsets that demonstrated Theory X tendencies.

A leader's belief system or assumptions as to how people will respond to particular cues or structures significantly defines the organizational parameters in which people work. The principal in this continuation high school had strong feelings about her students that embraced both sides of the McGregor paradigm, although it emphasized a Theory Y orientation. She felt that these students were competent individuals capable of success. She was working under the assumption that, while the students required higher degrees of structure based upon their unusual backgrounds and experiences, they had the capacity to perform successfully in order to achieve. Ultimately, she felt, and she structured her leadership style around this assumption, that by gradually providing them with sufficient support and validation, they would be able to arrive at their own decisions and guide and control their own destiny.

With respect to faculty, she realized that they, too, had to identify their own perceptions regarding these students in order to effectively teach and direct their academic, social, and emotional activities. Again, how the teachers perceived these students determined the atmosphere and climate in their classrooms. While they had to maintain certain expectations and academic standards, it was within the context of their appreciating their students' potential and extending the range of opportunities to accommodate them in order for them to succeed.

Finally, from an organizational perspective, this principal discussed her faculty's commitment to the school vision and her short- and long-term planning to improve student achievement. This discussion projected substantive school changes requiring 3 to 5 years of curriculum review and revision and more consistent and applicable pedagogical approaches. She also indicated the need for personnel changes more consonant with her vision and leadership direction.

Discussion Questions

1. What are some of the key issues this administrator raises in this interview?

2. What is the tone of this interview?

3. Why did she stress the role of parents in this community?

4. What is her perception of the district's educational philosophy and what drives that perception?

5. Could you explain this principal's philosophy regarding curriculum and how to apply it to students with significant behavioral problems?

6. What is her political view of the principalship?

7. What changes would this administrator recommend that would significantly change the effectiveness of teachers?

8. Do you find her comments consistent with other schools and districts you've experienced?

9. If you were appointed principal in this school, what would some of your 1st-year objectives be?

Student Activities

1. Write a letter to the superintendent requesting additional administrative support.

2. Write a letter of introduction to the community indicating your philosophy, background, and goals for the upcoming school year.

3. Write a letter of introduction to the staff regarding your philosophy, background, and goals for the upcoming school year.

4. What agenda items would you include for your first faculty meeting at the beginning of the school year?

5. What funding sources would you pursue to support your school program?

Interview Question

What additional interview questions would you direct to this administrator?

Simulations

Role-play a conversation this principal would have with a student who was just transferred to her school. How would she begin the discussion? What direction would she want the conversation to go, considering the student's background?

What would she say to the parent? What do you think her assumptions would be about the parent's ability to deal with her son or daughter? Would you want to meet with the parent individually or with the student? Please explain your points of view.

What would you say to the parent? Would your approach be different from this principal's? In what way?

Role-play a conversation you would have with a teacher who you felt was not approaching the students positively. Considering Theory X and Y, how would you structure your questions? What types of responses would you consider indicative of a Theory X or Y orientation?

Structuring a School Environment

The principal stated many areas that required a different strategy to improve the performance of her students. Consider the following:

1. How gradual should your decision making be regarding replacing faculty?

2. What process needs to be followed regarding curriculum development?

3. Would generating a faculty feedback questionnaire indicate a leadership Theory X or Y orientation? Please explain.

Principal Leadership Application

The principal states that there were several teachers whom she felt were being obstructionists. Most teachers, though, appeared to be taking on teacher leadership roles that would advance the strategies regarding student performance and achievement.

How does she say she would deal with those teachers who were not supporting these schoolwide initiatives? Would you approach them in the same way?

The principal talks about a conference with a student where she explains the hard facts about her expectations of this student. What do you think of this approach?

How would you

Convey the same information to this student, but with your particular leadership style?

Involve the mother in supporting the school structure and expectations of her son?

Consider generating additional funding sources to support the school program?

Whom would you approach? Why?

Why do you think it takes several years to constitute significant change in a school?

Why is understanding the theoretical underpinning of McGregor's work so important for a principal as she analyzes her leadership assumptions and how it affects the needs of her school?

Questions Related to ISLLC Standards

See Appendix for ISLLC Standards.

1. How does this principal address Standard #1? Based upon the interview, cite at least one example that demonstrated that this standard was met.

2. How does this principal address Standard #2? Based upon the interview, cite at least one example that demonstrated that this standard was met.

3. How does this principal address Standard #5? Based upon the interview, cite at least one example that demonstrated that this standard was met.

4. Do you find that she also responded to other ISLLC standards? If so, which ones would you identify she addressed, and please cite specific examples.

Readings and Resources

McGregor, D. (1977). The human side of enterprise. In M. T. Matteson, and J. M. Ivancevich, *Management classics*. Santa Monica, CA: Goodyear.

A compilation of management and leadership classics including, but not limited to, the following authors: Frederick W. Taylor, Max Weber, George C. Homans, Chester Barnard, Amitai Etzioni, Warren Bennis, Peter Drucker, Herbert Simon, Henri Fayol, Chris Argyris, and Abraham Maslow.

10

Addressing Organizational And Personal Needs: The Philosopher

Understanding the organizational and individual needs of the school is extremely complex and must be addressed from a variety of vantage points. How a principal balances the various expectations involving leadership direction, student academic performance objectives, community inclusion, and professional faculty growth while also acknowledging the personal needs of his faculty is the focus of this chapter. How can a principal model effective leadership practices that instill this holistic cultural ethos, or orientation, and perspective about life issues, while coordinating and directing the educational goals of the school?

Themes addressed in this chapter are

- Understanding both the micro- and macro-picture of education
- Developing an environment of predictability and stability
- Providing opportunities for personal growth and professional development
- Projecting a need to be physically healthy
- Anticipating reaction in order to be proactive

Profile of the Philosopher

Principal: male

Age: 50+

Ethnicity: African American

Experience: 6 years as principal; 1 year as assistant principal; 10 years related administrative experience

School: high school; student population: 1,100

That's often what is missing with inner-city kids, is that their minds are not being respected. . . . People say that there is institutional racism, and it may not be intentional, but the institutions don't expect them to reach AP classes or don't expect them to get into advanced literature classes, and so, for those reason, their minds never become challenged.

My first day as principal there was a teachers' strike. From Day 1, it was focused with staff, students, and so on. I was there for 6 years and didn't miss a day. I cared very deeply for my job, the school, and the goings-on there.

But, various things happened during that 1st year. For example, in addition to the teachers strike, in January a student was shot by an outsider: a Filipino student shot a Latino student. That made for a very hard 1st year as principal, yet it brought the school together a lot more. Each year, I learned a good deal in trying to deal with people, solving problems and dealing with conflicts.

So there are occasions, turning points for administrators, as to what direction they'll go. Once that becomes clear, I think schools are able to move ahead, particularly . . . from a site-based operation. I think once you discover that it becomes empowering. Frequently people assume that everything must go through downtown.

I think my philosophy about running a school is that you need to do what you say you're going to do. Regarding evaluations, we had, by contract, to conduct pre- and post-observation conferences in order to go through the entire evaluative review. The main thing with me was to meet every single timeline and not be late. I was to be there when I said I was going to be there. I found that it was important for the school to be very clear as to what was happening and this approach gave very little opportunity to become anti-administration, because you're managing a place that is very clear and responsive. What I wanted to do was to exceed the expectations of the teachers who could fall into a mode of always questioning the administration. I also wanted to include them as much as I could in site decision making.

In my 1st year, we had the CTBS [California Test for Basic Skills], and I made sure that every teacher in the school took the test. I didn't care what their grades were. I told them that they could take it and throw it away. But they must know what the kids are being tested on.

Each day you need to come in and feel that you could deal with anything that could come up, even the very toughest problems.

School Context

Leadership demands a personal philosophy and the ability to appropriately apply that philosophy to the school environment. Understanding who you are, your goals, priorities, and the organizational context underscore effective leadership. While there must be a clear sense of perspective, it must be married to the environment. In this way, school populations and cultures will be driven by clear purpose and a positive and relevant strategy.

The principal in this mid-sized high school entered the position with a rich and very diverse background. He was well traveled, philosophically clear, personally centered and had a definite sense of what his charge was and how he was going to achieve his goals. The school was extremely demanding. It had a highly at-risk population, which, from the 1st day he entered the school, challenged both his expertise as an administrator, his personal resolve, and his commitment as an educator.

School Characteristics

The school consisted largely of African American, Latino, and second-language learners. It had a history of disciplinary problems, dissention between faculty and administration, and under-achieving students.

School Climate

The previous administrator did not involve the faculty in decision making, although there was sufficient administrative support available to decentralize the school operations. The reliance upon downtown had been the weight upon which decisions were made, so a sense of frequent bureaucracy, inefficiency, and wasted time was ever present. Decisions were often delayed and deferred to the district level.

School Organization

The school had a principal, three assistant principals, a counselor for every grade level, and other administrative personnel. There were close to 100 certificated staff.

Interview

The following interview was conducted as a retrospective review of his administrative work in this high school and throughout his career.

Dubin:

Could you tell me a little bit about your background, training, and preparation in education?

Principal:

Well, basically, I never really saw myself going into teaching formally. I became a Peace Corps volunteer in Nigeria, which needed math and science teachers. And so, I taught math for 2 years in the British/Cambridge system, which initially didn't impress me very much. Afterwards though, I was impressed and thought very highly of it because I felt the best thinking in Europe and Africa put these exams together, which included very rigorous essays. The kids studied very hard; it was clear to them what they had to work for.

After returning to the States from the Peace Corps, I got married. My wife was a teacher. I applied for and received a California teaching credential. I first taught at a school for juvenile delinquents for 6 months, a log cabin-type school about 50 miles south of San Francisco. Afterwards, I was a beginning and advanced math teacher in a high school in the neighboring area. After about a semester there, because I had had a terrific experience in Africa, we decided to move to Nairobi, Kenya. I taught math there, and my wife taught in an elementary school outside of Nairobi in a rural area.

We returned to the same high school where I taught math and also worked unofficially as the assistant principal and remained there until 1977, when I was laid off. Prior to the layoff, the superintendent asked me if I was interested in becoming a school administrator, which I had never really thought about. I decided to take the national examination, passed it, and received my administrative credential. After a short time outside of education, I received a call from the district that they wanted to rehire me as principal.

I returned and accepted the position as principal and worked in that capacity for 6 years, from 1979 to 1985. Afterwards, I became supervisor of high schools at the district level from 1985 to 1992. In 1992 I retired and consulted in various capacities. I was consultant to the federal court as a member of the advisory committee regarding desegregation. I was an assistant to the superintendent from 1992 to 1999/2000. Since then, I've continued on as a consultant working with the state monitor focusing on consent decree and working on various task forces within the district. I've also served as an adjunct faculty member within the higher education arena.

At the time I was principal, the school consisted of approximately 1,600 students. It was the closest high school to a low-income area in the city. It was composed of primarily African American students, Latino students, and a large number of limited English-speaking students. My 1st day as principal there was a teachers' strike. From Day 1, it was focused on staff, students, and so on. I was there for six years and didn't miss a day. I cared very deeply for my job, the school, and the goings-on there as anyone, I would say.

But various things happened during that 1st year. For example, in addition to the teachers' strike, that January a student was shot by an outsider; a Filipino student shot a Latino student. That made for a very hard 1st year as principal, yet it brought the school together a lot more. Each year, I learned a good deal in trying to deal with people, solving problems, and dealing with conflicts.

Dubin:

Let me backtrack for a moment. What did the school's staff configuration, administrative support system, look like? You said that there were 1,600 students.

Principal:

Yes. There was about 90 to 100 certificated staff. There was a six-period day, and all students took six classes. At that time there were 200 units to graduate rather than 230-plus units that are required today. The school was more comprehensive, with more vocational classes than academics, as today. The technological courses were not as central to the curriculum then, although my high school did have a strong component of technology. We had a minicomputer schoolwide system. In fact, when I started the school, that 1st strike-ridden day, we had begun with a running start because we were able to computerize our master schedule. I had done a lot of work in this area in my previous high school and so we were very much up-to-date in getting students' schedules throughout the strike and never missed a beat. I'd say the 1st day of classes each year we always had a strong master schedule.

During my 6 years there, the school paid a lot of attention trying to be efficient and well managed. There were three assistant principals: curriculum, counseling, and groundskeeping/attendance. Generally speaking, the administrative team was all very dedicated; we had a common focus. We had dedicated teachers who wanted to take the kids from where they were. Many of the students came in with less than high-school-level reading and math, and so we worked very hard to get the kids to perform at a level that would enable them to graduate and go on to college.

Dubin:

You mentioned you had three assistant principals: curriculum, counseling and plant management. What about counselors? Did you have counselors at the school?

Principal:

Yes. Initially, we had a counselor for every grade level. When I left, they started consolidating counselors and questioned whether they needed counselors. But the years I was there, we had counselors at every grade. We also had special-education counselors for special-education students who were kind of teacher-counselors at that time.

Dubin:

You mentioned earlier that you had begun with a strike going on, which was something of an unusual way to begin an administrative assignment and must have been a particularly difficult period. Do you recall the district providing any kind of guidance or support that would have helped you to navigate through those very difficult political times?

Principal:

No. I think the district was working as hard as it could to deal with the teachers and the union. When I began as principal and spoke with the superintendent, he was very supportive. At that time I told him about my concerns about the school and his comment to me was, "You have to get in line, like everybody else." Well, I learned a lot from that statement because from then on I never really depended upon downtown. For example, I worked to attain a grant from a foundation that could be used for various discretionary needs. I tried to be as independent as possible at the school site. I developed that philosophy very early on as an administrator.

Dubin:

That's a very interesting comment because the range of administrative approaches with respect to their connections with the district and understanding of it is considerable. There are those who don't understand the workings of the district and are trying to find their way and those who are trying to be more independent and still be very successful. Again, it's very interesting the relationship that develops between site people on the front line and the district level.

Principal:

I recently visited a school as a consultant, and spoke with a principal who had been there 8 years. When she had first arrived at the school, the reading scores had been in the 30th percentile and within an 8-year period the reading scores doubled, to approximately the 60th percentile. One of her strategies involved asking the teachers about the kinds of reading programs they'd be interested in. They gave their input and, as a result, ended up with a particular reading program, which seemed to have met much of the concern the teachers had expressed. She then adopted that program, which included staff development appropriate for that school.

After the 2nd year, she called the district office to get some support from CIPD [curriculum-instruction-program department] for a reading specialist to come out and visit the school. The district response was that it didn't recognize or support that particular reading program. The principal did not expect that response and simply wanted someone to come out and speak to her parents and community regarding reading. Since the district didn't send anyone, the principal said that she never again depended on the district to support her along those lines.

So there are occasions, turning points for administrators, as to what direction they'll go. Once that becomes clear, I think schools often are able to move ahead, particularly when you can do as much as you can from a site-based operation. I think once you discover that, it becomes empowering. Frequently people assume that everything must go through downtown.

Dubin:

I see. That clarifies and explains an entirely different approach.

When you reflect back on that 1st year, I'm sure you consider it quite an unusual one. As you consider the years that followed, though, how did you determine your priorities and set in motion the process to communicate them?

Principal:

With respect to priorities, we had a high school proficiency test that was being developed for math. We were a Title I school for reading, so we had real focus on math and reading. I also felt that we had a staff very committed to low-achieving students; one-third of the student body was bilingual.

A lot of teachers were excited about the school and transferred here. I believe that once you give attention and are fully committed to a program of excellence, you get a lot of people who are supportive and want to be a part of it. People come into education to contribute. Unfortunately, there is so much bureaucracy, there are a lot of things in-between, lots of side issues that frequently divert people from their original ideas and visions. To be consistent, you must also consider what students want. Their creativity needs to be tapped into, and they don't want to be compared to other students.

The more energy that each person can bring into a school, seeing themselves as contributing, doing something that is significant, the more the school will bring into it things you never thought about. For example, in my 3rd or 4th year there, the girls' basketball team came in second in the state; there was tremendous staff and alumni support. Twice the boys came in third in the state in basketball, which produced additional and continuous energy. The bilingual students loved the school and being a part of it. There were a lot of people who were contributing and providing excellence in the school even though there were tough times. All this brought us closer together as a staff.

Dubin:

There was another response from a principal who mentioned having come into the school initially to create an environment for student success, since so many students had never realized success. She was trying to create something, for example, in the play yard for a few minutes where students could play basketball so they could begin to feel good. She was trying to institutionalize this. She wanted to change the climate of continual failure.

Principal:

A good example of that was the work of Jaime Escalantes [portrayed in the film] *Stand and Deliver*. [His] students who were doing essentially mediocre, routine work, for example, remedial math. He said that they could do better, achieve more than that. He felt that these students had a tradition of achieving more than that, particularly in mathematics. Where they were at was not enough; they had to push themselves more. They had to take two math classes one semester, or go to summer school or take algebra or take geometry. This is a pathway. So what happened with him was that when someone stated an interest, he followed up. Beyond simply stating success, he respected the minds of the students.

That's often what is missing with inner-city kids is that their minds are not respected either by the curriculum or by the institution. People say that there is institutional racism, and it may not be intentional, but the institutions don't expect them to reach AP classes or don't expect them to get into advanced literature classes and so, for those reasons, their minds never become challenged. I did many things as principal that addressed this need, but there were many areas that were equally as important.

Two areas dealt with safety and behavior and was something that was continuous. In working with my assistant principal in charge of counseling, we developed an approach of having high expectations with students in terms of disciplinary expectations. We were very candid and clear as to what we expected from them.

Let me mention a couple of other things that were important. With regard to health, personally, I ran 5 miles a day so I was in very good shape physically. I think it very important to be physically and mentally balanced as an administrator, just as it is for students. You must keep challenging students in that same way. The physical education program had to be just as important as the academic programs. We had tremendous PE teachers who believed in a balanced PE program.

I always tried to keep abreast of technology, computers, staying on the cutting edge with those kinds of things in the school. At one point, I wanted all the students to write a simple program, a Dartmouth model. So we always had some very good thinking along the line of technology using computers, going into computer labs. In fact, toward the end of my tenure, the superintendent appointed me to oversee an educational task force. I continued as principal as well as in charge of that task force. One objective of the task force was that no grade in the district was to be lower than a B. We came up with parallel kinds of curricula: kids being able to take an exam more than one time. There was a lot of excitement with the superintendent and other principals with what we shared along curriculum lines and along safety lines.

The budget I handled less because we had people from the federal and state [agencies] who were very capable, although I did my own personal balancing of the budget. There was discretionary money, and I made sure that the money was well spent. I've never gone along with the philosophy regarding the poor, urban, inner-city kids. While at times you may have a lot of money; you need to know how to use it. To me money was never as central an issue as my philosophy and running my school.

As far as safety, the budget, the curriculum, and the master schedule: how it looked and how it included people were the things we focused on from the very 1st day of school. Classes always started, were balanced; kids were not in the halls. It was a well-managed school.

I think my philosophy about running a school is that you need to do what you say you're going to do. Regarding evaluations, we had, by contract, to conduct pre- and post-observation conferences in order to go through the entire evaluative review. The main thing with me was to meet every single timeline and not be late. I was to be there when I said I was going to be there. I found that it was important for the school to be very clear as to what was happening, and this approach gave very little opportunity to become anti-administration, because you're managing a place that is very clear and responsive. What I wanted to do was exceed the expectations of the teachers who could fall into a mode of always questioning the administration. I also wanted to include them as much as I could in site decision making.

Dubin:

And so there was a range of priorities and critical strategies in which you provided leadership. You were to be consistent; meet when you said you were going to meet, be consistent, and predictable so as to engender trust.

Principal:

Right. And basically that went right through to the administrative team, that is, the assistant principals. We were very focused. When we asked teachers to do something it was not in isolation. We were doing our jobs very thoroughly; it was always laid out. What was very important to me in running the school resulted from my being the assistant principal before in that school. This was very fortunate. At that time, I was in charge of attendance, testing, and curriculum. From the very 1st day, we had a handbook that was thorough, complete, that had teacher evaluations, attendance procedures. And so, every year there was a very clear handbook, which indicated what was expected from everyone. The last few years, I came up with a one-page leaflet that I gave to the students which had all of their calendar dates, the athletic events, the testing dates. And so it was very important to globalize information, getting it out to the teachers and the students, what the needs were. We wanted the communication to be as clear as possible!

Dubin:

On another note, what would you say the issues are that new administrators face? As well, what would you say the issues are that face more experienced administrators?

Principal:

I think that to a great extent the issues really are the same. I am currently on a district task force with a high school and I am involved with some of the issues I faced 20 years ago as principal. The issues that were significant then are significant now. One of the things that makes it difficult for a new or experienced administrator is dealing with crisis. It doesn't matter what it is specifically. As I mentioned, I started with a strike crisis. We had a recent situation in a high school within the last few weeks that involved an experienced administrator and a problem between two students. That crisis involved an experienced administrator with 15 years of experience. Any and every administrator must learn to deal with crisis, which could happen at any time. What helped me was the fact that I had been an assistant principal at that site and I was working with an experienced, capable, confident principal who was grooming me to move into the principalship. He was there short term. I was able to watch him run the school operations. Many new principals are being put into situations that are entirely new, where they really don't know how the place operates, what is going on.

Another example of similar situations today and yesterday for me was dealing with the testing program. In my 1st year we had the CTBS (California Test for Basic Skills) test, and I made sure that every teacher in the school took the test. I didn't care what their grades were. I told them that they could take it and throw it away. But they must know what the kids are being tested on.

With attendance, we had in-services with every single teacher in the school, so they'd know exactly how to fill out attendance forms, excused absences, and what to expect. I had done all this as an assistant principal so I had some literacy with the school and its operations. You see, with a new person coming into a school, he or she can try, but it is difficult to immediately become literate, that is, the budget, attendance, and so on, all the things you've mentioned. If you have that to learn and there is also a crisis, it can be overwhelming for a new person.

For an experienced person coming in, it takes a lot of energy. For many experienced administrators, it is starting over when they are assigned to a new school. So, that energy I mentioned becomes very important. At my high school the teachers would tell me that the students stay the same age, but the teachers and staff get older each year. I've often asked that question to administrators and superintendents when they take on a new assignment. Do they have the energy to start again? How do you stay cutting-edge? How do you reach a situation where you see challenges for yourself and everyone else? Many people are in administration for 10 to 15 years and simply want to know what downtown wants and report that back to the staff. You've got to generate something.

At one particular district, the mission statement indicates that every student needs to be intellectually challenged, physically and mentally balanced, economically competent, culturally and linguistically sensitive to his or her greatest capability. You want that for every student. It's one thing to write that, but for that to happen to over 60,000 students takes a lot more energy and profound thinking. For the people who are able to get beyond that statement and see how that is working at their school and their classrooms, they will be empowered. So for a seasoned administrator who has come along, is familiar with the words and the terms of the district, who sees people come and go, that is, superintendents and such, in the end what they need to do is have their own goals and vision. What is it that they stand for? The seasoned administrator needs to stand for something, and the teachers need to know that. When they go into a school, they need to be more than a technician just knowing the rules from downtown. If they want a school that's vibrant, then people must be able to tap into their own creativity and energy.

Dubin:

I see. That is quite a demand, but a necessary one for a seasoned administrator.

Let me get back to a comment you mentioned before. You stated that they have to know how to deal with crisis. You alluded to a situation with a seasoned administrator. But how would you advise someone to deal with crisis, how does that work? What type of skills do you need when that kind of thing surfaces?

Principal:

Well, again, a lot depends upon the energy that you bring into the school every day. As an administrator, it is very important that you are physically fit. I had been in the Peace Corps and had a very positive experience. I had done many things at the grassroots level. To me, a teacher and administrator are very similar. I really felt as though I could deal with the toughest problems in the school, both in a classroom and as an administrator. I think it very important for you to be willing to take on anything and feel as though you can deal with any problem whether the crisis comes or whether it is trivial; you need to have the energy. And you cannot predict . . . you could go for 15 years and nothing ever happens. Each day you need to come in and feel that you could deal with anything that could come up, even the very toughest problems.

Of course, there may be other schools that could be more difficult than yours, and so it is important to have dialogue. I've had some good principal meetings where they held such dialogues and shared ideas as to what was working. I think it's extremely important that you demonstrate that you are capable of solving anything in the school. You don't want to duck anything and you want the teachers to know that. In fact, I felt that I could teach any class in the school. I might have had a little trouble with Spanish or French, but anything else I'd have been willing to take a crack at it or, if necessary, study for it. I went into it with that kind of energy with the teachers. I was the type who was willing to challenge them on anything. I was clear.

Dubin:

When you talk about energy, you're talking about confidence, having a vision and being willing to take on the challenge. Much of it is a real grounding and security in addition to physically having the energy to deal with the pressures of those crisis situations.

Principal:

You also must let people know that you are very serious about what you are doing. I communicated to the staff that I was not interested in gossip. It's academic achievement and it's about people doing their best; giving their best effort. People respect that.

It's amazing that people listen during a faculty meeting. You know that because they come back and say certain things that were said. They really want things; they're working hard, they want to see things moving. Even though they may complain, you find out that over the years people are really listening to the things you say, particularly if you are really serious.

Dubin:

I see. Let me ask you a different question now. Do you consider the principalship to be a political position and in what ways?

Principal:

Frequently it is. For example, a superintendent may want an African American or Latino at a particular school. It could be what the community wants. . . . If you start with the superintendent who might have a great educational vision and leadership but whose board is basically questioning a particular issue, that hiring decision becomes contingent upon the votes of the board. In this way, the superintendent's job is quite political. So if the superintendent's job is political, then it certainly translates down to the principal. Many times it could be the superintendent's idea, other times it might be the board pushing as to who might be a principal. So, certainly the principalship can be political.

On the other hand, you could get some who are a lot less politically driven, such as some schools being given the opportunity to have a selection committee and interview candidates. They could request and get their first, second, and/or third choice. So you can see cases where you do get the input from the staff; you do get those extremes.

I've seen cases, when I was assistant superintendent in charge of schools, where the committee got exactly what they wanted, and the person was disastrous. The person had come from outside the district. The parents got what they wanted but the person never connected with the teachers. The teachers felt that the person was not academic enough. So what I am saying is that, at times, it is political and works well because the person can be very competent. Sometimes it can be political and disastrous; the person is not well rounded enough. Other times the person will come in and act as they feel the superintendent wants them to act, but not with their own voice. That also can be a problem in that they're conforming to a particular type of leadership. Schools are very complicated. You have the union, the superintendent, your supervisors, the students, the parents. . . .

And so, survival alone is a critical aspect. For this reason, you must have your own personal vision and goals, and people need to be able to see that in you. It's amazing how that can bring a school together. At my high school, we did a great deal with our curriculum. We had done a lot of creative things in terms of curriculum and responding to the kids' needs.

Dubin:

With respect to the incredible complexity of the job, the energy, commitment, and so many other things that constitute an effective leader, how do you deal with avoiding burnout?

Principal:

I think that burnout is a tough problem. At the end of my 6th year, I had put a whole lot in. When I changed to the district level, I had been asked to accept the district position earlier on, but I wanted to continue my work at the high school. In any event, I have stayed in various positions for 6 or 7 years on average. I was a teacher for 6 to 7 years and a principal for 6 years and an assistant superintendent for 6 years. For me, I run a cycle.

In urban inner-city schools, there are overwhelming tasks. People work hard, but the job seems to be getting harder. If kids came in more prepared, it would take less energy.

An administrator needs to enter a school, work hard, look at all the different areas that need attention in order to be effective and be able to meet the students' needs. What we have now though is a school modeled like factories. We just process people. They sit there for 6 hours. Generally, students are very passive and the teachers provide most of the knowledge, educational leadership, and direction. It's like the pitcher in baseball: they do most of the work, 80% to 90% of it, and that's a fact. For that reason, the burnout is there, like in baseball. You can go so far with a pitcher. It is the same with the administrator as with the teacher.

Dubin:

So what is the answer? In schools where these conditions exist, what changes would you make? What changes would you implement to make them more able to survive? Is it possible?

Principal:

You need to look at the configuration of the school. If schools are designed as factories where students sit there and are processed, this has to change. Some students can do it: sit there for 6 hours and survive. You need to look at different models of schools.

Let me give you an example. One school with which I am familiar specializes in the arts. They have academics in the morning and arts in the afternoon.

It is much more humanistic to run a school that way. I have seen their dance classes. I've seen kids dance for an hour and one half every day. They are at their maximum ability. Not only that, they are developing personal discipline. Schools have got to operate in ways where students are not sitting there for 6 hours a day, they're actually involved, particularly at this point in their lives. They're pursuing interests. Teachers need to love their subjects, kids have to be able to pursue things in which they're interested, and they must be disciplined.

I've always said that there are three things that are necessary for schools to have significant things going on. One thing is good teaching. The one essential thing about good teaching is that students need to know that a big part of teaching is that they must teach themselves. The teacher needs to transmit that to the student, otherwise you're just being given something. You've got to be able to teach yourself and learn yourself.

The next thing that a school needs is rigorous courses. Why? This is because you've got to be able to be challenged, to be disciplined, focused. You need to be able to take things on. With respect to crisis, which was mentioned before, anyone would be more able to take on crisis when they have been disciplined, have more stamina, more stick-to-it preparation. There must be a mental attitude toward any problem that you come up against. The rigor is very important.

A good example of how inner-city students, in particular, were pushed dealt with an outdoor program I had been involved with some years ago. When you talked to kids in the program, the kids who were failures in other situations turned it around in that setting. They explained that this outdoor program allowed them to test their own limits, to feel empowered, worked with a group, a team. They said that they were actually doing something physical and not sitting around. Some kids who were smokers mentioned that they hadn't smoked for 30 days. They would take on life kinds of issues, rather than artificial situations that were made up from textbooks or workbooks and the like.

The third thing an effective school has to offer is the environment where there are other motivated people.

These are the things that have to happen for significant learning to go on. You can have these outdoor programs and schools with a more creative scheduling and course-work. You've got to have those elements in mind on a more profound level as you look at how students are going to learn. Even if you're going into a traditional school, you've got to ensure that kids are taking tough courses. You've got to make sure that there's a balance, and they're not sitting around all day.

It happens with teachers as well. One school I'm working with has developed the outdoor program I alluded to before, and there are people who are interested in developing other programs. When you look at kids at private schools, which are very expensive, you'll find that those students are involved in these kinds of activities during the year and the summer. They find out about these programs, that is, being physically fit and being able to test the limits of endurance. All kids need these kinds of experiences of being challenged rather than sitting down for 6 hours a day.

Dubin:

Research tells us that the curriculum must be in the mind and body of the learner, which is precisely what you just captured.

Principal:

Absolutely. I certainly agree. In the end, the students do create their own curriculum. In the Outward Bound programs, for example, they develop their own journals. They should be as creative as possible, synthesize their experiences, develop new kinds of directions that wouldn't be in a formalized book, and be encouraged to do that.

Dubin:

In light of your response, which focused on learning and the need to understand and implement it, in your experiences how can that philosophy direct the actions and direction of the school? How does that happen when ultimately the decisions are derived from the principal's office? And as an offshoot of the concept of the principal as sole decision maker, what are your thoughts regarding isolation and being the lone decision maker?

Principal:

It's very true, and for that reason you find many principals seeking help and decision making from downtown. They then convey that to their teachers, that their decisions were based upon what they were told to do. A prime example, as I mentioned earlier, regarding the experienced principal who was not able to handle the crisis at her school and ultimately resigned, was that she was continually calling downtown for guidance. Teachers were asking what they were to do, who was going to make the decision. Again, some are fearful that they'll get their hands slapped, so it does come down to the question. . . . In that particular situation, you had 2,000 students which required coordination, and it was very serious.

While I mention this situation, let me say that for new administrators there is much in the way of routine that needs to be established with clear coordination. While it is important to understand the existing culture when they first assume the position, they need not be controlled by that culture but seek the changes which need to be made. I have found that those entering the profession coming from different districts, reflect attitudes that typify the ethos of that particular district-level leadership, be it suburban as opposed to urban, that either fosters this dependency and dysfunction or not.

But clearly it is a pressure-cooker job.

Dubin:

So lonely can be defined in a number of ways. Ultimately, it's the principal who must understand and determine how the decisions should best be made, be it in a crisis or not. Understand the relationship with the district and [that] districts are different; understand your particular leadership style and when you draw the line.

Principal:

Exactly. Let me give you another example, and it also relates to the political assignment we spoke of earlier. There was an assistant principal who was placed in a school. As you know, many times the principal has no decision as to placement. And as I mentioned, for political reasons, assistant principals can be either placed or moved as a result of poor evaluations or whatever. In any case, there was a particular case where, for about 1 or 2 years, there was a great deal of tension between two administrators. They simply couldn't get along. As assistant superintendent and their supervisor, I was supposed to write them up. Well, I wrote that they were both doing their jobs. Well downtown said that they were going to remove one of the administrators from the job. My comment was that if they were going, I was going, because I didn't see it that way. Downtown did step back, but they were shocked that I was willing to challenge them.

There are a lot of people I have seen who would do anything to keep their administrative contracts, whatever it may take. All of that becomes part of how people react in those jobs, what they do. In the end, you're right; it is a lonely job. They do what they can to sustain it, to survive. There are a lot of things people can't help you with. You have to see it as part of the job. I don't think you can get away from that.

I would refer back to my thoughts about those three important features of a school that are doing significant things. You need to be involved with rigorous things, you're learning new things. When I mentioned about the student who was shot, one of the things I did was become a member of the community board to teach a conflict resolution model throughout the city. I'd go out to the city and work to resolve conflicts. You need to stay in touch with things that are going on and have the energy to do that.

Dubin:

So, in other words, it's important to involve yourself and be stimulated. Also you must be clear about your vision. In this way, you can deal with the pressures that are associated with that sense of isolation and your being the singular person in making those decisions.

Principal:

Yes. I can think of yet another example. I was working with a superintendent who had worked very hard during his tenure in a district: received an advanced degree, studied the curriculum, and learned to address the myriad of issues associated with the district. He lived for problems. He tried to educate the board rather than be dictated by it. People need to look at this type of attitude as they enter these positions.

Another superintendent I worked with was extremely politically astute; he understood the politics involved. Some understand it less. You really see this at the principal level. They don't like to get involved necessarily, but when they do, they get so overwhelmed they can't get out of it.

Dubin:

Yes, I see. With respect to the overall, is there anything else you'd like to add that new administrators should consider, or experienced administrators for that matter?

Principal:

Yes. I would say in my case, I really felt as though the 1 year as assistant principal was extremely important. I was able to see the job; it wasn't theory. Again, in my case I ended up moving right into that school even though it was a very difficult situation. I felt as though I was aware of the complexity of the job. Now there are so many young people interested in administration, but they have a lot tougher time while they are limited to the classroom, teaching. Unless they have an opportunity to be involved in administration in some capacity, it will be more difficult. You want people to be in situations where they have running starts, where they don't come into these situations cold. . . .

You want young people who want to become administrators to have these opportunities. In a sense what I am saying is that you want them to exceed expectations of what it takes for the job. That's what people need to think of and not just survive. . . . The more things they can do in seeing what it takes to be a leader when they get there will give them more energy, more confidence, more capability.

Dubin:

Thank you very much for your very thoughtful and comprehensive feedback. It will certainly help those interested in pursuing leadership in our public schools.

Analysis

This very experienced and seasoned principal was responsible for organizing, reorienting, and ultimately redirecting the activities of an under-performing school. He needed to implement an alternative decision-making process at his school in addition to creating a more progressive, researched-based school environment that would address the needs of his student and teacher population. He wanted to build trust in his staff, provide legitimacy, consistency, and a supportive and meaningful culture for his students. He also had to begin to distance himself from the politics and dependency of the district in order to direct the school with greater autonomy and self-purpose. During the interview, he addressed many of the general leadership areas involved in administration, for example, school goals and priorities, personnel, budgetary decisions, participatory management strategies, politics, ethics, personal goals, physical and mental preparedness as well as a host of other leadership considerations specific to his educational philosophy.

The leadership of a school must be approached from many perspectives, as evidenced in this principal interview. There were a multitude of district expectations demanded of the principal: high test score results, school security, disciplinary procedures and student behavior regulations, maintenance considerations involving school plant and grounds, coordinated outreach projects with community members, and fiscal management and responsibility. As a result, the vision and strategies needed to effectively address these school processes and roles were vested in the principal and required expert decision making and organizational skills.

One human relations framework that embodied the philosophy of this principal was drawn from the work of the sociologist Abraham Maslow, whose theory of a hierarchy of needs attempted to explain the underlying needs that drive and motivate individuals. Applying Maslow's framework to this school case, it can be said that the principal was attempting to provide an atmosphere for individual growth and development in order for them to function at their highest level. The levels of need and the ability of the school to satisfy them would produce secure, capable, productive, and self-actualized human beings.

Discussion Questions

1. What are some of the key issues this administrator raises in this interview?

2. What is the tone of this interview?

3. Why does he not identify or stress the role of parents in this community?

4. What is his perception of the district's educational philosophy and what drives that perception?

5. Could you explain this principal's philosophy regarding curriculum?

6. What is his political view of the principalship?

7. What changes would this administrator recommend that would significantly change the effectiveness of teachers?

8. Do you find his comments consistent with other schools or districts you've experienced?

9. If you were appointed principal in this school, what would some of your 1st-year objectives be?

Student Activities

1. Write a letter to the superintendent requesting additional administrative support.

2. Write a letter of introduction to the community indicating your philosophy, background, and goals for the upcoming school year.

3. Write a letter of introduction to the staff regarding your philosophy, background, and goals for the upcoming school year.

4. What agenda items would you include for your first faculty meeting at the beginning of the school year?

5. What funding sources would you pursue to support your school program?

Interview Question

What additional interview questions would you suggest to this administrator?

Simulations

Role-play a meeting between the principal and his staff during a faculty retreat prior to the beginning of the school year. Considering the leadership philosophy of this administrator, what would be on his agenda?

If you were to develop icebreaking exercises, what would they be that would

develop a strategy for staff inclusion

connect the veteran faculty with those just hired.

If you were to develop physical exercise activities during the retreat, what would they be? Would you organize them yourself or would you hire a consultant?

Creating a Consistent School Philosophy

Effective schools have an overriding philosophy and procedural approach that is accepted and followed by faculty. Whether it focuses on disciplinary processes, grading standards, staff meetings, or back-to-school-night presentations, the school acts as a unit. This approach creates an atmosphere of connectedness, efficiency, and unification.

1. How do you create this uniform approach?

2. If faculty disagrees, how do you create consensus?

3. What are the greatest challenges to consensus?

4. How do you measure the effectiveness of an overall school philosophy?

Principal Leadership Applications

In the course of the interview, the principal indicated an important strategy that emphasized leadership preparedness. He felt that by being efficient, on time, and behaving as you state you will he would be relieved of the possibility of faculty dissent or questioning.

What do you think of that strategy?

How realistic is this approach?

In another instance, the principal stated that it was important for teachers to take a basic achievement test the students would be taking.

What do you think of that approach?

What impact would that make on you?

Could a consequence of that strategy change the testing process? How?

The principal indicated that he learned an important lesson regarding decision making and his reliance upon the district for validation and confirmation.

What was the lesson he learned?

Would you respond to that superintendent's comment in the same way?

How would you define his leadership style?

Questions Related to ISLLC Standards

See Appendix for ISLLC Standards.

1. How did this principal address Standard #1? Based upon the interview, cite at least one example that demonstrated that this standard was met.

2. How did this principal address Standard #2? Based upon the interview, cite at least one example that demonstrated that this standard was met.

3. How did this principal address Standard #3? Based upon the interview, cite at least one example that demonstrated that this standard was met.

4. How did this principal address Standard #6? Based upon the interview, cite at least one example that demonstrated that this standard was met.

5. Did you find that he also responded to other ISLLC standards? If so, which ones would you identify he addressed, and please cite specific examples.

Readings and Resources

Lunenburg, F., & Ornstein, Allan. (2004). *Educational administration: Concepts and practices*. Belmont, CA: Wadsworth.
An overview of the literature in educational administration that identifies and summarizes various frameworks and theories.
Cunningham, W. G., & Cordeiro, P. A. (2000). *Educational administration: A problem-based approach*. Boston, MA: Allyn & Bacon.
An educational administration text that focuses on popular and current theories and frameworks that apply to K–12 school environments. Chapters can be used to isolate learning areas and, cumulatively, provide a complete student portfolio.

11

Group Dynamics and Multinationalism: The Internationalist

A principal's leadership in an American International School whose population consists of students from all around the globe requires a unique set of skills. The K–12 American school in Lahore, Pakistan, was supported by the U.S. Department of State and offered American and internationalist curricula geared for student entry into the educational system in the United States and elsewhere. How does a principal negotiate the academic and social needs of a culturally and internationally diverse student and community body? How does she integrate a multilevel, pre-K to 12th-grade curricula collaboratively, so that all the disparate voices can be heard? This principal-superintendent discusses the many challenges she faced during her tenure in the American International School in Lahore, Pakistan.

Themes addressed in this chapter:

- Orienting and working with an international board of directors
- Principal and superintendent leadership
- Supporting diverse points of view
- Safety issues, political and physical
- Expectations of teachers

Profile of the Internationalist

Principal/Superintendent: female

Age: 65+

Ethnicity: Caucasian

Experience: eleven years as principal

School: K–12; country: Lahore, Pakistan; student population: 250

I was looking for people who enjoyed teaching. I was looking for people who were flexible. I was looking for teachers who felt that children came first. Having international experience was important and would allow them to survive some of the overseas challenges. For example, when the American embassy in Islamabad was set on fire in 1979, many teachers were over-whelmed by the experience and left. Several though stayed, who had had overseas experience and a different perspective. Let me add: Honesty and confidence are important traits that I look for when hiring teachers. . . .

The board president was French; the vice president, American; the trea-surer and secretary were Pakistani; the three members-at-large were British, American, and Swedish; and the ex officio member was the consulate gen-eral. It was quite a mix of educational backgrounds. . . .

It is an incredible, wonderful, life-altering experience. [A teacher or administrator] will never be the same educator or leader afterwards. They will view education, leadership, culture, the world, and people in an entirely different way.

School Context

The American International School in Lahore, Pakistan is one of hundreds of K–12 American schools throughout the world. Each school is unique and represents American values and educational policy, procedures, and curriculum expectations but with the companion cultural orientation of the host country. The Lahore American school reflects a strong American presence that underwent unusual changes during the period of this superin-tendent's tenure. She was an American woman in a Muslim country, which was highly unusual. Indeed, at that time, she was one of only a handful of women superintendents overseeing an American International School.

Assuming such a leadership position successfully requires a clear under-standing of the complex needs of the school and community. She identified the needs of the student population, the parents in the community, the political nature of the board, and the evolving political climate within the country as all those factors affected the American school. She was also acutely aware of the high expectations of the school, which were predicated on Western values but also acknowledged the rich cultural heritage of Pakistan.

The superintendent was hired initially as a teacher and later as principal/superintendent. The school was extremely well structured and predictable, had high rates of student success, and was supported by the community. Indeed, for many of the parent constituencies it represented an extremely important base for values and a connection to their country of origin.

School Characteristics

The school consisted of Americans, Pakistanis, British, French, and other nationalities. It was considered a hybrid school, being tuition-driven yet supported by the Department of State for those Americans whose families worked in the diplomatic sector. They were afforded an education allowance, enabling their children to attend the school for virtually no cost. There were 250 to 350 K–12 students. The school had few disciplinary problems. Faculty and administration had cooperative working relationships and represented different educational backgrounds and nationalities from around the globe.

School Climate

The superintendent had been a teacher at the school for many years and was in the formative stage of developing a leadership style she hoped would be accepted by the faculty and community.

School Organization

She was the principal/superintendent of the school. Enrollment was low, so no additional administrator was supported by the board of directors.

Interview

The following interview was conducted as a retrospective of her 15 years as superintendent.

Dubin:

Could you tell me a little bit about your background, experience, and training with respect to your educational career?

Principal:

I was living in Pakistan and became a teacher in the American International School. After several years of teaching, an opportunity presented itself for me to take on a stronger leadership role. I gradually came to assume the principalship and superintendent of the school.

Dubin:

What is an American school overseas? Tell me more about the school. How large was it and what types of students were in the school? What were their backgrounds? Tell me about the teachers in the school as well as your administrative support. Give me a sense of the school.

Principal:

Well, first let me give you a little background. I started teaching there in 1964. At that time a war broke out and our student population went from 320 students to 5. Each year after that, more students enrolled. By the time I left, 20 years later in 1984, there were over 350 students.

American International Schools originally began because American diplomats stationed in that area had children who required an American education. It started in 1956 in Lahore, Pakistan and was also affiliated with the United States Department of State and the Overseas American Schools Office.

Dubin:

I see. What types of kids went to that school?

Principal:

All types of children went to that school. Well, interestingly, in 1964 there was only perhaps a handful that was not American. When we reopened, there was one American student, who happened to be my son, some missionary children, and the rest were Pakistani children. Because of the war with India and all the foreigners were evacuated, it was a long time before the population of children returned. The British returned first, and over time the other nationalities ultimately returned. It took considerable time before the American population increased to even 50%, as it had been before.

Otherwise, it functioned as a private school in that many families were not missionaries nor from the diplomatic corps. All these other parents had to pay full tuition. It was an interesting blend of private and public families, very diverse culturally and financially. The children of the diplomatic or military families as well as the missionaries were funded by their respective organizations to allow them to attend the school; thus, free education. The United States government was required to provide education for American citizens. Alternatively, the local families were responsible for their own tuition costs.

Dubin:

How many faculty and staff did you have?

Principal:

When I left there were 28 teachers. There were several aides. We had an assistant principal. We had a counselor, a special education teacher. We also had many servants, drivers, and others who were indigenous to the culture.

Dubin:

And so you began as a teacher and then, due to need, evolved to administration.

Principal:

I became the principal and superintendent because, well, there was another war. Again we were without students, paying students, and so the board decided to have one of the local teachers assume that role.

Dubin:

And because you had demonstrated leadership and interest, they selected you.

Principal:

Yes, and it was scary, but I wanted to do it!

Dubin:

What made it scary?

Principal:

It was a lot of responsibility. I also did not know all the ins and outs of the schools in the many countries we had dealings with. I knew I was going to be learning a lot. It was a big problem initially because the teachers and the parents were to vote in order to decide whether to recruit for a superintendent in the United States or select me. And so, at the outset there were a few ill feelings during the 1st year I started in the school.

Dubin:

The politics of schools has surfaced in many interviews I've conducted which dealt with hiring from within or without, that is, within the state or outside the state, or in or out of the country, which was your case.

Did you find that, as a result of coming from the teaching position at the school, there was any conflict in your own mind? Your relationships with your teachers were changing, since you essentially were going from a colleague to a supervisor. Do you recall that situation?

Principal:

Oh, yes, I was aware of that and knew before I started that that was going to happen, on both sides. I was feeling uncomfortable. I still wanted them to be my friends. I wanted to let them know that I was on their side. If a conflict arose, I wanted them to come to me.

I had one such episode with a teacher where I was being criticized for being partisan, and so I made a point of explaining the process to her: how I went through the steps in order to make an objective decision, why these things happened. I don't know if she ever accepted my explanation. And so the 1st couple of years were really hard.

Dubin:

Did you find that because it was such a close-knit community, an international community, and everyone knew each other, there was balance between you, the board, the faculty, and the parents?

Principal:

Not in the beginning. As the years went by, the parents became more involved in the school, which I had been promoting. I had been promoting the idea that parents needed to be more a part of their child's learning and participate in the school activities. Ultimately, I regretted that approach because it made life very difficult for me. When they had been invited to my home for a social dinner prior to my new administrative role, they related to me as a friend and teacher. They often had different expectations of me as a superintendent. They felt that I should be giving them whatever they requested, favors as a result of our previous relationship.

Dubin:

Such is the nature of politics. Before I ask you about favors overseas, let me ask you about general priorities. When you think back on your decision-making priorities as you began the school year, how did that process work? How did you organize?

Principal:

I had prepared a document, which outlined my role, priorities, a timeline, goals and objectives, essentially my blueprint for the school operation and direction. It was my philosophical and practical plan to lead the school, and I presented that to the board.

Dubin:

So, as part of this job description, you identified the specific programs you felt would most benefit the school, for example, math, reading, and so on.

Principal:

Exactly. And because this was a K–12 school, I had several levels to consider, and the curriculum had significant vertical articulation streams that I was planning. I had approximately 300 to 350 students, which ran the entire spectrum, that is, nursery, elementary, middle, and high school. It was extremely individualized and personalized. Classes were small and there was considerable attention given to each child.

Dubin:

How did you spend your time during the day, week, month, that is, parents, instruction, students, school plant, budget, and so on? There were so many different areas.

Principal:

There wasn't enough time. In the beginning I was trying to spend most of the time in the classroom. I was hoping to visit and observe each teacher at least three times a year. As an aside, when there was a message for a teacher, I brought the message directly to the classroom. I would wander in and visit informally. Later, as I became more sophisticated, the paperwork became more time-consuming, so I was not as available for the teachers and the students as I had been. It helped a lot that I had taught and had known at least half the kids before.

Dubin:

Your background, previous experience, the school location, your evolution as an administrator all are highly unusual characteristics that separate you from most other administrators. That being said, when you think about education today and your sense of issues here in the United States, what do think the problems are that new, prospective administrators face as they assume a leadership role?

Principal:

Here in America it seems to me that the issues are really not very different from the way it was in Pakistan. I have done some specialized teaching in the United States since my superintendency, and the problems are pretty much the same. There are diminished resources for the many educational needs. There is parent dissatisfaction. The power of the parent is even greater today with respect to the legal issues, and so there are issues of encroachment. They are very comfortable coming into the schools and challenging teachers. The legal battles, court cases have grown enormously.

Dubin:

What about diversity issues, which drive much of American public education today? In your experience, was this not an area with which you had to contend, considering the rich international population of your school? How did you work with these children of different backgrounds in order to develop sensitivities and understandings about their respective cultures, religions, and nationalities? Can you tell me how you addressed this area and how you communicated this?

Principal:

Well, yes. I think about the 3rd or 4th year I was principal/superintendent, we hired a Pakistani teacher part time, who happened to be the cousin of the former president of Afghanistan, to orient the children to these cultural differences. She developed a program whereby she would help the children understand about Pakistan and, in so doing, help them understand their own backgrounds. She taught everyone in the school about the cultural dances, singing, foods, clothing and embroidery, geography, history, arts, and went on field trips to better inform them about the country. Essentially, it was a culturally enriched curriculum course that became a part of the entire school curriculum. It really was a very comprehensive academic, practical, and experiential curriculum that dealt with the entire subcontinent.

She was a very dynamic and caring human being who loved Pakistan and communicated that to the children. I believe that many of the parents would have benefited by being in her class.

Dubin:

I would think so.

Principal:

Let me add that this class also lent itself to breaking down some of cultural and economic differences among the children. As you know, the school population consisted of the very wealthy Pakistani children from powerful families, children from many, many other countries throughout the world, and the powerful American diplomatic and corporate children. This was a very unusual mix of children. This class helped to bridge the differences in their backgrounds.

Dubin:

In light of these considerable cultural and economic differences among these children, could you be more specific as to any conflicts that presented themselves and how you managed them?

Principal:

Well, the most common situations that would arise had to do with name-calling and stereotyping. The Pakistani children would speak in Punjabi, the regional language of Pakistan, in classrooms or the playing field, and insult the Americans; and, of course, this was returned by the Americans, who insulted the Pakistani children.

Dubin:

What were the languages there?

Principal:

Well, Punjabi and Urdu. I would say that the Pakistani children were quite reluctant to respond to insults and taunts unless they felt really pushed. Then they would respond in kind. I was somewhat remiss over the years when the population changed and there were over 50% Pakistani students and 50% all other. At that point, the Pakistani children became more powerful in the school. They relied upon each other since they became greater in number and could seek revenge that they didn't dare do before when there were fewer Pakistani children.

Dubin:

Did this find its way into the community?

Principal:

Oh, yes, on both sides. The children would tell their parents that they had a fight today in school. . . .

Dubin:

Then they'd call you and ask what you'd do about it?

Principal:

Exactly.

Dubin:

How then would you categorize this? In terms of the basic cultural differences, would you consider this racism or attitudes of superiority brought in by the Americans or assumptions or resentments made by the Pakistanis toward Westerners?

Principal:

Well, I really didn't get any complaints from the Pakistani parents about Americans unless their own children were attacked.

Dubin:

Why do you think that was the case? Is it because they were unaccustomed to coming to the school with those issues, as opposed to non-Pakistanis who might have been more aggressive and comfortable approaching and voicing their points of view?

Principal:

Well, frankly, the timid ones I don't know about. The Pakistani parents could be quite aggressive and articulate their points of view, although, once voiced, they became less angry and assertive. We were usually able to smooth things over and get people to understand about what was happening. When it came to an expulsion, though, things became far more difficult. Parents would offer me bribes. They would really play up to me and tell me how wonderful I was and so on. When I didn't respond to them and the expulsion would stand, they were very unhappy.

Dubin:

When you mentioned bribes before, could you be more specific about that. What was a bribe exactly?

Principal:

Mostly money.

Dubin:

Well, tell me more. How did that work?

Principal:

Let me give you an example. One of our extremely wealthy families had several of their children and cousins in the school. One of them had a child who was not very bright or hard working. His grades continually went down. In addition, he had very poor attendance; he simply did not come to school. Every week he missed at least 1 day of school, and I knew that the child was perfectly healthy. I finally found out that the child was playing golf and going to golf tournaments. And, at times, he would simply not attend school at all. The parents could not make him come to school. I informed them that I had tried many different approaches, but their child simply did not care enough about school and his own education and was going to be expelled. I had not been able to find a way to interest him; he was only interested in his golfing.

When they heard this they were pretty angry. After a few days they requested a meeting. At this meeting, they told me that they knew how hard I'd worked and thought that they could help me with the work if they knew how much more money I could use. They alluded to additional money being made available to hire someone else to do some of my work or some ways of supplementing the budget or my salary.

Dubin:

Someone who could help you? These were subtle ways to influence you.

Principal:

Yes. They were extremely subtle. I did not realize how I'd get myself in situations somewhat sideways. It was hard to know how I got myself in certain situations.

Dubin:

Do you think that this was a cultural thing? Do you think that this was acceptable in Pakistan? As Americans, do you think that we don't recognize this as part of the process? Or do you think that this happens in the United States?

Principal:

Oh, of course it happens in the United States, but not to the degree that it happens there.

Dubin:

As you think about your career there, is there any particular issue that was particularly difficult for you as a principal or superintendent?

Principal:

When I was superintendent, there were challenges to my leadership based upon my ascension to the position. At one point, there was a petition that came to the board for my removal. There were teachers who challenged my authority throughout and took the opportunity to approach the board. Fortunately, I had support on the board and one in particular who came to my defense. He really argued and questioned the truth of some of the allegations and saved the day. He stated that this was the best American school his children had ever attended, and he had been stationed throughout the world. He was also highly respected in the community.

Dubin:

And so it was very important to have the board support you in order to do your job and be free, somewhat, of the political maneuvers typical of the schooling enterprise, particularly at your level.

Principal:

Indeed. But, understand, that was not always the case. There were years when I had boards whose membership did not always support me.

Dubin:

Such is the nature of relationships between board members and superintendents. In the context of this school's uniqueness in location and size, did you find that there were more issues of encroachment on the part of the board members? Were there problems with their not being able to distance themselves from the daily operational decisions of the school?

Principal:

Interestingly enough, it started off that our Scandinavian board member, who really meant to be helpful, became more involved than he should have. Their educational system was quite different from the American and Pakistani schools, and so I think that he really was somewhat baffled at our approach, curriculum, teaching, and so on. He meant to be helpful and made suggestions but was quite insulted when they weren't accepted. I had to be extremely tactful in my response and work closely with him and the community. That wasn't easy. Let me add that the board itself was composed of five nationalities. The board president was French; the vice president, American; the treasurer and secretary were Pakistani; the three members-at-large were British, American, and Swedish; and the ex officio member was the consulate general. It was quite a mix of educational backgrounds.

Dubin:

Did you have to teach them about the American educational system?

Principal:

Oh, yes. I had to teach the parents and the board.

Dubin:

Did you have to set aside time and have special meetings to do this? All the systems—Pakistani, American, British, Swedish, and French—are so different.

Principal:

Yes I did. For the first 10 years I would have special orientation sessions for parents. I would talk about customs and ask them to orient me about theirs. If there was something I needed to know to better understand them and their children and culture, to please approach me. Later on, unfortunately, I simply didn't have time for that. While the orientation sessions no longer were scheduled, I did communicate to the parents that they could approach me at any time and talk with me about whatever concerned them, something of an open-door policy. This process worked all right. We did rely upon our Pakistani teacher to explain some of the customs of the school when questions arose about the country and social mores.

As for the board, I also had special sessions with them and we had a rotating election process so that the replacements were staggered over time. The learning process was continued and flowed reasonably well over the years. That didn't change the educational differences, but it made the transition less dramatic.

Dubin:

And so the differences that surfaced were successfully managed in this way.

Principal:

Yes. With respect to the parents, over the years we hired a principal and counselor who also significantly assisted in this open-door approach. Let me add we provided information to all the import teachers, that is, those coming from the United States, who were given a packet of information that dealt with cultural differences, environment, people, language, travel, money, food, health, and virtually everything they would need to understand life in Pakistan. That helped enormously in preparing them for their adjustment and change in working here. Still, there were some teachers who had great difficult adjusting and would approach me in November or December and tell me that they planned to return to the United States during Christmas and not come back.

Dubin:

The culture shock was so severe. What traits did you look for as you recruited for teachers to work in Pakistan? What were the types of personal and professional traits you would focus on as you determined whom you would hire for an overseas faculty position in this part of the world?

Principal:

I was looking for people who enjoyed teaching. I was looking for people who were flexible. I was looking for teachers who felt that children came first. Having international experience was important and would allow them to survive some of the overseas challenges. For example, when the American embassy in Islamabad was set fire in 1979, many teachers were overwhelmed by the experience and left. Several, though, stayed who had had overseas experience and a different perspective. Let me add: Honesty and confidence are important traits that I look for when I recruit for teachers.

Dubin:

Well, your hiring strategies are somewhat different from those of administrators in the United States. Clearly, in the United States, if a teacher did not work out, they have but to call a district, and there would likely be other candidates available. You, on the other hand, were hiring someone to work on the other side of the world. You did not have the luxury of many mistakes in your perception of your teacher choices. In a small school, a teacher-hire could have many preparations. Indeed, they could have been an academic department, since they were teaching in so many different areas. And, of course, while considering the strength of their academic training, you also had to consider how emotionally equipped they were for life in a developing country. This was quite a balance.

Principal:

I wanted people who were adaptable, resilient, and calm in a crisis situation. I wanted teachers who would take the appropriate steps to deal with conflict. I was astounded by teachers I'd hired, thinking they would deal with adversity. And yet in a crisis some absolutely panicked. One particular case involved a husband who had actually been in a war as a younger man and yet was unable to deal with some school crises that did happen. In retrospect, I guess he was still traumatized by his previous experience, which came to the surface when our conflict occurred.

What had happened was a student mob was approaching the school. You see, the United States policy regarding Pakistan was changing, and the local press was writing very negatively about Americans. When United States/ Pakistani politics was in flux, it affected all American interests abroad.

And so our operational safety plan was that if the school was threatened, the teachers were to stay with their students and not leave them. Well, unfortunately, he did. He wanted to be with his wife and left his students. It was both a leadership and personal breakdown for him.

Dubin:

I understand. Those are critical leadership moments; literally, life-and-death situations. It places an enormous amount of pressure on your judgment when recruiting for teachers. Would you be thinking of these potential issues when you were hiring teachers? Of course, it's not possible to really know how people will react in given situations, but I would think you would want as accurate a gauge of these possibilities as possible.

Principal:

Of course. That was of paramount concern to me.

I also considered how able a teacher was to be self-sufficient, that is, they needed to have interests that would allow them to be self-contained, since the outside social opportunities and activities would be more limited in Pakistan. If they enjoyed reading, hiking, music, writing, that is, less socially engaging and more personally rewarding; these were also traits I looked for. On the other hand, being able to socialize and join in community events and activities, that is, picnics, sporting activities, day trips with other teachers was also important. They needed to integrate themselves into the community. And so, a prospective candidate had to offer both sides of the coin; they had to be very adaptable and flexible.

Another consideration focused on single teachers as opposed to married couples. While again one can't generalize a person's stability and adaptability, but I did consider the married couple as more likely being self-contained, since they had each other to rely upon, emotionally and with respect to activities and interests. The separation from home, being far from those things with which they were most familiar, would not likely be as traumatic for a couple or family for that matter if they had children than for a single individual.

Dubin:

It certainly does make the recruitment process very complex.

On another note, yet quite in the flow of our discussion about hiring, it has been said that the position is one of isolation. While this can be more relevant for teachers in an overseas format, rather than in the United States, did you find that to be true for you when you were principal and superintendent?

Principal:

It was far more isolating than I anticipated. I thought that I could continue as I had before I became principal. But after you've had to say no a few times to someone you had a friendly relationship with, it did something to the relationship. You realize that it is very isolating. It was very painful when you had to explain yourself over and over again as to why you had to decide in a certain way. People often did not understand or did not want to understand. Saying that it had nothing to do with how I felt about them, but rather it would be better for the kids and the school, was quite difficult and isolating. So it was, and particularly for me. I was learning and struggling to become an administrator and in an entirely different culture.

Dubin:

You were struggling in a different role and culture. I could see this leading to unusual types and levels of distrust, wanting to use you because of your position.

Principal:

And sometimes they got away with it. I would say that many, many teachers had come into my office, weeping and terribly upset about something, some sincerely, and others because they wanted to manipulate me.

For example, staff development conferences were something that was of great interest to many teachers because it would involve the school supporting and paying for their attendance at these conferences. Understand, these were international conferences, and so they were very sought after by the teachers because they were held all over the world, for example, Athens, Rome, Madrid, and so on, and so they were very desirable.

Dubin:

In other words, it was hard to differentiate their behavior, the legitimacy of their requests as being in the interest of the school or for their personal enjoyment.

Principal:

Yes. The buck did stop with me in all these respects, and many teachers were not pleased if I did not select them to attend the conference.

Dubin:

Did you find that you were able to connect with other international educators, that is, principals, superintendents, who could support you and advise you about leadership and all these cultural or administrative nuances? Was there anybody you could call and ask what they would do?

Principal:

Well, no, not really. I did call once or twice to other international educators but not often. My husband and I had friends in the consulate with whom we consulted and asked advice. They gave me some valuable feedback.

Dubin:

But other than that contact, there was no one else you relied upon or consulted?

Principal:

No, not really. I did enjoy attending the administrative conferences in various places in the world. That helped. In the beginning, I felt guilty using the money for these conferences, but I soon realized that it was quite important for the school, teachers, and my own personal growth. The fact that I was a woman, and one of the few principal/superintendents in the world, added another factor that made my work and isolation even more profound.

Dubin:

Your administrative experience was truly unique.

A general question I usually reserve for the end of the interview asks you to add any information that we haven't covered in this interview. But let me be more specific since your administrative experience had been highly unusual because of the international overseas format. Is there anything you would like to convey to those administrators who are interested in international education leadership in countries throughout the world? What would you wish to communicate to either young aspiring administrators or experienced administrators interested in this career pursuit?

Principal:

Well, they should first think about what it is going to be like, what they are getting into. Be sure they do as much as they can to learn about the culture, the country, the school!

Dubin:

In other words, they need to know about the people, the teachers, recent history of the country, politics, economics?

Principal:

Absolutely. Particularly in today's times with all the worldwide crises. They should really ask why it is that they want to go, why in this school, specifically.

Dubin:

Should they find other administrators who have had international experience or experience in this particular country or school to get feedback from them?

Principal:

Yes, that would be very helpful. Get as much information before they go. They really have to be extremely flexible. Are they flexible enough? They need to be clear about family, friends, and separation issues.

Dubin:

Should they be aware of time and the need to allow the cultural shock of the experience to be processed before they make decisions or determinations about how the experience would be affecting them? It's been said that there is a correlation between the number of photographs a new arrival in a culture takes and the cultural adjustment. When you stop taking so many pictures, generally, you've begun to see the environment in more normal and acceptable terms.

Principal:

That is really true. Once they arrive, they need to give the experience time before they make any final decisions about what they want to do and how comfortable and happy they are there, particularly the 1st year.

Let me say that it is an incredible, wonderful, life-altering experience. They will never be the same person or leader afterwards. They will view education, leadership, culture, the world, and people in an entirely different way.

Analysis

The principal/superintendent identified in this interview was unique in that she was dealing with an international American school, multinational community and board of directors. As well, she was selected as principal/ superintendent from within the organization, which presented a number of unusual issues with which she had to contend. She also addressed some of the cultural issues of living in Pakistan with respect to the foreign and local populations and their perceptions and understandings of American and Pakistani education. She also spoke of the unusual pressures by the local community on her decision making.

This interview captured many unique issues involved with this international principal/superintendent as she considered her school goals and priorities, personnel, budgetary decisions, participatory management, politics, ethics, as well as a host of other leadership areas.

One of the most pressing leadership challenges provided in this international school format deals with a principal creating an inclusive system that moves the school forward efficiently, accommodating the diverse educational backgrounds of the entire school community. When we examine the educational research that frames this school setting and leadership decisions, the work of several prominent theorists surface. The work of Kurt Lewin, one of the significant contributors to the human relations movement, identified the use of group dynamics as fostering involvement, participation, and greater productivity in organizations. In this setting, it is clear that active participation by all group members was crucial in moving the school forward. Without such inclusion, the various groups would have felt detached from the school setting, which served as the hub of the community.

The work of Carl Rogers in the fields of counseling and psychotherapy, as well as Elton Mayo's Hawthorne studies, identified the power and influence of personal experiences and internal group affiliations as significant factors affecting organizational effectiveness and the enhancement of the human condition. Their insights offer a deeper understanding regarding individuals and group participation.

The principal in this international American school wished to develop the process that would enable all the participants to be engaged in a meaningful but defined way. While offering a curriculum whose content core was from the United States, she also had the international baccalaureate courses available for international students. As she stated, one of her courses dealt with the Pakistani culture, the country, its language and customs in order to better acquaint all students with the national heritage of Pakistan. In addition it was a means to break down barriers that existed among the students. Finally, working with the international board of directors, she oriented them to the American curriculum and also incorporated other curriculums from other countries. Her ability to negotiate these multifaceted needs within this international school setting was truly impressive. In the light of our multicultural student population in the United States, many of her issues are extremely relevant to the issues administrators contend with in this country.

Discussion Questions

1. What are some of the key issues this principal/superintendent raises in this interview?

2. What is the tone of this interview?

3. Can you identify the roles of the different parent groups and board of directors in this international community?

4. What is her perception of the school's educational philosophy and what drives that perception?

5. Could you justify the position she has taken regarding curriculum?

6. What political changes have transpired in this school and why?

7. What changes would this administrator recommend that would significantly change the effectiveness of teachers?

8. Do you find her comments consistent with other schools or districts you've experienced?

9. If you were appointed principal/superintendent in this school, what would some of your 1st-year objectives be?

Student Activities

1. Write a letter of introduction to the students of the school.

2. Write a letter of introduction to the community indicating your philosophy, background, and goals for the upcoming school year.

3. Write a letter of introduction to the staff regarding your philosophy, background, and goals for the upcoming school year.

4. What agenda items would you include for your first faculty meeting at the beginning of the school year? How would you develop that agenda?

5. What funding sources would you pursue to support your school program?

Interview Question

What additional interview questions would you suggest to this administrator?

Simulations

Role-play what you would imagine to be a conversation between this superintendent/ principal and her board of directors regarding the philosophy of an American international school.

Role-play a parent night at your school involving many parents from different countries throughout the world where, as principal, you explain the American curriculum objectives. What types of questions would you expect them to ask? What would your expectations of them be?

Developing a Supportive School Environment

The principal talked about several experiences involving teachers, her ascension to the superintendency, the community, culture, the board of directors and other matters. What did you find to be the most important strategies she discussed regarding the following:

1. students
2. parents
3. faculty
4. the board of directors.

She spoke of the politics of the country and issues of safety. What characteristics would you consider important when you consider hiring faculty members to work at the school?

Principal Leadership Applications

At one point in the interview, she described a teacher as not following the safety rules regarding evacuation drills. This could have been an extremely dangerous situation. What tact would you have taken regarding disciplining the teacher? What additional strategies would you employ with respect to safety issues when

1. recruiting for teachers
2. offering orientation regarding the school plant
3. communicating with your community
4. communicating with the student body in preparation for a crisis
5. preparing a student and parent handbook identifying these issues and procedures.

In light of the school being international, do you think that a particular leadership style would be more appropriate in this setting? Why?

Questions Related to ISLLC Standards

See Appendix for ISLLC Standards.

1. How did this principal address Standard #1? Based upon the interview, cite at least one example that demonstrated that this standard was met.

2. How did this principal address Standard #3? Based upon the interview, cite at least one example that demonstrated that this standard was met.

3. How did this principal address Standard #4? Based upon the interview, cite at least one example that demonstrated that this standard was met.

4. How did this principal address Standard #6? Based upon the interview, cite at least one example that demonstrated that this standard was met.

5. Did you find that she also responded to other ISLLC standards? If so, which ones would you identify she addressed? Please cite specific examples.

Readings and Resources

Mayo, E. (1933). *The human problems of an industrial civilization*. New York: Macmillan.
Details the Hawthorne studies, one of the original studies that initiated considerable thought and additional research regarding the human relations movements of the following decades.
Rogers, C. (1942). *Counseling and psychotherapy*. Boston: Houghton Mifflin.
A theoretical review of Rogers's framework regarding individuals and their view of reality based upon their own personal experiences, which are ever changing and adjusting.

PART IV

No Child Left Behind

12

A Principal's Approach to the No Child Left Behind Act

Political pressure can have enormous influence on the culture and operation of a school. Generally, individual states have enjoyed the sovereignty to initiate legislation that affects school programs. Funding, curriculum, testing, credentialing, philosophy and other important aspects of the schooling enterprise have emanated from state and local initiatives. Departing from this historical backdrop, the federal educational initiative called the No Child Left Behind Act has assumed a more vital role in public school operations, funding, and expectations.

In light of this federal mandate, this K–8 middle school principal described the philosophy and leadership decisions she had to make at her school site. How was she to reconcile the expectations of No Child Left Behind regarding credentialing, employment, testing, teacher performance, and community reaction? How was she able to develop the leadership skills necessary to analyze test data and adjust her curriculum to address deficiencies in student performance? How did she maintain the morale of her faculty as they reacted to the pressures and demands of No Child Left Behind? How did she approach her community when they felt that their children would be compromised by under-achieving transfer students?

Themes addressed in the chapter:

- Leadership vision
- Communication: faculty, parents, public

- Short- and long-term planning
- Developing a supportive environment
- Special education students

Profile of NCLB: The Principal

Principal: female

Age: 40+

Ethnicity: Caucasian

Experience: 6th-year as principal; 1 year as assistant principal;

School: K–8 middle school; student population: 800

I think that is a reasonable response to No Child Left Behind. I think that most people see it as rigorous standards, ambitious results but with no resources. That's been the bottom line. We know that there are no resources, but we still are accountable to the rigorous standards and the ambitious results. So you have to forget about it. You literally have to take a staff of people and say to them, "We have no money."

You're constantly involved in the conversation where you're attempting to manage this legislation. The biggest part involves trying to meet your academic performance index and your adequate yearly progress. So it's not just a number but all your subgroups that you have in your school, which could be significant. It just depends on meeting the 5% improvement every single year. If they don't meet that, the first people who are blamed, according to my understanding of the legislature through the conversations I've had with my teachers, are them, the teachers.

I enjoy working with statistics and data and understand that the application of it and analyses are important tools in assessing student performance. It is somewhat isolated, and I don't ever see it as understanding the child completely. But one portion of that is certainly an important part in seeing any person's educational experience. They are always going to be scrutinized based upon some kind of standards-based assessment. That doesn't paint the entire picture of the child's intelligence or achievement, but it does play a part in public education or institutions for the rest of their lives, that level of assessment.

So, you have to be able to break it down into smaller chunks for your staff, to prioritize it, and that's what I do. I take the areas of need and break them out. . . . It's very interesting because you can look at some groups and then overall performance but then you can break it down further to grade levels, particular students, and ultimately to exact areas of need. Within math or language arts, or reading, or writing, these are the areas where you have the need. It's not a one-size-fits-all machine. You'll be able to, literally, take one level of your curriculum to focus on in order to identify the needs of that child.

It makes your job easier. I explain this all the time. Teaching 500 kids as a group, is much more challenging than teaching 500 kids as individuals.

The planning for instruction, implementation of programs comes out in a completely different way because you understand the data. You understand what the needs are and find out that a very small portion of these students have extreme learning needs, a very small portion. You have to exercise your expertise in dealing with those particulars . . . to keep breaking that down in order to identify your priorities.

School Context

This principal had been in that position at this middle school for 6 years. She knew her student population quite well and exercised a very flexible yet structured leadership style.

The school was in a very exclusive area of the city and had a very diverse student body. During her tenure the school underwent considerable change in terms of her leadership style and the student population. Prior to her assuming the principalship, the student population had been quite homogeneous. During the past several years, it has become far more diverse, representing more ethnic backgrounds.

School Characteristics

The school consisted of approximately 700 students: 25% Caucasian; 30% Asian; 25% African American; 15% Latino; 3% Samoan; 1% Chinese, and a few others. On an API (academic performance index) scale, they had very high test scores.

School Climate

The administrator was well prepared to deal with the considerable demands of the No Child Left Behind legislation. She was, though, very concerned about parent and teacher reaction to the demands of the law and focused much of her attention on information gathering and communication with her teachers and parents.

School Organization

The school district had a student population formula that provided some administrative support, for example, an assistant principal.

Interview

The following interview was conducted with a K–8 principal who has been actively involved in implementing the No Child Left Behind legislation in her school. It was conducted in early March 2005, soon after the Bush administration hired the new secretary of education, Margaret Spellings. The interview focused on the impact of the legislation on her school site and on what leadership approach she found most effective.

Dubin:

I very much appreciate the time you've allowed for this interview, which will focus on No Child Left Behind and how it has impacted your school. First, though, please tell me a little about your educational background and experience.

Principal:

Sure. Actually, I started my career in education a little later in life, first having begun in private industry but then, in my early thirties, decided that I would pursue education. My main objective, though, would be to become a school administrator. I took the foundational courses to become a teacher and at the same time, completed my master's degree and credential for administration in the evenings. I've spent the last 6 years serving as a public school administrator in this large inner-city school district. I started my tenure as an assistant principal and then the following year as a principal in this K–8 school. I plan to move on from site-level administration to district-, state-, or federal-level leadership in administration.

Dubin:

Please tell me about your school.

Principal:

Well, it's something of an anomaly in this district. There are actually six K–8 schools out of 177 K–12 schools. We have 77 elementary schools here. We fall within the purview of the assistant superintendent who oversees the elementary schools. She takes the K–8 schools as her responsibility and supervision. Therefore, we don't fall into any prescribed models because of the uniqueness of our expanded grade levels. We essentially glean our understanding and expertise from our colleagues, although it is a rather small group of us. The advantage of being a K–8 administrator, and I was also a teacher on this grade level at this site for 1 year, is to build a community and culture having those children and their families for 9 years, hopefully also having some level of staff stability. You build relationships that you wouldn't necessarily have in an elementary, middle, or high school where there are more isolated divisions. It's been a great experience in that regard because I am in a position to manage the school, but I can dabble into other areas that I'm really interested in, which are policy, new program implementation, and things like that.

Dubin:

How large is your school?

Principal:

We have 703 students with a tremendous amount of diversity. Prior to expanding into the K–8 model, we were a K–5 school with only six classes, one per grade level with 180 students, predominantly Asian or Caucasian. Now our population is comprised of 25% African American, 15% Latino, 30% Asian and other subgroups, an American Indian population, and Caucasian or other nonwhite and European populations.

Dubin:

It sounds like you've got a global school. I appreciate that background information.

Now let me ask you specifically about the No Child Left Behind initiative. It's impacted our national educational system for approximately 5 years now, and I'd like you to explain how it has affected your school.

Principal:

When the legislation was initiated in California, the greatest impact on the site level, rather than the district level, dealt with the level of scrutiny regarding teachers and programs. The result of that scrutiny was a significant push toward very ambitious standardized testing. This rubbed up against many schools, and my K–8 school, from a budgetary perspective. There was also a feeling initially that the impact would be greatest on teachers because one of their overriding forces or stipulations in that legislation dealt with high-quality teachers, ensuring that you have that level of teaching at your school site. Then the definition of that needed to be considered. At my site I have 36 certificated staff members. The majority is designated classroom teachers but some are support staff, that is, special education teachers, resource teachers, and a counselor who is certificated.

The challenge is to go into every grade level, not to marginalize, but [to] level all the teachers at each grade or the most critical grade levels and ensure that they have the same educational background, mastery of skills, and expertise. That's where it became a dog-eat-dog situation, where teachers were suddenly scrutinizing each other in order to save themselves in some ways because the goal was, ultimately, to have all teachers have a certain level of credentialing.

They are now being pushed to higher levels of education, which is quite interesting, because in California it's not a requirement to have a master's degree to be a teacher: a valid and content-specific credential certainly, but not a master's or higher levels of education. You will not be supported financially, that is, you will not get incremental raises or compensation for higher levels of education, so there is no push to raise that level of experience for teachers. So initially that was the first challenge.

Then the support personnel had to experience a higher level to at least an associate degree and also take some child education units. Furthermore, if they were special education paraprofessionals, they had to be trained within those areas in order to support those students. So there was the adult impact initially, not so much the child, and primarily because our school is a high-performing school. We've also improved our achievement as we've increased our diversity. So in some senses the programs that we have at our school are not under scrutiny as much as the teacher quality and the support staff.

Dubin:

So the element of testing, which is a part of the criteria, has not been the critical area but rather credentialing and high-quality teacher preparation are factors that have impacted your school.

Principal:

Well, actually it impacts every school in the district according to many discussions I've had with my colleagues in the field. The challenge is . . . and this is something I've experienced over the years in trying to build a culture and understanding and compassion in working with teachers in my school . . . is the idea of being blamed, that is, it's the teacher's fault that the students are not achieving. You're constantly involved in the conversation where you're attempting to manage this legislation. The biggest part is trying to meet your academic performance index, and your adequate yearly progress. It's not just a number, but all your subgroups that you have in your school, which could be significant, have to meet the 5% improvement every single year. If they don't meet that, the first people who are blamed, according to my understanding of the legislation through the conversations I've had with my teachers, are them, the teachers. Whereas, their perspective would be focused on the students, that is, their home environment, their socio-emotional conditions, learning challenges like learning disabilities.

On the standardized testing there's a range of scores you can receive for special education students or ELL students. One hundred percent of all the students in California are required to take an English-only, standards-based test, which is pretty rigorous and ambitious. It's one of the highest standards in the nation. But we have a tremendous number of students in our general public school population that are English language learners. Then there are the special education students, none of whom are exempt. As soon as they take a test of this nature and it's modified to a certain level, it's already scored below the average and essentially already skewed to the negative, no matter what the results. Then the scores are matched with the general population, and even though they're modified, they're already skewed below, so it's kind of a double whammy.

Dubin:

How do you develop a greater understanding of what these tests mean, what the scrutiny of the legislation means to teachers?

Principal:

Well, basically, what I do is a lot of counseling through my staff meetings, through my professional development, as to how to strengthen my teachers' understanding of this legislation. It's not about blaming them but, honestly it's about giving them more responsibility because of the fiscal state of educational funding. That's what's happening. That's a reality. Recently, I had a great conversation with a couple of my staff members. They said that what they needed was additional support because certain kids in their classes were being identified or targeted because of their particular needs. It could be a variety of strategies that we use for these kids. Their learning styles or needs are completely different, absolutely different, all over the dial. What we need is so much, but we know we're not going to get the resources. That's basically because of the funding cuts. So we must be self-reliant; it's on the teacher, it's on you. Their response is that it is not fair, this level of responsibility.

There are other components, which lead to compacts or contracts with families, parents, teachers, and students. We go down a very prescriptive path with a lot of these kids. I believe it develops a support system for them and helps define their level of education. This is all we have left.

We have 75% of our student population who can be independent learners. They have a more progressive, open-ended type of educational experience, still using the core curriculum, but beyond that because of their life experiences and what they bring to the table. Now we've taken this group of kids and kind of marginalized them because we're under so much pressure to move them and ensure that they improve because of that legislation.

So there is this essence of blame for teachers. That's where you start losing people no matter how qualified they are. Actually, the most highly qualified teachers, because they have the most free time on their hands, and by that I mean free time figuratively. I mean that they can walk into a classroom, and, because of their level of expertise, they don't need to rely upon lesson plans and standards of curriculum because they know them, they are embedded in their practice. They've had years and years to do this and they've had wonderful success. They're the ones who are challenging this legislation, not the new teachers. The new teachers are scared to death because they're being looked at. They're just out of teacher education, 1 or 2 years of education under the belt ostensibly, perhaps their 1st year in the classroom. They feel that they'll be scrutinized first and see themselves as under the chopping block all the time. They hold fast to all of this. Their minds are not open. They are not going to have that developmental period that perhaps they would have had a few years ago before this legislation. Now they are being scrutinized on this level.

I think it's even more that they don't have that high morale we should have. Teachers should have high morale. They should feel, every single time they come into the building in the morning, that life is great and they've got the greatest job in the world, but they don't. It's bad enough that their salary has always been so low and continues to be so low, but the flip side of this side now is that if you don't meet your mark, you don't meet this match for 3 consecutive years, you just fall.

I feel it. I feel the weight only because in our school, the overall group performance is high. But we're hiding a group of children that we're all aware we've targeted, we've identified. They've all got names. We know exactly who they are and what programs we're using for them, but it has not been adequate because we've been focusing on all the children, collectively. So now we have to shift our focus, teach all children more individually: our accelerated children, our general education children, our lower-end children in order to move them, and not even a tremendous amount of movement.

You see, the issues of equity are the key issues that we're talking about now in my school. I think that that is a reasonable response to No Child Left Behind. I think that most people see it as rigorous standards, ambitious results but with no resources. That's been the bottom line. We know that there are no resources, but we still are accountable to the rigorous standards and the ambitious results. So, you have to forget about it. You literally have to take a staff of people and say to them, "We have no money."

Dubin:

So as a site person, while on the one hand you recognize that you're asked to do something that is perfectly reasonable, that is, an environment should be created where every child should succeed, on the other hand, there are very legitimate extenuating circumstances, as you mentioned: background, resources, and so on that make it very difficult for that to happen. And so your leadership perspective is that this is what we have to deal with, we have to move forward and do the best we can do at this time. That is how you're treating this. Program improvement, that 3-year hammer hanging over your head, is a reality, and so you're saying this is what we have to do.

Now regarding that 25% of those students whom you mentioned are hiding, 95% of those students in these subcategories have to be identified. That is one of the problems that recently surfaced with schools nationwide, that very effective schools were found to have as few as 10 students within a subcategory who were not tested and then the school was identified as a program improvement school. Now how do you deal with that potential issue in your school?

Principal:

Yes, well this is where you talk about ethics. It's an ethical issue, not only when you work with staff but your schoolwide community; when you're talking with parents. I must tell you that there is an understanding. The majority of my parents come to community meetings, and I have several a year as well as parent education workshops, to talk about all these issues. In fact, I had a parent education workshop specifically on No Child Left Behind just to explain to them how this will impact our school. Mostly, the parents saw this as bringing in students from under-performing schools. As you know, one of the stipulations in No Child Left Behind legislation was that if parents were not satisfied with their district-identified under-performing schools, they were granted permission to leave them. They then had access to any high-achieving schools they wished to send their child to. And so we were impacted. We had roughly about 20 to 25 students taken from schools identified as under-performing schools and placed in our schools. These children were perceived as under-performing students. Our parents perceived these children as being dumped in our schools, which was one of the most horrific statements you could imagine. It's like they were coming into our place and messing up our thing here. That is what was going on. It's like they were going to impact our achievement, our performance results.

And so, you have to get over that first step with your community; that's the real challenge. You have to have them realize that these are children, first of all, and they are somewhat responsible for their education, but for the most part are not, especially as it concerns their achievement. That is really our job. So, it's breaking it down to almost de-personalizing the legislation and really getting the hard cold facts. I say it's the kids; the challenge is that when they come in they obviously have certain learning needs. Maybe they don't feel so successful in school. They've been impacted by peer pressure, by community pressure, by other parents, things like that. This is the constant conversation. We're a very conversation-based school, which is a good place for me.

It is really important to educate people to have them understand that there are reasons why these things happen. Most important, we have a level of program intervention, things that might better support these children in the public's mind. That's what we're here to do, that's our purpose as a public institution is to serve these children, to take away that stigma of their being dumped. There is a classification of student populations in my school, as perceived by certain members of my community, that these children are less worthy of receiving the level of education that they need. I believe it is really an issue of equity. I've used that word a thousand times. It has nothing to do with equality. It has to do with equity. These children need these services more and are going to get it. Seventy-five percent of our children of my school are advanced or accelerated.

Dubin:

This sounds very controversial.

Principal:

Oh yes. Absolutely.

Dubin:

They're also saying that there are limited resources and are asking where these resources can best be applied. They appear to be suggesting that there are diminishing returns here, and if they are redirected to the other population, they would argue that the resources would go further. Thus, you have this conflict and the issue of equity.

Principal:

Yes. That's exactly what it comes down to. In their minds it's literally looking at resources. They feel that they'd rather build our accelerated population than spend any time on this. In my mind, this is really the flip side of this legislation. The emphasis must be on the lower-performing population. Their accelerated students can only go so far statistically. We're maintaining them regardless of what happens. We end up reviewing this ideology each year, so we really have built a culture in this school. It took me, finally, with a select group of parents, taking them into my office and explaining to them what closing the achievement gap meant. It means focusing on those lower-end students. In essence, we're improving all our groups of students; but we've really been moving the achievement gap, not closing it. That's all inherent in that legislation as well, as it concerns the AYP and API.

Dubin:

So you need to communicate and educate parents in order to convey your overall philosophy and leadership. You also need to identify and accept this new population coming in that will be perceived as lowering the test scores, which could ultimately affect the program improvement status. But that's an issue and reality you're willing to take on and, in fact, feel is extremely important. That's something they have to buy into and you feel that is a part of educating your parents.

Principal:

Statistically, it doesn't really work that way although, as you point out, parents panic and perceive that to be the case. They feel that the accelerated levels are lowered in order to raise the lower-achieving students. But these children have taken these standardized tests for years and performed successfully, and I, having worked at this school for years, observed the teaching and understand the quality programs, and so on. It is not based solely upon these school offerings but rather the total life experience of these children. We have a variety of educational experiences in our lives: schools, families, cultural opportunities, traditions, support systems at home [that] value and support the goals of education. These families and children will continue to get high grades and perform successfully on standardized tests, not because of my school, teachers, or programs, but because of many other factors. So, even more to the point, this group will never fall behind. I have no worries about my highest-achieving group.

Dubin:

Another argument regarding these children's educational deficiencies and overall test scores, however justified or understandable, is that they will seriously threaten the entire school population. The legislature mandates that the funding would be affected, or even a leadership takeover of the school, if the school does not meet expectations. What about that argument? How do you deal with that? This is clearly an important leadership issue.

Principal:

Yes, absolutely. There are two separate scrutiny levels, AYP, which is adequate yearly progress, which is essentially the more important piece of this, not the API. The API is just a formula, which takes every single score of the school and then determines an overall [academic] performance index. That is really not meaty, not important, because the AYP really looks at the disaggregated data and tells you, in particular, within these subgroups, how you are making improvements. So, we made our AYP this year for all of our groups. We made our API for our overall groups, but we did not make our API for our subgroups; most importantly, our African American students.

Dubin:

Therein lies the real teeth of the legislation.

Principal:

That's what people have to see. They can't just see this number. That's where the leadership piece is so important. I bring it out. I tell them to look at our school. It looks perfectly fine when we have an overall API of 853. Actually, that's a little low to me because we've had that for about 2 years, in that range. We may have reached an apex and we've got to get past this; we're leveling now. But the problem is then with my African American group, their API, their general score as a subgroup is 690; thus my achievement gap. That's been consistent throughout. Before, when it was 700+ for the overall school, the African American population was 500+, so we continue with this 180- to 200-point achievement gap on our overall test scores between, most particularly, the Caucasian-identified group and our African American group. The African American group would not be considered a significant group because the percentages of the testing population is at 18%.

I have about 25% to 30% of students in my school kindergarten, first graders who are not tested. There is no scrutiny for those particular grade levels, which is another case in point. What are we doing with those kids in those two grade levels to get them ready for the upper primary grades and then upper elementary and then, ultimately, middle school levels? What are we doing? Are we all just sitting back, holding fast, because we don't have any kind of standardized testing or statewide level of scrutiny? . . . .

The problem, ultimately, is that you have to constantly educate your population. These are needs that have to be met. We can pretend that they don't exist because they're covered by our overall school score, but when the stats are in and the overall results are there, our overall work of the day is to analyze that data, that disaggregated data, in order to serve those populations. They'll just come back next year with the same results.

Dubin:

Everyone is supportive of the idea that every child should succeed. There is nothing wrong with that aspect of the legislation. What is pointed out is the funding issue. The schools are being asked to do things that may not be possible and is unfair. Under the present initiative a shadow could be cast on the entire school. What I'm hearing from you is that it is extremely important that, as a school leader, you provide education going forward, understanding test data and instituting intervention strategies. That is your attitude and approach.

Principal:

Yes. It also begs the question to me, To whom is it unfair? I think that answer is that every single adult might tell you that it is unfair to him or her. But not one child will tell you that it is unfair.

Dubin:

By fair, I mean that there could be a change of the school leadership in such a draconian way. The schools could feel that they have a wonderful school, most of the students are succeeding and that they are doing everything they can, but the consequence seems to be so dramatic. The effort to reconcile this may be greater than the actual problem. That seems to be unfair.

Principal:

What you have to do is look at additional resources and management of your resources particularly, as you're placed at this level of scrutiny. As I've heard more about that aspect of the initiative, I thought that there would be many schools that do a wonderful job on paper, that are accelerated and [are] the highest-achieving schools, but I know from my personal experience, working with those administrators and having a child enrolled in the public school system, that there are schools in the same position that I'm in. This is not a small population. Twenty-five percent is not a small percentage; it is pretty substantial and it is growing because of the No Child Left Behind legislation.

When I look at my budget each year, I see it as a piece of paper. I don't see it as cash in the box. It has to be fluid in some ways and flexible in other ways. I'm constantly on the phone with my budget director to really negotiate. . . . Not only do you need to look at fund-raising organizations within your community but you need to write grants and establish relationships with community-based organizations who would be willing to fund certain programs for your school. I constantly network with people who have these resources and have intentions of supporting those program initiatives I have in my school. That is a crucial aspect of my job and has little to do with my site-based leadership but more of how I create a presence in my community.

Let me give you an example of this. I have a Korean immersion program in my school, which is quite unusual for a K–8 school, but very successful and a great cultural addition to our school. Those students, as second-language learners, are predominately Caucasian, African American, and other ethnicities other than Korean . . . Well, those children actually are some of my highest-achieving students based upon second-language acquisition and proficiency. It's a luxury of a program and it's growing in demand and, in fact, we have a waiting list. It's kindergarten through fifth. So I spend a good amount of time during the year in conversations and meetings with the Korean consulate general, who has funded a portion of my program, because I can't afford to pay my teachers in the program. So they help me with that.

I also get assistance from the director of multilingual programs in order to help me get support personnel because I don't [have] enough funds in my budget. I am constantly working my way through the channels downtown establishing these relationships. I never want to give the parents or teachers or anybody else the feeling of complete loss or hopelessness. That's what you can encounter when you confront these kinds of things. I think it's a matter of being flexible and access this level of change without terrible division or destruction within your school community. . . . I try to build a community culture where you're not relying on people so much. We're relying on structures and systems within our community and organization. So anybody can take over.

Dubin:

It is clear that you are extremely positive, aggressive, and assertive in identifying ways in which you can compensate for the educational programs, alerting parents to this, issues of equity, seeking additional fund-raising, being entrepreneurial in so many ways.

How do you become educated in interpreting data? It is very complex and has become a very important part of all of this. Is this something you take on yourself or do you get support in understanding this data from the district?

Principal:

Well, some of the data and various assessments we receive regarding our test results come in different forms: some comprehensible, some more difficult to grasp. Fortunately, one of the very competent and accessible departments in our district deals with testing and assessment. They really help break it down for me. We start with that and also have instructional leadership seminars during the summertime prior to school starting. Years before, we had binders that disseminated data, that is, ethnic background, learning styles, special education, socioeconomic backgrounds, that sort of thing.

Dubin:

Some feedback I've received suggested that larger districts had strong support personnel that helped principals understand the data as opposed to small districts where the resources were limited, thus offering less data training for their principals.

Principal:

I enjoy working with statistics and data and understand that the application of it and analysis are important tools in assessing students' performance. It is somewhat isolated and I don't ever see it as understanding the child completely. But one portion of that is certainly an important part in seeing any person's educational experience. They're always going to be scrutinized based upon some kind of standards-based assessment. That doesn't paint the entire picture of the child's intelligence or achievement, but it does play a part in public education or institutions for the rest of their lives, that level of assessment. So you have to be able to break it down into smaller chunks for your staff, to prioritize it, and that's what I do. I take the areas of need and break them out.

It's very interesting because you can look at some groups and then overall performance, but then you can break it down further to grade levels, particular students, and ultimately to exact areas of need. Within math, or language arts, or reading, or writing, these are the areas where you have the need. It's not a one-size-fits-all machine. You'll be able to, literally, take one level of your curriculum to focus in on in order to identify the needs of that child. It makes your job easier. I explain this all the time. Teaching 500 kids, as a group, is much more challenging than teaching 500 kids as individuals. The planning for instruction, implementation of programs comes out in a completely different way because you understand the data. You understand what the needs are and you find out that a very small portion of these students have extreme learning needs, a very small portion. You have to exercise your expertise in dealing with those particulars. You need to keep breaking that down in order to identify your priorities.

Dubin:

With respect to special education, there seem to be conflicts because of the way in which the federal government is addressing this population of children. Have you had any issues with special education students? How are you dealing with those students, particularly in light of No Child Left Behind?

Principal:

I have a relatively large population of identified special-education children in my school. I have 68 students, 44 of whom are learning disabled, mild to moderate disabilities. Their IEP goals are not quite as strategic as my more severe populations of students, which involve inclusion students who have moderate to severe disabilities. Actually, these lean toward the more severe disabilities, such as visual, hearing, mobility challenges, autism, cerebral palsy, and other issues. I have 24 students in my school who are fully included. They are part of the general education spectrum. I have no special day classes. I don't have any students who are isolated based upon their learning needs or abilities.

That has a considerable impact on the overall scrutiny of data because we break out that population of students as a subgroup, as special education students. The challenge is that the most severe students cannot participate in the California Standards Test or California achievement tests. It simply is not appropriate, just from the standpoint of accessibility of the visually or hearing impaired or mobility issues dealing with fine motor skills. There are also cognitive issues involving deficiencies of 4 to 5 or more years with some of these students. At times, it is even difficult to establish a cognitive ability or grade level. So they are simply not able to participate in that assessment.

What is tricky is that No Child Left Behind states that 100% of student populations must be experiencing this level of assessment, that is, the most ambitious and rigorous level of assessment, which would be the California Standards Test. But we need to make modifications for these kids. We give them the accommodations as they need and have a right to by law, and yet we're dinged for it. As a school, we take their results and deal with the various levels of modifications. If you pass certain levels, you're placed in different levels of modifications, severe or excessive. The students who experience those tests, regardless of what the result is, even though they have a legal right to those accommodations, will still be scored and skewed automatically below basic because they were given the edge, in the public's mind. To me that is where the ethical question comes in. They do not have equal access. They do not have access to this material or level of instruction, but they're expected to reach this standard, which will never happen.

Major legislation must be enacted that will deal with this issue. . . . In any case, what I do with my staff and parents of special education students is that I simply explain that this is the way it is, and we have to accept and participate. They can write letters to request to be exempted from this, but we'll still be dinged anyway. To me, ultimately, it doesn't really matter. I need to tell them that they have to decide what they think is appropriate for their child. They can take the test or not. If they take the test and we modify it to deal with their level, we're going to get dinged on the under-performing index or statistical range, so it doesn't matter. So I ask them to make the choice. We're going to get dinged on the exemption or dinged on the under performance.

Dubin:

Let me ask you about the press. How do you deal with community perception of your school as it is assessed by No Child Left Behind mandates regarding testing, achievement, and overall success and failure? Could this affect various fund-raising initiatives, bond measures, and so on?

Principal:

The challenge with the press, unfortunately, is a reactive rather than proactive response because your school's name appears in the paper. Suddenly you need to make your community understand what those test scores mean after you've been designated, and according to this statistical analysis only, rather than a total overall school assessment. They're simply basing this on the test scores, Grades 2 to 12 essentially. That's what you're looking at. . . . In this city it appears that the press gets the information out first so we're always responding. We're created a reactive culture.

Beyond all the data, which I believe is suspect, people come to me immediately. I always have meetings in the beginning of the year to discuss and review the data and our overall performance goals. I have both leadership-administrative goals and goals set forth by No Child Left Behind, that is, the AYP and API. I try to explain all that beforehand, which I believe is the answer. Some of those principals that know, are aware, and understand the data should meet with their community before, perhaps the 1st week of school. They should tell them all those things that are happening and what level of scrutiny is involved and take a more proactive approach. The district tries to initiate this, but there are a variety of things they are contending with, particularly at the beginning of the year.

You see, at the beginning of the year when all this information comes out, that is, the AYP and the API, we are mainly dealing with enrollment issues. We are bombarded with that. Placement and full-enrollment capacity are our focus, and that is very distracting.

Let me relate a good example of how the media deals with the perception of good and bad schools. One of our high schools has a fantastic principal who truly turned his school around by developing many of their programs. Statistically, the test scores are still quite low, and they are considered a lower-performing school. But it has a great student body, the programs are sound, the principal is extremely effective, there is teacher leadership, and I'm certain the school will turn around. But they get very bad press. The area has a good deal of criminal activity, which is not coming from the school. While some of the students may be connected to it, it is not a part of the school. Nonetheless, anything that happens regarding criminal activity is put into the press as coming from the high school. This is what the principal has to struggle with all the time, always reactive to the press.

Dubin:

The idea of funding or support that could be adversely affected by the type of publicity generated about a school could further fuel the fires for vouchers. In this regard, what are your thoughts about vouchers?

Principal:

Yes. I was going to mention this. As we've discussed earlier, low-performing schools must notify all the parents that they have the right to access any high-performing school of their choice in the city. . . . The media released this information as essentially the parents' walking papers. Not only does it address the public sector but also allowed parents options for their children's needs. In some cases they were relocating from under-performing schools to high-performing schools because their children's needs were not being met in those schools. This was particularly true of the special-education children. They would challenge the district for them to attend nonpublic schools. They would use a portion of the public money they were allotted by the state per pupil and apply it to a charter or private school.

The biggest impact has been the charter schools where there is a significant competition for enrollment. When you consider all the major cuts in funding, that is, categorical funding, Title I, consent decree, school improvement funds, and so on, the decrease in enrollment [average daily attendance], which is our bread and butter and determines student allocation, has had a dramatic effect on public education. Already there are thousands of students who have taken advantage of this because the parents have little faith or trust in the public schools. This is based upon the No Child Left Behind initiative, which has allowed them to do this.

Dubin:

And that suggests the rationale for this legislature, according to many educators. While ostensibly No Child Left Behind suggests a detailed, positive, and aggressive plan to improve our public schools, there appears to be an unwritten agenda to undermine the public school system and legitimate vouchers. If it is determined or perceived that the schools are not providing an adequate education for our students, should there not be alternatives, private education, for example; thus, the vouchers. At the moment, it is a very fluid situation. In fact, many states are challenging this legislation as encroaching on states' rights. What is your sense of this?

Principal:

I know this has been an incredible and highly charged district issue here and elsewhere. They have been relying upon those funding sources. I also see this as an ethical question because of the particular needs of the diverse student populations that we experience in this city.

With regard to the politics, I believe we have state officials who are committed and determined to fight for the rights of our students and our school system. It affects K–12 education and universities as well.

Dubin:

If you had an audience of principals, how would you recommend they approach this legislation? What would your leadership strategies be?

Principal:

I would suggest that they know the legislature, focus on the needs of their schools and the overall assessment of their school, that is, data analysis, public relations, and so on. You must maintain a level of feedback that is continual. You must match the pressure from the legislature with your school's strengths and weaknesses in order to give you focus.

You should also lobby for your district on the state level. . . .

From the site level, it is extremely important to manage the legislation. It becomes a job rather than an emotional attachment to something you say is unfair. You must downsize it.

Dubin:

Downsize it. Know your student population. Understand and analyze the data so you are informed. Being aware of your parent reaction and educating them before it happens.

Principal:

When you've done your analysis and talked with your staff, because you'll always talk to your staff before your parents, then you talk to the parents. This is done in the beginning of the year, so you're preparing early.

You can project your particular situation and how it will impact your school. Those conversations should begin early with the school site council, academic plan, and with the budget. How will this impact our programs, our activities, the needs of our students, our instructional program? I relate this to my community in September. They will have the information directly. I will also put it in my community newsletter in April, a state of the school address. This is our plan and the anticipated impact.

Dubin:

Being proactive rather than reactive. And as you mentioned, validating your teachers. Also being entrepreneurial, since the money available to schools will be affected.

Finally, what do you project will be the situation with No Child Left Behind in the coming years?

Principal:

From a historical point of view, the many legislature initiatives over the past years have had various levels of impact, some positive and negative, and then put on a pile. There was nothing that was capacity building. In this state, I can see this happening after the initial impact.

I also see state-by-state flexibility to bring out the major issues like special education, working with diverse populations, and other areas. We need to pull out certain portions of it to create separate legislation for these needs. We also need to scaffold this legislation. . . .

We really don't have the kind of emphasis about education in this country that there needs to be. It is initiated by political cycles rather than being constant.

Dubin:

So No Child Left Behind could serve as a legislative blueprint, a flexible guide to follow.

Principal:

Yes.

Dubin:

Thank you so much for your insights and feedback.

Principal:

My pleasure.

Analysis

The principal focused on how she was going to implement the No Child Left Behind legislation at her school site. She explained about the range of issues that impacted her school and the various groups that would be affected. She stated that the teachers needed to be supported because they appeared to be the target of the legislation. She indicated the parent reaction to the legislation and how they perceived it to undermine their school programs and utilization of resources. She identified the news media as being an extremely important delivery system to convey accurate and timely information to her parents. Finally, while she understood the complexities of the legislature, she was quite clear in citing important elements of it that could serve the interests of all her students.

Principal Leadership Applications

At one point in the interview, the principal talked about the need to support her teachers and that the legislature seemed to point the finger of responsibility at the teachers for not being effective with the students. She explained how she continually supports and reinforces her teachers.

Did you feel her approach was correct? Why?

Were there other ways she could have supported her teachers?

Role-play a meeting with her teachers reinforcing her feeling that they were extremely capable and hard working and not responsible for some of the problems the students were having.

During another exchange in the interview, she talks about communicating to parents the importance of their acceptance of the transfer student.

What suggestions does she make regarding these students?

How would you handle this level of pressure if you were the principal of this type of school?

What advice does she offer the inexperienced administrators that would help them cope with the demands of applying No Child Left Behind to their school sites?

Another very important message regarding her leadership strategy was the need to connect with the news media.

What did she plan to do to control and direct the information flow in the community?

How was she able to maintain her professionalism and focus, knowing that some of the demands seemed to be unjustified and under-funded?

Do you feel that this would be a difficult role for you in assuming the principalship?

Questions Related to ISLLC Standards

See Appendix for ISLLC Standards.

1. How did this principal address Standard #1? Based upon the interview, cite at least one example that demonstrated that this standard was met.

2. How did this principal address Standard #2? Based upon the interview, cite at least one example that demonstrated that this standard was met.

3. How did this principal address Standard #4? Based upon the interview, cite at least one example that demonstrated that this standard was met.

4. How did this principal address Standard #5? Based upon the interview, cite at least one example that demonstrated that this standard was met.

5. How did this principal address Standard #6? Based upon the interview, cite at least one example that demonstrated that this standard was met.

Readings and Resources

U.S. Department of Education. (2002). *The No Child Left Behind Act.* http://www .ed.gov/nclb

13

A Superintendent's Perspective on NCLB

President George W. Bush identified educational reform as his number one domestic priority. On January 23, 2001, he sent his No Child Left Behind (NCLB) education plan to Congress and asked it to consider ways in which the federal government can be far more involved and effective in working with our public school system. It is hoped that this federal role would close the achievement gap between those students who have historically realized success in our system and those disadvantaged and minority children who have not. There are essentially four principles that provide the foundation for Bush's comprehensive education reform plan:

Stronger accountability for results

Expanded flexibility and local control

Expanded options for parents

An emphasis on teaching methods that have been proven to work

While this initiative has already made a significant impact on the schools in the United States, at the time of this writing, the plan is still undergoing considerable revision, and its application to schools remains very fluid. Nonetheless, it offers an important vehicle for an analysis of administrative leadership as principals approach and enact various aspects of the plan at their respective school sites.

Goals of the No Child Left Behind Act

- All students will reach high standards by 2013 to 2014
- All limited-English proficient students will attain language arts and math proficiency
- All students will be taught by highly qualified teachers by 2005 to 2006
- All students will be educated in safe environments
- All students will graduate from high school

Themes addressed in this chapter:

- Principal responsibility and leadership
- Assessment and accountability
- Expectations
- Requirements
- Funding and tax impact
- Parent and community reaction
- School reaction
- Future legislation
- Vouchers

The No Child Left Behind Act is a federal measure designed to bring accountability to education nationwide.

Profile of NCLB: The Superintendent

Superintendent: female

Age: 45+

Ethnicity: Caucasian

Experience: 10+ years as superintendent and assistant superintendent; 5+ years as principal; 4 years as assistant principal; 5 years as a teacher

County/District: office of education; county student population: 28,000

If you step back, or up into a helicopter, I think because of No Child Left Behind, schools and districts are paying far more attention to data. They are learning how to look at student performance data in ways that they had not been forced to look before. On that level, there is something good that is happening.

> . . . One of the critical arguments against No Child Left Behind [is that] every school would want a highly qualified teacher in every classroom; everybody does want students to be proficient. The expectation is that the federal government would provide the funding to help states and school districts do this work. The federal government simply has not provided the funding.
>
> We have all said, from the very beginning, that this is in fact going to highlight the public schools as failing and that vouchers will be the solution.

County Context

County- and district-level leaders must assume a wide-ranging perspective regarding the individualized needs of schools within their educational organizations. This veteran and highly experienced, former award-winning principal, assistant superintendent, and superintendent had several extremely important roles to perform in her county. It is quite clear from her interview that she understood the political dynamics of the No Child Left Behind legislation and the implications for each district, school-site principals, parents, and students. She also conveyed a deep concern regarding the impact it would have on public perception about public schools and future consequences.

County Characteristics

The County had two unified districts (K–12); 15 elementary districts (K–8); two high school districts (Grades 9–12), totaling 19 districts. There were 45 elementary schools (K–8); 11 middle schools (Grades 6–8), 8 high schools (Grades 9–12), three continuation schools, six alternative education/independent study schools and four charter schools for a total of 77. There were 28,000 students consisting of 68% Caucasian, 17% Hispanic, 6% Asian, 3% African Americans, with Filipino and Native American representation. There was a very high graduation rate (more than 95%) and a low dropout rate (0.7%). A significant portion of the student population scored above the national averages for the SAT (Scholastic Aptitude Test).

County Climate

The county had a very strong educational program reflected in each district and considerable financial backing, which supported the overall county program. A significant percentage of the parent population were well educated and had very high expectations of the schools. There were grant opportunities and various outside funding sources that augmented the per-student allotment for each school.

County Organization

The county office was organized with a superintendent, several assistant superintendents, and a number of administrative support staff overseeing services and programs to meet the needs of the districts including alternative education, business, education, general services, personnel and administration, information, a regional occupational program, special education and outreach programs. Each district had a superintendent and support staff, as appropriate to the needs of the district.

Interview

The following interview was conducted with a superintendent/assistant superintendent and principal who is expert in understanding, extrapolating, and conveying the No Child Left Behind legislation to upper-level leadership in districts and county offices as well as to site-level principals. The interview was conducted in early March 2005, soon after the Bush administration replaced U.S. Secretary of Education Rod Paige with Margaret Spellings.

Dubin:

I appreciate the time you have given me to answer questions about No Child Left Behind legislation, as to its impact on schools in your district and county office, as well as its effect on school principals.

First, let me ask you to tell me about yourself, your background, professional position, and administrative role regarding No Child Left Behind.

Superintendent:

Certainly. Currently I have two roles: assistant superintendent of education in this county office with a focus area in educational services, that is, teaching and learning for students, staff, and the community. As well, I serve as superintendent in a small K–8 district. I have also been trained and certified as a curriculum auditor. I have been a distinguished school principal, a blue-ribbon school principal on the middle school level. I have been a K–8 principal and was a teacher and high school administrator for many years. I have had a broad range of administrative experiences and responsibilities.

Most recently, I have been a superintendent/principal on the K–8 level, so I've had a good deal of hands-on experience with accountability measures as they have been unfolding within the last few years.

Dubin:

So you know what an initiative like No Child Left Behind will mean to schools across the nation.

Superintendent:

I've watched it unfold almost a page at a time.

No Child Left Behind is a federal measure designed to bring accountability to education nationwide. The unique part of No Child Left Behind is that it is the first initiative that makes the assumption that in the year 2013-2014, all students in our nation will be proficient in English, language arts, and math. That includes socioeconomically disadvantaged students, English language learners, as well as students with special needs served by special education programs.

Dubin:

That's quite an ambitious initiative.

Superintendent:

That is the challenge that people are now looking at. In addition, never before have we had an accountability measure that requires 95% of our students to participate at every test at every grade level. That has created significant problems. First and foremost, people did not have the overall understanding of No Child Left Behind because they have been interpreting it section by section as to what it means each year. So we've been getting information for the last 3 years in bits and pieces. It's only been within the last year that California has had its final plan approved by the federal government that we clearly understand what the current requirements are.

It is important to note that California has a different way of doing business from many of the other states. California requires legislative action to implement education policy. In many states the superintendent of public instruction or their designee can make decisions about what happens in schools. In California, the legislature is involved and the education code is then written and implemented. California has struggled considerably within the last 2 years to overcome the bureaucratic obstacles and network to, in fact, pass pieces of legislation that the federal government will approve. There have been many situations where you pass one piece of legislation, but then it has to be revised in cleanup legislation because the federal government said it wasn't good enough. That's why, in California, we're having a particularly difficult time. This state might be unique in this respect relative to the national situation.

Dubin:

This need for additional time, was this not woven into the initiative as to its potential impact on the uniqueness of various state districts and schools and how they respond?

Superintendent:

There are two issues. There is the requirement that you address the many elements of the initiative. Each state must design a workbook, and the Federal Government must approve it in order to increase student achievement. But there is no additional funding that would need to take place to support districts to, perhaps, pay staff to do some of the data analysis, for example, or to have small instruction groups for under-achieving students at different levels. There is no funding source for that. So what districts are doing nationwide, depending upon the state, is trying to provide resources to support the implementation of No Child Left Behind.

Dubin:

That was not explained?

Superintendent:

That was one of the critical arguments against No Child Left Behind. Every school would want a highly qualified teacher in every classroom; everybody does want students to be proficient. The expectation is that the federal government would provide the funding to help states and school districts do this work. The federal government simply has not provided the funding.

Dubin:

In light of that reaction, have they revisited that issue and are now saying that they will provide that funding?

Superintendent:

No. In fact at this time, one state, Utah, is currently questioning the federal government's legal position and challenging the right of the federal government to tell the states how they will implement education. Essentially, they are questioning the federal government's right to tell a state what to do in an area where the state believes it has the right to determine school accountability measures.

Dubin:

In other words, they're challenging the constitutionality of it.

Superintendent:

Correct.

Dubin:

And also for special education?

Superintendent:

Now with special education, issues are most significant. In California, a student is required to have an IEP, individual education plan, which determines what work they will do, what grade-level work, what interventions and everything so related. In No Child Left Behind's requirement in California, it states that regardless of what the grade level the work is that the student is completing, he must be tested at his age-appropriate grade level. So, if you may have an IEP that says that, for example, a sixth grader is to be doing third-grade work because that is what his testing is, that's where his ability is to be successful. Although actually placed in the sixth grade, the No Child Left Behind requirement says that if you test him on the third-grade level, his scores will not count for participation, and he'll be given an automatic default of the lowest score for performance.

So, in other words, there's a conflict here immediately with the federal law requiring us to provide a program that is academically appropriate as determined by a team of people from specialists to school staff to parents. They made those decisions. But then the federal government says that you can't follow that decision when it comes to testing.

So there are imminent challenges within the special education arena.

Dubin:

That seems so obvious. And yet, how was this overlooked? It seems as if the federal law regarding special education mandates that special education children be tested according to a specifically designed plan by educators and parents yet that policy is not regarded as legitimate within the context of No Child Left Behind. That seems to be a basic conflict of mandates on the federal level.

Superintendent:

Yes. I think there has been a draconian implementation of No Child Left Behind. And at each point with these topics, the federal government has not backed down at all. We have a new secretary of education, Margaret Spellings, and many people are hoping that she will more reasonably implement the No Child Left Behind principles.

Dubin:

What is the issue that deals with accountability?

Superintendent:

If a school or a district is found not to meet their adequate yearly progress, their participation rate of 95% or more in multiple categories, their academic performance index—and each state has a different phrase for that statewide accountability measure that is used to measure performance and graduation rates—there are four categories. If they don't meet adequate yearly progress in these four categories 2 years in a row, they enter what is called program improvement. There has already been much publicity about many of the highest ranking schools in various districts, in Florida for example, who are beginning to enter program improvement.

In my district, we have schools where students were testing at the highest level statewide, above the statewide average, yet are entering program improvement because they did not have the participation rate in the special education subgroup 2 years in a row. So what is required is you take a portion of your Title I money, and this is the money that is designed to serve the lowest-performing students in your school district, and provide professional development with that money. Many districts have other sources of providing for professional development but No Child Left Behind says that you must take your Title I money and pay for professional development. And you have to use some of that money in the event parents want to transport their children to another school district. You have to allow for that.

In the 2nd year you must provide for tutoring for students who fall below grade level. So Title I money, designed to service those lowest-performing students, is now being pulled away from that role and spread out into program improvement efforts. And these efforts may or may not have as much value as what schools have been able to do with their Title I money previous to this.

Dubin:

In your experience, what has been the reaction of the schools, and specifically the principals, to this? Are they knowledgeable of these expectations and what the consequences will be?

Superintendent:

No Child Left Behind criteria are incredibly complex. What I am doing in my role here at the county office is spending a good deal of time with the superintendent helping her understand what the different criteria are and why her district is heading into program improvement. I just spent 2 hours with her. She is afraid that her principals do not have the time to hear this information. I, of course, was able to meet with her one-on-one, go through the various processes, and it took several hours. Well, principals most often have only minutes to devote to topics at the school-site level. There are probably a few who have the ability to do the research to understand the enormous breadth of No Child Left Behind, and there are regulations in every facet of what we do. Currently the state has taken the No Child Left Behind regulations and interpreted them for our consolidated application, and every state has a way of giving their school districts their categorical funding.

I believe most states are aligning their reporting on that to No Child Left Behind. So that's invisible, and most principals are getting to know that that's happening in many cases. But they do have to be very aware— and [this] is a problem in our county and I suspect in many places—that they're not providing good data alongside the student test data. There are many sheets of paper that come with the student testing, where you have to explain whether it's a special education student, whether they get new national free-lunch programs, all these specialty boxes. STAR (standard testing and reporting) test data had been ignored by many schools. So for the principal who knows the importance of good data and good information in addition to test-taking procedures, their schools will do better. A principal who has no clue that all of these things interrelate will do poorly.

Dubin:

So if the districts do not provide the expertise that you're providing, for example, or the person power to convey that to them, this will create a considerable problem for these principals.

Superintendent:

Especially in the smaller districts. Big systems have curriculum administrators who are interpreting the information and feeding it to their principals, and that is the ideal situation. It's important to look at big-district principals and small-district principals because that will have an impact nationwide. There is no measure that I have seen, and I have been working in education since 1970, that is as complex as No Child Left Behind.

Dubin:

How can a parent know what is involved with No Child Left Behind? As you explain the incredible detail and need for principals to become better informed and understand the initiative, how do they convey this to parents? What do they say to parents who are asking questions about it?

Superintendent:

That is absolutely fascinating. When a school becomes a program improvement school, one of the main provisions of No Child Left Behind is that principals must tell parents everything that may be wrong. So principals then respond that they understand and know they're in trouble and send a letter to the parents. Parents are often puzzled because of the letter, which is required, yet they will tell you every time that they love their school. There have been continual newspaper articles that show that when given an opportunity to change schools because their school did not meet adequate yearly progress, parents stay in the community they're in. So not as many people have availed themselves of the opportunity to do that.

So I don't think many parents really understand as much as the harried principals understand. The information they get is at the level when there is a problem.

Dubin:

That sounds very interesting because one of the rationales behind this legislation is to provide parents the opportunity to change schools if they want to. Yet somehow that connection, that is, that other kind of relationship between the parent and the school seems to transcend the feedback and assessments.

Superintendent:

Any time you have a piece of legislation that is this complex and is evolving as frequently as it has evolved, there is a lack of clarity. The schools can't explain it to parents because they can barely understand it. The state can't explain it to the schools because they're constantly having now to go back to the federal government to make sure what they think is happening is, indeed, what is happening. We've never had any kind of a regulation that makes the states march to the federal government this frequently to clarify points. The lack of clarity has been the issue with No Child Left Behind.

Dubin:

So in other words, the awareness level now is still in its beginning stages, and with a different secretary of education you may have other possibilities.

Superintendent:

Opportunities to completely revision it: that is either good or bad. Remember the constitutional piece that you mentioned earlier, which is an extremely important one, that No Child Left Behind assumes that the states will follow the national educational mandate at this moment. And the struggle that school districts have is, in principle, [that] no one would disagree with high goals but the practical implementation has been so challenging that states are now having to find themselves spending precious resources in legal interpretations to work with the federal government.

Dubin:

Now let's play the devil's advocate for a moment. If the states identify their testing and their measure for accountability as their choice and the federal government, essentially, is encroaching on the historic territory and role the states have played, could they not reject it and say no, we're not going to adhere.

Superintendent:

Absolutely. But here's the catch. The federal government is saying that you will not get any of our federal funding unless you comply.

Dubin:

That's Title I funds?

Superintendent:

That's Title I and Title II, and there are many Titles.

Dubin:

Yes, and that would have significant implications.

Superintendent:

That would have significant implications for states not to comply. That is the answer to the question as to why we're doing all this silliness. They have us, here in California and in most other places, in a position where you must move forward. If you step back, or up into a helicopter, I think, because of No Child Left Behind, schools and districts are paying far more attention to data. They are learning how to look at student performance data in ways that they had not been forced to look at before. On that level, there is something good that is happening. We are nationally trying to make sure that all of our teachers are credentialed properly. The dilemma that we will face very soon is that parents, teachers, principals, and schools districts will find this to be a farce because it is impossible to have students perform at 100% level of proficiency.

Dubin:

Of course.

Superintendent:

Each year more students in each state will be identified as program improvement, and it will not be long before something will change. Public perception regarding public education again will be damaged because it's one more thing that public education has attempted to do but has been inadequate. People who have no knowledge of education, they will see this blow up in the future on some level.

Dubin:

That's a well-taken point. So in thinking about the principal, the site level, what advice would you give to principals at this point?

Superintendent:

Principals must become informed. They must be able to look at their individual student achievement data. That's not across the school, that's classroom by classroom and student by student. We owe it to all of our students to find out what it is we hold as achievement objectives for each student and what plans we have to help students get there. And we have students of every ability level in every classroom. We are going to have to provide research-based instructional strategies that are different for interventions, and this really highlights the importance of looking at your special populations and trying to see what you can do to help students be more successful in the school program. So if you place all those other stakes aside, the key kernels that we have to pay attention to is looking at student achievement data in a more specific manner and breaking it and desegregating it in as many ways as we can.

Dubin:

Yes, and as you said before, this is a good thing to really look and focus in ways that are data driven. That could really help improvement and help kids succeed.

Superintendent:

Oh, absolutely.

Dubin:

Now, in your judgment, would you say that there might also be a more positive, agreeable, and balanced relationship that ultimately will evolve between the federal government and the states?

Superintendent:

I would hope that the opportunity to rethink some of the challenges to implementing No Child Left Behind would be available with the new education secretary. We will see whether that person is willing to face some of these significant issues such as special education, for example. The worry I have, having been at the school site and participated in special education IEP meetings with parents who already feel horrible that their child is not able to perform at the grade level, [is that,] in essence, we slap the face of that parent and that student one more time with a measure like this. It breaks my heart to watch, and I've sat in meetings where parents, no matter what they know, still choose to pull their child out because they won't have their child's self-esteem damaged one more time. I, as a district superintendent and principal, understand and am willing to go through the school program improvement process because when it's all over and done, we have to be able to educate the students that we serve in the best manner, with the simple level of dignity that should be afforded to every child, [no matter] who they are and where they're at.

Dubin:

In your experience, when you think of other initiatives, can this be compared to anything else?

Superintendent:

I think that there have been many different initiatives that have come and gone. This almost looks like you've collected something from each one of them and made it part of this one. For example, we have to identify the research-based practices now when we get money for programs like alcohol, tobacco, and other programs. They're making you do everything. If we had staffs and schools to do this kind of research thoroughly we might be able to identify some intervention strategies. But we don't have the people power to implement this. So what I think they've done is taken every good idea that's ever come along and made it part of this bill.

Dubin:

And implemented it without understanding completely the ramifications of it.

Superintendent:

Unfortunately, many of the people who are policy makers on the local, state, and federal levels never enter the classrooms. So they are not watching how students perform daily to see how an initiative like that fits in. When you have as many components as this legislation has, you have to give it something to get to this. And what we have to be able to do is to continue to teach more than English, language arts, and math to students.

Dubin:

Well, you have covered a considerable amount of information regarding No Child Left Behind clearly, concisely, and expertly. I also suspect that you represent a small number of knowledgeable people in the country who are aware of and understand this extremely important initiative.

Superintendent:

Well, it is my perspective. I just hope that, somewhere in the process, there will be more reasonable people involved in No Child Left Behind.

Dubin:

If you saw it in a positive way, it is safe to say that you would see some compromise where districts and states can be responsive to what they would agree would be the objectives that underscore it, with resources and reasonable time, and without this hammer held over their heads for consequences.

Superintendent:

Correct. Correct.

Dubin:

From that logistical vantage point, within a 3-year period, if so many top schools—and that's been part of this problem nationwide—or a significant portion of them are identified as needing improvement, what would they do?

Superintendent:

There is no way any state can provide the intervention necessary for this many schools.

Dubin:

Not possible, and they've got to realize that.

Superintendent:

And I also think they know that. I think this is one of the most extreme pieces of legislation I have ever seen or could imagine. And how can they gracefully get out of this?

Dubin:

Could this drive a movement for the vouchers?

Superintendent:

We have all said, from the very beginning, that this is in fact going to highlight the public schools as failing and that vouchers will be the solution. That has been Bush's agenda from Day 1.

Dubin:

We see one consequence could be a compromise or agreeable solution where there would really be an attainable, viable solution that everyone would agree upon., And yet another outcome could possibly be where that doesn't happen, resulting in placing more pressure in legitimating vouchers.

Superintendent:

You have got it. That is the bottom line.

Dubin:

What else did I not ask you that would be helpful?

Superintendent:

Well, there really is so much to it. I can't add much more to what I've already mentioned. But this is really the type of initiative where you could get lost in the details of implementation and forget the overall structure of what we're trying to do in the schools. Aside from the two possible outcomes that we just touched upon, I think another thing that could happen is that if schools continue to be reported and identified as program improvement schools, then local taxpayers will react. All the communities throughout the United States who give to their schools because they think they're supporting good schools and it's raising their property values, well it's going to be harder and harder for individual school districts to pass tax levy measures in the states involved. In no way does that reflect the teaching and learning that's actually taking place in those communities, but in fact reflects some compliance measures on somewhat difficult-to-attain models.

Dubin:

I understand. And that is what could very well be advertised to the public. That information would be sent out to the public, who would have a limited understanding of how functional and successful the schools are.

Superintendent:

The other place that would have a lack of understanding is the press. They are guilty of misquoting schools and districts and creating a degree of chaos when it need not exist, locally and across the state. I recently talked with someone at the state department about this earlier, and they were talking about the headlines in cities with high-performing schools, and so I know that all these things are going on and these concerns are real.

Dubin:

That's another piece that we can't explore at the moment, but certainly articulating these issues and insights to the press who write articles; for them to convey to their communities and parents what is really going on, to educate them.

Superintendent:

Right.

Dubin:

Thank you very much for your comments and sharing your expertise.

Analysis

The superintendent provided an insightful overview of the No Child Left Behind legislation and the impact it is having on our schools nationwide. She identified the rationale behind the legislature, the perspective from the county-district level, and the effect it was having on principals at the site level. She provided a wider lens in which to understand the initiative and how she felt principals needed to effectively respond to the law on the site level. It may be very useful to compare her comments with all of the principals interviewed, particularly the interview of the principal that specifically focused on her interpretation and implementation of the No Child Left Behind initiative at her school site.

Readings and Resources

U.S. Department of Education. (2002). *The No Child Left Behind Act*. http://www .ed.gov/nclb

Appendix

Interstate School Leaders Licensure Consortium Standards for School Leaders

Standard 1

A school administrator is an educational leader who promotes the success of all students by facilitating the development, articulation, implementation, and stewardship of a vision of learning that is shared and supported by the school community.

Knowledge

The administrator has knowledge and understanding of

- learning goals in a pluralistic society
- the principles of developing and implementing strategic plans
- systems theory
- information sources, data collection, and data analysis strategies
- effective communication
- effective consensus-building and negotiation skills

Dispositions

The administrator believes in, values, and is committed to

- the educability of all
- a school vision of high standards of learning
- continuous school improvement
- the inclusion of all members of the school community
- ensuring that students have the knowledge, skills, and values needed to become successful adults
- a willingness to continuously examine one's own assumptions, beliefs, and practices
- doing the work required for high levels of personal and organization performance

Performances

The administrator facilitates processes and engages in activities ensuring that

- the vision and mission of the school are effectively communicated to staff, parents, students, and community members
- the vision and mission are communicated through the use of symbols, ceremonies, stories, and similar activities
- the core beliefs of the school vision are modeled for all stakeholders
- the vision is developed with and among stakeholders
- the contributions of school community members to the realization of the vision are recognized and celebrated
- progress toward the vision and mission is communicated to all stakeholders
- the school community is involved in school improvement efforts
- the vision shapes the educational programs, plans, and activities
- the vision shapes the educational programs, plans, and actions
- an implementation plan is developed in which objectives and strategies to achieve the vision and goals are clearly articulated
- assessment data related to student learning are used to develop the school vision and goals
- relevant demographic data pertaining to students and their families are used in developing the school mission and goals
- barriers to achieving the vision are identified, clarified, and addressed
- needed resources are sought and obtained to support the implementation of the school mission and goals
- existing resources are used in support of the school vision and goals
- the vision, mission, and implementation plans are regularly monitored, evaluated, and revised

Standard 2

A school administrator is an educational leader who promotes the success of all students by advocating, nurturing, and sustaining a school culture and instructional program conducive to student learning and staff professional growth.

Knowledge

The administrator has knowledge and understanding of

- student growth and development
- applied learning theories
- applied motivational theories
- curriculum design, implementation, evaluation, and refinement
- principles of effective instruction
- measurement, evaluation, and assessment strategies
- diversity and its meaning for educational programs
- adult learning and professional development models
- the change process for systems, organizations, and individuals
- the role of technology in promoting student learning and professional growth
- school cultures

Dispositions

The administrator believes in, values, and is committed to

- student learning as the fundamental purpose of schooling
- the proposition that all students can learn
- the variety of ways in which students can learn
- lifelong learning for self and others
- professional development as an integral part of school improvement
- the benefits that diversity brings to the school community
- a safe and supportive learning environment
- preparing students to be contributing members of society

Performances

The administrator facilitates processes and engages in activities ensuring that

- all individuals are treated with fairness, dignity, and respect
- professional development promotes a focus on student learning consistent with the school vision and goals

- students and staff feel valued and important
- the responsibilities and contributions of each individual are acknowledged
- barriers to student learning are identified, clarified, and addressed
- diversity is considered in developing learning experiences
- lifelong learning is encouraged and modeled
- there is a culture of high expectations for self, student, and staff performance
- technologies are used in teaching and learning
- student and staff accomplishments are recognized and celebrated
- multiple opportunities to learn are available to all students
- the school is organized and aligned for success
- curricular, cocurricular, and extracurricular programs are designed, implemented, evaluated, and refined
- curriculum decisions are based on research, expertise of teachers, and the recommendations of learned societies
- the school culture and climate are assessed on a regular basis
- a variety of sources of information is used to make decisions
- student learning is assessed using a variety of techniques
- multiple sources of information regarding performance are used by staff and students
- a variety of supervisory and evaluation models is employed
- pupil personnel programs are developed to meet the needs of students and their families

Standard 3

A school administrator is an educational leader who promotes the success of all students by ensuring management of the organization, operations, and resources for a safe, efficient, and effective learning environment.

Knowledge

The administrator has knowledge and understanding of

- theories and models of organizations and the principles of organizational development
- operational procedures at the school and district level
- principles and issues relating to school safety and security
- human resources management and development
- principles and issues relating to fiscal operations of school management
- principles and issues relating to school facilities and use of space
- legal issues impacting school operations
- current technologies that support management functions

Dispositions

The administrator believes in, values, and is committed to

- making management decisions to enhance learning and teaching
- taking risks to improve schools
- trusting people and their judgments
- accepting responsibility
- high-quality standards, expectations, and performances
- involving stakeholders in management processes
- a safe environment

Performances

The administrator facilitates processes and engages in activities ensuring that

- knowledge of learning, teaching, and student development is used to inform management decisions
- operational procedures are designed and managed to maximize opportunities for successful learning
- emerging trends are recognized, studied, and applied as appropriate
- operational plans and procedures to achieve the vision and goals of the school are in place
- collective bargaining and other contractual agreements related to the school are effectively managed
- the school plant, equipment, and support systems operate safely, efficiently, and effectively
- time is managed to maximize attainment of organizational goals
- potential problems and opportunities are identified
- problems are confronted and resolved in a timely manner
- financial, human, and material resources are aligned to the goals of schools
- the school acts entrepreneurially to support continuous improvement
- organizational systems are regularly monitored and modified as needed
- stakeholders are involved in decisions affecting schools
- responsibility is shared to maximize ownership and accountability
- effective problem-framing and problem-solving skills are used
- effective conflict resolution skills are used
- effective group-process and consensus-building skills are used
- effective communication skills are used
- there is effective use of technology to manage school operations
- fiscal resources of the school are managed responsibly, efficiently, and effectively
- a safe, clean, and aesthetically pleasing school environment is created and maintained
- human resource functions support the attainment of school goals
- confidentiality and privacy of school records are maintained

Standard 4

A school administrator is an educational leader who promotes the success of all students by collaborating with families and community members, responding to diverse community interests and needs, and mobilizing community resources.

Knowledge

The administrator has knowledge and understanding of

- emerging issues and trends that potentially impact the school community
- the conditions and dynamics of the diverse school community
- community resources
- community relations and marketing strategies and processes
- successful models of school, family, business, community, government, and higher-education partnerships

Dispositions

The administrator believes in, values, and is committed to

- schools operating as an integral part of the larger community
- collaboration and communication with families
- involvement of families and other stakeholders in school decision-making processes
- the proposition that diversity enriches the school
- families as partners in the education of their children
- the proposition that families have the best interests of their children in mind
- resources of the family and community needing to be brought to bear on the education of students
- an informed public

Performances

The administrator facilitates processes and engages in activities ensuring that

- high visibility, active involvement, and communication with the larger community is a priority
- relationships with community leaders are identified and nurtured
- information about family and community concerns, expectations, and needs is used regularly

- there is outreach to different business, religious, political, and service agencies and organizations
- credence is given to individuals and groups whose values and opinions may conflict
- the school and community serve one another as resources
- available community resources are secured to help the school solve problems and achieve goals
- partnerships are established with area businesses, institutions of higher education, and community groups to strengthen programs and support school goals
- community youth family services are integrated with school programs
- community stakeholders are treated equitably
- diversity is recognized and valued
- effective media relations are developed and maintained
- a comprehensive program of community relations is established
- public resources and funds are used appropriately and wisely
- community collaboration is modeled for staff
- opportunities for staff to develop collaborative skills are provided

Standard 5

A school administrator is an educational leader who promotes the success of all students by acting with integrity, fairness, and in an ethical manner.

Knowledge

The administrator has knowledge and understanding of

- the purpose of education and the role of leadership in modern society
- various ethical frameworks and perspectives on ethics
- the values of the diverse school community
- professional codes of ethics
- the philosophy and history of education

Dispositions

The administrator believes in, values, and is committed to

- the ideal of the common good
- the principles in the Bill of Rights
- the right of every student to a free, quality education
- bringing ethical principles to the decision-making process
- subordinating one's own interest to the good of the school community

- accepting the consequences for upholding one's principles and actions
- using the influence of one's office constructively and productively in the service of all students and their families
- development of a caring school community

Performances

The administrator

- examines personal and professional values
- demonstrates a personal and professional code of ethics
- demonstrates values, beliefs, and attitudes that inspire others to higher levels of performance
- serves as a role model
- accepts responsibility for school operations
- considers the impact of one's administrative practices on others
- uses the influence of the office to enhance the educational program rather than for personal gain
- treats people fairly, equitably, and with dignity and respect
- protects the rights and confidentiality of students and staff
- demonstrates appreciation for and sensitivity to the diversity in the school community
- recognizes and respects the legitimate authority of others
- examines and considers the prevailing values of the diverse school community
- expects that others in the school community will demonstrate integrity and exercise ethical behavior
- opens the school to public scrutiny
- fulfills legal and contractual obligations
- applies laws and procedures fairly, wisely, and considerately

Standard 6

A school administrator is an educational leader who promotes the success of all students by understanding, responding to, and influencing the larger political, social, economic, legal, and cultural context.

Knowledge

The administrator has knowledge and understanding of

- principles of representative governance that undergird the system of American schools

- the role of public education in developing and renewing a democratic society and an economically productive nation
- the law as related to education and schooling
- the political, social, cultural, and economic systems and processes that impact schools
- models and strategies of change and conflict resolution as applied to the larger political, social, cultural and economic contexts of schooling
- global issues and forces affecting teaching and learning
- the dynamics of policy development and advocacy under our democratic political system
- the importance of diversity and equity in a democratic society

Dispositions

The administrator believes in, values, and is committed to

- education as a key to opportunity and social mobility
- recognizing a variety of ideas, values, and cultures
- the importance of a continuing dialogue with other decision makers affecting education
- actively participating in the political and policy-making context in the service of education
- using legal systems to protect student rights and improve student opportunities

Performances

The administrator facilitates processes and engages in activities ensuring that

- the environment in which schools operate is influenced on behalf of students and their families
- communication occurs among the school community concerning trends, issues, and potential changes in the environment in which schools operate
- there is ongoing dialogue with representatives of diverse community groups
- the school community works within the framework of policies, laws, and regulations enacted by local, state, and federal authorities
- public policy is shaped to provide quality education for students
- lines of communication are developed with decision makers outside the school community

References

Behrman, J. N. (1988). Values underlying capitalism. In J. N. Behrman (Ed.), *Essays on ethics in business and the professions*. Englewood Cliffs, NJ: Prentice Hall.

Berger, L. P. & Luckmann, T. (1966). *The social construction of reality: A treatise in the sociology of knowledge*. Garden City, NY: Doubleday.

Blau, P. (1964). *Exchange and power in social life*. New York. Wiley.

Boles, K. & Troen, V. (1992). How teachers make restructuring happen. *Educational Leadership*, 49(5), 53–56.

Colby, A. & Kohlberg, L., et al. (1987). *The measurement of moral judgment:* (Vol. 2). Cambridge, England: Cambridge University.

Cushman, K. (1991). The essential conversation: Getting it started, keeping it going. *Horace*, 8(2).

Darling-Hammond, L. & Ancess, J. (1996). Authentic assessment and school development. In J. Baron & D. Wolf (Eds.). *Performance-based student assessment*. Chicago: University of Chicago Press.

Dubin, A. E. (1991, Spring). The power of the second in command. *The San Francisco State School of Education Review*, 3, 43–46.

Dubin, A. E. (1995). Emerging educational structures: The impact on leadership "culture." In S. W. Rothstein (Ed.), *Class, culture, and race in American schools: A handbook*. Westport, CT: Greenwood.

Elmore, R. F. (1992). Why restructuring alone won't improve teaching. *Educational Leadership*, 49(5), 44–48.

Fullan, M. G. (1992). Visions that blind. *Educational Leadership*, 49(5), 19–20.

Fullan, M. G. & Hargreaves, A. (1991). What's worth fighting for? In *Total schools*. Ontario, CA: Ontario Public School Teacher's Federation.

Goffman, I. (1963). *Behavior in public places*. London: Collier-Macmillan.

Hoerr, J. (1991.) What should unions do? *Harvard Business Review*, (May-June) 30–45.

Johmann, C. Sex and morality: Mind. *Omni, 20*, 4–5.

Leithwood, K. A. (1992). The move toward transformational leadership. *Educational Leadership*, 49(5), 8–12.

Lieberman, A. & Miller, L. (2001). *Teachers caught in action*. New York: Teachers College Press.

Lutz, F. W. & Iannaconne, L. (1995). The governance of local schools as influenced by social class, race, and ethnicity. In S. W. Rothstein (Ed.), *Class, culture, and race in American schools: A handbook*. Westport, CT: Greenwood.

Matteson, M. T. & Ivancevich, J. (Eds.). (1977). *Management classics*. Santa Monica, CA: Goodyear.

Relevant policies from the American Association of School Administrators Code of Ethic in *Ethics and the school administrator*. (1970). G. Immegart & J. Burroughs (Eds.) Danville, IL: The Interstate Printers & Publishers, Inc.

Rothstein, S. W. (1984). *The power to punish: A social inquiry into coercion and control in urban schools*. Lanham, MD: University Press of America.

Rothstein, S. W. (Ed.). (1993). *Handbook of schooling in urban America*. Westport, CT: Greenwood.

Index

Academic Performance Index (API),
    5, 30, 241, 244, 250, 255, 268
Accountability, 132, 138, 244–246
    See also No Child Left Behind Act
Adaptability, 162–163, 228–229
Adequate Yearly Progress (AYP),
    a 244, 249, 250, 255
Administrative issues:
    addition support personnel,
        12–14, 133–134
    administrative support, 171
    autonomous decision-making
        focus, 197–198
    isolation, 59–63, 79–80, 144
    mentorship programs, 184
    school district policies, 32–33,
        76, 87–91, 133–134,
        137–139, 197–198
    team building, 113
Advocacy, 56
After-school programs, 40, 132–133
Alternative language programs, 32
Alternative schools, 48, 51, 88–89
American International School
    (Lahore, Pakistan), 215–236
Authority, 77, 226

Balance:
    burnout, 160–161
    community-building
        approach, 158
    importance, 123
    personal life, 14–15, 137, 201
    politics, 56–57

    test scores, 34–35, 161–162
    time management, 117
    trust, 126
Belief systems, 27–45, 53, 188–189
Benchmarks, 11
Bilingual programs, 71–72, 131
Bribes, 224–225
Budget issues, 13, 31–32, 36,
        54, 153, 201, 251–252
Bureaucracy, 53–55, 115,
        136–137, 156
Burnout:
    administrative support, 91–92
    balance, 160–161
    creative solutions, 206–208
    job demands, 115–116
    prioritization, 14–15
    solutions, 145–146
Bush, George W., 261

California Standards Test, 254
California Test for Basic
        Skills (CTBS) test, 203
Charter schools, 256
Coaching:
    See Mentorship programs
Collaboration, 60–62, 76–77,
        121–122, 159, 187–188
    See also Decision-making process
Commitment, 124
Communication, 18–19, 73,
        94–95, 117, 202
Community day school,
        178, 180

Community issues:
  community-building priorities,
      8–10, 58, 158, 242–243
  international environments,
      222–227
  No Child Left Behind Act, 247–249,
      251–252, 255–256
  special interest groups, 119–120
Comprehensive high schools, 172–175
Compromise, 185–186
Confidence, 202–204, 228
Conflict management, 57–58
Consistency, 201–202
Continuation schools, 170–192
Continuity, 53
Counselors, 134–135, 152–153,
      171, 180–181, 196–197
Creativity, 39, 157–158, 199,
      203, 206–208
Credentialed teachers, 36–38,
      131, 243–244
Crime effects, 256
Crisis intervention abilities, 57–58,
      97–98, 120–121, 141–143,
      197, 202–204, 228–229
Criticism, 12, 118
Cultural conflicts, 36, 222–229, 233
Curriculum
  American International School
      (Lahore, Pakistan), 221
  collaborations, 121–123
  data interpretation skills,
      252–253, 269–273
  demographic effects, 111–112
  discipline issues, 10–11
  No Child Left Behind Act,
      245–246, 267–268
  reading programs, 173–176,
      197–198
  success strategies, 206–208

Data interpretation skills, 173,
      252–253, 255, 257, 269–273
  See also No Child Left Behind Act
Decision-making process:
  collaborative style, 40–41, 77,
      153–154, 185, 187–188
  cultural conflicts, 222–229

  judgment, 96–98
  leadership styles, 85–103
  parental involvement, 151
  prioritization, 123, 135–136, 185
  responsibility, 77
  school district policies,
      195, 208–210
  student-centered focus,
      116–117, 186
  teacher buy-in, 175–177
  team building, 157, 175–177
  timeliness, 187–188
Delegation, 185
Demographics:
  American International
      School (Lahore, Pakistan),
      217, 218–219
  county school system, 263
  elementary schools, 5, 30, 48, 51,
      71, 87, 89
  high schools, 171, 196
  middle schools, 109–112, 130, 132,
      151–152, 241, 243
  school boards, 226–227
Determination, 55–56
Discipline:
  after-school programs, 39–40
  community day school, 178, 180
  conflict management, 57–58
  as curriculum, 9–11
  detention program, 138–139
  student expectations, 200
  suspension rates, 136
District policies:
  bureaucratic decisions, 53–54
  control issues, 32–34
  decision-making process, 195,
      208–210
  educational support, 173–175
  See also Administrative issues
Diversity, 138, 222–223, 233, 241

Drucker, Peter, 100–101
Educational reform
  See No Child Left Behind Act
Elementary schools
  demographics, 5, 30, 48, 51,
      71, 87, 89

ethical considerations, 27–45
school culture development,
    3–26, 58
social interactions, 69–84
stabile environments, 46–68
Empowerment, 89, 207
Energy, personal, 203–204
English-only programs, 32
Escalantes, Jaime, 200
Ethical considerations, 27–45, 247–249
Evaluations, 12, 19–20, 135–136, 201
Expectations, 15, 201–202
Experience, 35, 94

Family system model, 162–163
Feedback, 18, 19, 20, 176–177
Flexibility, 15, 75, 92, 161, 228–229
    See also No Child Left Behind Act
Fun, 9
Funding, 13, 31–32, 36, 54, 135, 153
    See also No Child Left Behind Act
Fund-raising activities, 52, 251–252

Gangs, 120–121, 141
Government legislation
    See No Child Left Behind Act
Grant opportunities, 118–119,
    251–252
Group dynamics, 233

Individual Education Plan
    (IEP), 254, 267
Inner strengths, 55–56
In-service training, 174–176, 203
Institutional racism, 200
Instructional reform facilitator, 11
International environments, 215–236
Internship programs, 38, 49–50
Interstate School Leaders
    Licensure Consortium (ISLLC)
    Standards, 278–286
Intuition, 96
Isolation:
    collegial support, 78, 98–99,
        121–122, 143–144, 159
    community involvement, 209–210
    international environments,
        230–231

knowledge assumptions, 187
special education students, 253–255
support issues, 17–21, 40, 59–60,
    78–79

Judgment, 96–98, 228–229

Leadership:
    belief systems, 188–189
    characteristics, 65–66, 157–158
    importance, xiii–xiv
Leadership styles, xvii–xviii
    balancer, 69–84
    community activist, 3–26
    ethicist, 27–45
    experienced leaders, 107–236
    international environments, 215–236
    intuitive leader, 85–103
    multitasker, 169–192
    philosophical leader, 193–214
    politician, 128–148
    sage leader, 107–127
    traditionalist, 46–68
    veteran, 149–166
Legislative impacts:
    See No Child Left Behind Act
Lewin, Kurt, 233
Loneliness:
    See Isolation

Management issues, 40, 116–117,
    156, 178–182
Maslow, Abraham, 211
Maturity, 15–16
Mayo, Elton, 233
McGregor, Douglas, 189
Mentorship programs,
    21, 49, 61, 184
Methodology, xv–xvi, xix–xx
Middle college, 179, 181–182
Mission statements, 203
Morale, 61–62, 246
Motivational environments,
    207–208
Multinationalism
    See American International School
        (Lahore, Pakistan)
Multitasking ability, 156, 169–192

Networking programs, 60–63, 78, 81,
    121–123, 145
News media, 255–256, 276
No Child Left Behind Act
    accountability, 265, 268, 271
    California legislation,
        243–245, 265–266
    funding, 251–252, 256–257,
        263, 266, 271
    goals, 262
    parental support, 247–249,
        256, 270, 273
    principal perspective, 239–260
    resources, 246–248, 251
    special education students,
        253–256, 267, 273
    superintendent perspective, 261–277
Nurturing environments,
    155–156, 171

Open enrollment, 111

Paige, Rod, 264
Pakistan:
    See American International School
        (Lahore, Pakistan)
Paraprofessionals, 244
Parent involvement:
    activism, 33, 41
    community-building priorities, 119
    continuation schools, 183
    cultural conflicts, 222–227
    decision-making process, 151
    importance, 31
    No Child Left Behind Act,
        247–249, 270
    parent-teacher conferences, 156
    parent-teacher organizations,
        52, 92, 96
    as priority, 73
    support issues, 137–138, 220
Parent-teacher organizations (PTOs),
    52, 92, 96
Personnel issues, 178–179, 181–182
Perspective, 15–16, 64, 94, 123, 145,
    188–189
    See also No Child Left Behind Act
Physical environment, 13–14

Planning, 107–127, 189
Politics:
    balance, 56–57
    community-building approach, 158
    constituencies, 16–17, 36, 78, 95–96
    hiring decisions, 118–119, 205,
        209, 219–220
    leadership styles, 128–148
    No Child Left Behind Act, 257
    parental involvement, 220
    power issues, 77
    school district policies, 32–33
    team building, 185–186
    See also No Child Left Behind Act
Power, 77
Predictability, 46–68
Preparation process, 38, 64, 72
Pressure issues:
    See Burnout
Principals, importance of, xiii–xiv
Prioritization:
    American International School
        (Lahore, Pakistan), 220–221
    burnout, 14–15
    consistency, 53, 201–202
    creativity, 157–158
    data interpretation skills, 252–253
    decision-making process, 116–117,
        135–136, 153–154, 185
    elementary schools, 7–9, 19, 73–75
    flexibility, 92
    hiring decisions, 228
    parental involvement, 73
    student-centered focus,
        123, 199–202
    team building, 113–115
    test scores, 8–9, 53, 199–200
Proactive behavior, 138–139, 257–258
Professionalism, 8, 18
Program improvement schools
    See No Child Left Behind Act
Publicity effects, 255–256, 276

Racism, institutional, 200, 224
Reflection, 41, 55–56
Respect, 143, 200, 204
Responsibility, 77, 184, 245
Rogers, Carl, 233

Safety issues, 120–121, 200–201
School boards, 141–143, 180, 226–227
School culture development
    community-building approach,
        3–26, 58
    conflict management, 57–58
    stabile environments, 53
School district policies:
    bureaucratic decisions, 53–54
    control issues, 32–34
    decision-making process,
        195, 208–210
    educational support, 173–175
    See also Administrative issues; No
        Child Left Behind Act; Support
Secretarial support, 59, 79–80,
    114, 160
Sense of humor, 55, 123, 159
Sensitivity, 56
Skill requirements, 157–158
Socialization, 22–23, 69–84, 229
Special education students, 244–245,
    253–256, 267
Spellings, Margaret, 242, 264, 268
Stability, 46–68
Staff development
    See In-service training; Training
        programs
Standardized testing, 203, 243–245,
    249–250, 254
Standards, 11, 93–94, 278–286
STAR schools, 7
Stress:
    See Burnout
Structure, 9–10, 58, 162–163, 171
Student-centered focus:
    decision-making process, 116–117,
        123, 155–158, 163, 186
    prioritization, 19–20, 199–202
    school environment, 155
    See also Continuation schools; No
        Child Left Behind Act
Summer school programs, 182
Support:
    administrative support, 144
    collegial support, 59–63, 78, 117,
        121–123
    decision-making process, 99

educational support, 173–175,
    245–249
importance, 80
international environments, 231–232
internship programs, 50
mentorship programs, 49, 61, 184
parental support, 138, 220
school district policies, 12–14, 33,
    59–63, 76, 79–80
secretarial support, 59, 79–80,
    114, 160
staff support, 20, 94, 114,
    196, 244
student programs, 132–133
team building, 113
See also Administrative issues;
    School district policies

Team building skills:
    community-building priorities, 8
    decision-making process, 157,
        175–177
    politics, 185–186
    trust, 94, 113, 159
Technology instruction, 197, 201
Test scores:
    accountability, 138
    achievement gaps, 135–136, 249,
        250, 261
    balance, 34–35, 161–162
    California Test for Basic Skills
        (CTBS) test, 203
    demographics, 89
    No Child Left Behind Act, 255, 267
    as priority, 8–9, 53, 132–136, 151,
        154, 199–200
    reading programs, 197–198
    special education students, 254, 267
    standardized testing, 243–245, 249
Theory X/Theory Y, 189
Time management:
    American International School
        (Lahore, Pakistan), 221
    availability, 114–115
    balance, 117
    bureaucratic paperwork, 53–54,
        115, 136–137, 156
    classroom observations, 92–93

district programs, 177–179
parent-teacher conferences, 156
prioritization, 14–16
troubleshooting, 74–76
Title I schools, 30, 110, 114, 134,
    199, 256, 268
Title VII schools, 118, 134
Training programs, 50–51, 77, 88,
    174–176, 230–231
Troubleshooting, 74–76
Trust:
    definition, 126
    importance, 124
    lack of, 143–144, 230
    networks, 41
    team building, 8, 94, 113, 159

Underperforming schools:
    belief systems, 27–45
    continuation schools, 170–192
    No Child Left Behind Act, 247–249
    prioritization, 196–211
    school culture development, 3–26

Vision:
    community-building priorities, 158
    continuity, 53
    educational opportunities, 173
    importance, 28, 73, 203, 205–206
Vouchers, 256–257, 275

Weber, Max, 65
Well-performing schools, 46–68

About the Author

Dr. Andrew E. Dubin is Professor of Educational Administration in the Department of Administration and Interdisciplinary Studies (DAIS) in the College of Education at San Francisco State University (SFSU). He received his Ph.D. from Claremont Graduate School and has worked as teacher, dean of discipline, and grade adviser in New York City; as a teacher and drama specialist at Colegio Nueva Granada in Bogota, Colombia; and as a principal and superintendent for the American International School in Lahore, Pakistan. In 1994 he was headmaster for the American International School in Rome. He has published numerous articles and several books on educational leadership nationally and internationally, has worked as an educational consultant, a lecturer at California State University, Fullerton, and as program coordinator in educational administration at University of California, Irvine. He also wrote *How To Remember Anything* (1971, Memory School Publishing) and has served as a memory consultant for schools and nonprofit agencies. He directed a teacher training program for returning Peace Corps volunteers at SFSU. He has developed the educational administration leadership institutes in San Francisco and San Mateo County and is currently directing the Marin County Leadership Institute.